Brazil on the Global Stage

Brazil on the Global Stage

Power, Ideas, and the Liberal International Order

Edited by
Oliver Stuenkel and Matthew M. Taylor

BRAZIL ON THE GLOBAL STAGE
Copyright © Oliver Stuenkel and Matthew M. Taylor, 2015.

Chapter 7 is drawn from Togzhan Kassenova, *Brazil's Nuclear Kaleidoscope: An Evolving Identity* (Washington, DC: Carnegie Endowment for International Peace, 2014).

First published in 2015 by PALGRAVE MACMILLAN® in the United States—a division of St. Martin's Press LLC, 175 Fifth Avenue, New York, NY 10010.

Where this book is distributed in the UK, Europe and the rest of the world, this is by Palgrave Macmillan, a division of Macmillan Publishers Limited, registered in England, company number 785998, of Houndmills, Basingstoke, Hampshire RG21 6XS.

Palgrave Macmillan is the global academic imprint of the above companies and has companies and representatives throughout the world.

Palgrave® and Macmillan® are registered trademarks in the United States, the United Kingdom, Europe and other countries.

ISBN: 978-1-137-49164-0

Library of Congress Cataloging-in-Publication Data

Brazil on the global stage : power, ideas, and the liberal international order / edited by Oliver Stuenkel and Matthew M. Taylor.
    pages cm
  Includes bibliographical references and index.
  ISBN 978-1-137-49164-0
  1. Brazil—Foreign relations—21st century.   2. Brazil—Foreign economic relations.   3. Brazil—Foreign relations—United States.
  4. United States—Foreign relations—Brazil.   I. Stuenkel, Oliver, editor of compilation.   II. Taylor, Matthew MacLeod, editor of compilation.
  JZ1548.B74 2015
  327.81—dc23   2014040766

A catalogue record of the book is available from the British Library.

Design by SPi Global.

First edition: April 2015

10 9 8 7 6 5 4 3 2 1

Contents

List of Figures and Tables

Figures

Tables

Acknowledgments

A volume such as this one incurs many debts, which we can only partially acknowledge here. All of the chapters benefitted from extensive and stimulating comments offered by our workshop participants, colleagues, and external readers, including Amitav Acharya, Leslie Armijo, Robert Blecker, Brandon Brockmyer, Ken Conca, Frank DuBois, Johanna Mendelson Forman, Louis Goodman, Dan Jacobs, Miles Kahler, Luciano Melo, Cristina Pacheco, Claudia Tomazi Peixoto, Carlos Portales, Tim Ridout, Sharon Weiner, and an anonymous reviewer. Matias Spektor has been a guiding force behind this project from the very beginning, and helped to brainstorm the project and encourage the participation of a diverse set of contributors.

The volume originated in a joint workshop of the American University and the Fundação Getulio Vargas, held at the School of International Service in Washington, DC. The workshop was made possible by financial support from the Center for Latin American and Latino Studies (CLALS) and the School of International Service (SIS), allowing for two days of deep conversation between scholars hailing from a variety of locations in Brazil and the United States. James Goldgeier, Dean of SIS, and Eric Hershberg, Director of CLALS, have been enthusiastic supporters from the outset. Their intellectual contributions, and their particular emphasis on drawing us beyond our comfort zone as scholars of Brazil, are also on keen display in the Foreword and Afterword to this volume.

Inés Luengo de Krom and the staff at CLALS kept us well-fed and single-mindedly focused on the task at hand. Our meetings were also facilitated by Kristi-Anne Caisse, Alicia Cummings, Amy Gillespie, and the staff of SIS. Tyler Evans' excellent assistance has been vital to pulling together the workshop findings and the final manuscript. We are indebted to Farideh Koohi-Kamali,

Sara Doskow, Chris Robinson, Dharmendra Sundar Devadoss, and all of the editorial staff at Palgrave for the support they have provided from our initial brainstorm through publication. Together, all those thanked here bear the bulk of the credit for what is now in your hands.

Matthew Taylor
Washington, DC

Oliver Stuenkel
São Paulo

Foreword
Eric Hershberg

As the global order has become increasingly multipolar in recent years, Latin American countries that were historically portrayed as the backyard of the world's foremost power have drifted away from American influence and grown less inclined to follow Washington's lead on an array of governance challenges. Greater autonomy has been encouraged by steady economic growth, fueled by the commodity boom that began around 2003, and by a significant diversification of partners for South American trade. It also reflects the determination of increasingly confident elected civilian leaders throughout the region to assert national sovereignty on matters of governance in domestic, regional, and global arenas. Sometimes the shift away from the American orbit has occurred without rancor and with minimal discord regarding the provision of global public goods or the institutional architecture needed to manage their supply. In other instances, Latin American distancing from Washington comes accompanied by confrontational language and actions. The intentionally provocative rhetoric of some of the more contestatory governments in the region annoys but does not perplex American diplomats, who see in the Venezuela-led ALBA alliance either a particularly illiberal version of twentieth-century populism or an anachronistic form of Cuban-inspired authoritarianism. But there is considerable puzzlement in Washington about the unwillingness of otherwise respectable Latin American governments to embrace US-supported positions on matters of international affairs that, from an American perspective, appear basic to how democracies engage one another and reinforce common-sense global norms. Brazil, Latin America's largest country and an emerging middle power in the international system, represents a signal example of this disjuncture between American expectations and Latin American attitudes and behaviors. This volume provides a clear and insightful interpretation of how Brazil engages the international arena and, in so doing, the volume offers important clues as to how Brazil will relate to the United States as it continues to advance its interests as an increasingly relevant actor in global affairs.

Brazil today exercises greater influence on the Latin American and global stages than at any previous point in history. As Stuenkel and Taylor note in their introductory chapter, it now represents the world's seventh-largest economy, a significant source of finance and investment in the Americas and Southern Africa, and the anchor for a number of meaningful multilateral institutions, such as the Mercosur customs union and the Union of South American Nations (UNASUR), a political alliance borne of Brasília's interest in establishing a leading role in a South America detached from the US orbit. On several occasions in recent years Brazil has led multilateral efforts to defuse potentially dangerous inter-state conflicts within South America or to mediate between governments and opposition in polarized polities. Beyond its own region, Brazil is also an important voice in the increasingly influential Group of 20 and, alongside India and South Africa, it represents a promising beacon of democratic politics among the emerging powers known as BRICS (Brazil, Russia, India, China, and South Africa).

Brazil will, and indeed already does, play a vital role in global governance, at times in ways that dovetail neatly with American preferences, as in its ongoing contributions to the United Nations peacekeeping mission in Haiti and its leadership in the Open Government Initiative championed by former Secretary of State Hillary Clinton. These examples point to ways in which the emergence of Brazil can lend support for key planks of a global liberal order, very much in keeping with US interests and values. And Ralph Espach may be correct to predict, in his contribution to this book, that over time converging interests between Brasília and Washington will increasingly lead to heightened cooperation on issues such as security. But for the moment Brazil's positions frequently clash with those of Washington on a wide range of issues, encompassing global and regional security, principles of non-intervention, democracy promotion, trade liberalization, the role of international financial institutions in promoting economic development and transparent governance, and, most recently, frameworks for governing the Internet and data protection. Divergences over such questions arguably are growing in both number and depth, and this book provides grounds for expecting that this will continue to be the case for the foreseeable future.

To some extent tensions may have become deeper owing to more than a decade of left-wing administrations in Brasília, as the Workers Party (PT) that has governed since 2003 traces its origins to labor and popular mobilizations against a military regime that came to power in 1964 with active support from Washington. Memories of American ties to unsavory security forces were perhaps rekindled by revelations of National Security Agency monitoring of private communications among Brazilian leaders, including President Dilma Rousseff, consternation over which triggered the cancellation of a state visit to the White House in 2013. But this book makes clear that divergences pre-date the PT's rise to power and reflect core ideas and values that are shared across the political spectrum in Brazil and that, because of their deep historical roots, will surely prove more enduring than any particular administration. At the same time, in the pages that follow I suggest that American reticence about growing Brazilian influence, and resentment over stances adopted by Brazil on quite a few global issues, is also a function of core ideas and values that are no less rooted in its own history as a hegemonic force shaping the global liberal order.

A product of a collaborative effort between American University and the Getulio Vargas Foundation, this book draws on contributions of prominent experts from both universities as well as several other institutions to offer a wide-ranging and nuanced account of Brazil's relationship to the US-led global liberal order in general and to several critical policy domains in particular. It will be a useful resource for international relations scholars concerned with the impact of emerging powers on the international system, as well as to Brazilianists and Latin America specialists keen to better understand how the increasingly assertive countries of Latin America may pursue a world order more in keeping with their perceptions of what is desirable for a twenty-first century that will be marked by a logic of multipolarity that they wholeheartedly endorse. The book should also interest students of the American role in the world who need to better understand the perspective of potential allies that nonetheless perceive the world in terms that differ fundamentally from those articulated in Washington.

To be sure, some of the international governance issues that have catalyzed divisions between Brazil and the United States evoke divergent perspectives among Latin American countries themselves. Stances regarding trade liberalization are a noteworthy example. Yet Latin American distancing from the American-led version of the global liberal order is widespread. Even discounting the proudly Yanqui-defying ALBA (Bolivarian Alliance for the Americas) countries and Argentina—with regard to which Brazil has played a moderating role that has diminished the sway of those in Latin America who would consciously undermine the liberal international order that the United States constructed in the post–World War II era—differences of view are particularly evident with regard to collective military intervention, the use of sanctions against misbehaving states, and, in the Western hemisphere itself, the appropriate approach to democracy promotion.

From a US government perspective, however, Brazil is perhaps the most frustrating of contemporary Latin American states in this regard. It has the size and prestige to matter, certainly in South America but arguably elsewhere in the hemisphere and extending to other regions of the Global South.

Its economy has the scale and capabilities that enable it to have an impact on developments far beyond its borders, for example, through spearheading the Mercosur customs union as an alternative to a US-led hemispheric free trade sphere, and through deploying the capital of state development banks, such as the Brazilian development bank (BNDES), as an alternative to the international financial institutions (IFIs) with which Washington shares a vision of market-driven economic growth. Politically, UNASUR has repeatedly been used by Brazil as an alternative to the Organization of American States (OAS) in taming regional conflicts, and Brazil has been at the forefront of a broadly shared Latin American acceptance of the legitimacy of ALBA governments that, particularly in the case of Cuba and Venezuela, the United States considers anathema and worthy of sanctions rather than support. Moreover, unlike any Latin American government, with the exception perhaps of Cuba during the 1970s in Sub-Saharan Africa, Brazil has not hesitated to project its differences with the United States onto the global stage in meaningful ways. Former President Lula's joint effort with his Turkish counterpart to broker a nuclear non-proliferation deal with Iran was particularly galling to the Americans, for whom that sort of leadership role on a major global security issue was not one to be assumed by aspiring middle powers. These are the departures from liberal orthodoxy that led one prominent commentator to criticize Brazil as being, in the words of former Mexican Foreign Minister Jorge Castaneda, Latin America's most reliable echo of American sentiment, "not ready for prime time."[1]

Readers of this volume will come away with a clear sense that this is not a particularly useful way of understanding a changing international order. A more multipolar world is one in which the "prime time" lineup will look somewhat different from that which aired at the height of the Cold War or during the brief interlude of unipolar hegemony experienced by the United States following the collapse of the Soviet bloc. From the Brazilian and broader Latin American perspective, a multipolar order is one in which scripts are prepared in multilateral fashion: while the institutional end product will not be identical to a single-authored version, if the drafting process is sufficiently collaborative, the result may come out looking like a friendly amendment to the original rather than a thorough rewrite.

In this respect, editors Stuenkel and Taylor provide a useful reflection on how competing perspectives in the mainstream international relations literature envision the likely stance of emerging powers vis-à-vis hegemonic liberal order. Whereas constructivists would observe that much that is dear

---

[1] Jorge G. Castaneda, "Not Ready for Prime Time: Why Including Emerging Powers at the Helm Would Hurt Global Governance." *Foreign Affairs*, September–October, 2010.

to international liberalism involves norms and regimes to which Brazil would find it natural to adhere, particularly if it is granted a seat at the decision-making table, realists predict that emerging powers will exhibit greater assertiveness in the global arena, seeking to expand national power in ways that will undermine the hegemonic order itself. But neither of these ideal typical positions properly captures the implications of Brazil's rising confidence and influence or the particularities of its positions in comparison to other middle powers that similarly exhibit what Stuenkel and Taylor refer to as "an ambiguous relationship to current international governance structures."

Contributors to this volume demonstrate that to understand that "ambiguous relationship" one must acknowledge the historical and ideational forces that shape Brazil's relationship to US-defined and led international regimes. This insight, in turn, calls particular attention to Brazil's aspiration to step forward as a voice for Latin America and for the Global South, collections of states with which it identifies and perceives a shared sense of legitimate grievance over inequalities in the global economy and in the historical configuration of international governance. It is Brazil's overarching identity as a developing country in the specific context of Latin America that both orients its actions in the international arena and generates antagonistic postures toward the United States that are widely shared by other countries in the region. This dynamic often bewilders US pundits and diplomats who do not grasp the sense of historical injustice that permeates Latin American visions of the region's relationship with the United States and thus the long-standing resentments that arise in response to Washington's defense of the status quo. As Tourinho rightly points out in his chapter, Brazil and its neighbors criticize the United States for seeking to preserve in the twenty-first century a hegemonic order that it imposed at a historical moment marked by yawning asymmetries. Especially rankling for increasingly self-confident and proud governments in the region is what they perceive as the persistence of double standards whereby the United States demands adherence to a given liberal regime even while exempting itself from sanctions for violating agreed-upon norms.

Indeed, underlying much of Washington's angst regarding Latin America's widening estrangement is the enduring trope of American exceptionalism and benevolence, qualities that are deeply ingrained in political discourse and bureaucratic cultures in the US government but alien to their counterparts in foreign ministries across much of Latin America. If during the past decade Brazil has come across as especially skeptical of US leadership in ventures that Washington takes for granted as an unequivocal plus for international order—consider trade liberalization, military intervention in the

Middle East, or exclusion of Cuba from inter-governmental institutions—this is not strictly a reflection of the rise of an anti-American left. Quite the contrary; as Maia and Taylor argue compellingly, the career diplomats of Itamaraty share a profoundly rooted nationalism that does not square easily with an American vision of universal adherence to norms that were made in and refereed by Washington. That this emerges especially vividly in Brazil's interactions with the United States—more so, for example, than in those of Mexico or Colombia—is in part a reflection of Brazil's relative size compared to other Latin American states, but it also derives from the ubiquity of developmentalist thinking that Maia and Taylor identify as influential across the political spectrum in Brasilia.

A fundamental challenge for US efforts to strengthen its relationship with Latin America, and first and foremost with Brazil, will thus be to leave behind a mindset anchored in an era of uncontested hegemony that is now a phenomenon of the past. United States interactions with the region will have to acknowledge legitimate differences regarding governance in the Americas and the broader world. Undoubtedly, there are currents in the American foreign policy apparatus that are aware of this imperative, and this generates powerful statements of principle that are warmly welcomed in Latin American capitals. President Barack Obama's eloquent pledge at the 2009 Americas Summit to enter a new era of partnership, equality, and reciprocity is perhaps the most noteworthy example. But good intentions cannot overcome fundamental differences in worldview which come into evidence once the niceties communicated during summits give way to substantive aspects of international diplomacy focused on tangible resources and impactful norms. Moreover, discrepancies over the proper role of the United States are not limited to regional governance but instead pertain to the broader international system. This last point is critical. Whether the topic is counter-terrorism or war and peace in the Middle East or countering China's growing influence in East Asia or management of the global financial system, the American assumption remains that the world looks to Washington for global leadership. To the extent that Latin American priorities and preferences lie elsewhere, what the United States is offering is not considered by much of Latin America, including Brazil, as essential global public goods. Nor are those goods seen as being provided neutrally in a non-self-interested manner.

Seen in this light, a central message of this book concerning Brazil may be applicable to Latin America more broadly. Brazil is by no means hostile to the notion of a global liberal order, yet it chafes at a version of such an order put forth at the behest of the United States. Over time, common imperatives may emerge to bring about a greater degree of convergence around shared needs, but just as ideational factors account for Brazilian reluctance to accept American leadership, no less deeply rooted ideational currents make it unlikely that the United States will soon join Latin American states in the stewardship of a global order in which it is not recognized as the leading force.

CHAPTER 1

Brazil on the Global Stage: Origins and Consequences of Brazil's Challenge to the Global Liberal Order

Oliver Stuenkel and Matthew M. Taylor

The global liberal order emerged triumphant from the Cold War, consolidated under the aegis of US power. But international institutions are increasingly under review, with a variety of nations challenging the implicit hierarchy of the global order, the dominant role of the United States within that order, and the essential foundations of global liberalism. Some challenges were widely anticipated: governments in China and Russia, for example, do not share the basic political tenets of the global liberal order, and China's rise poses the most obvious long-term challenge to today's US-led order.

A more curious case emerges from Brazil. In the past generation, Brazil has risen to become the seventh-largest economy and fourth-largest democracy in the world, yet its rise challenges the conventional wisdom that liberal capitalist democracies will necessarily converge to become faithful adherents of a US-led global liberal order. Indeed, Brazil demonstrates that middle powers, even those of a deeply democratic bent, may offer important challenges to the world order, differing in their views of what democracy means on the global stage, as well as to how international relations should be conducted among sovereign nations. As such, it is a powerful example of the potential challenges that middle powers—even the capitalist democracies among them—pose to the dominant patterns of international politics in the twenty-first century. Contrary to China's more recognizable and clear-cut challenge, which has many parallels to the history of US contestation of British dominance in the nineteenth century, the role of middle powers such as Brazil is often less easily understood in the realist terms that dominate US foreign policy circles. Perhaps as a result, especially when they challenge US positions, Brazil's foreign policy stances are often portrayed by frustrated Washington officials as quixotic and naïve, or ridiculed as puerile and petulant third-worldist jabs at a stereotypical Uncle Sam, intended only to win popular approval from a nationalistic and anti-American electorate. Washington policymakers often seem "to consider Brazil an interloper in world affairs, a nation that does not quite measure up to the status and power it has achieved and whose foreign policy judgments are often uninformed and misguided" (Hakim, 2014). While these perceptions may capture important elements of reality, this volume points to the fact that Brazilian foreign policy positions often have more enduring origins, embedded within a deeply held set of beliefs that together shape the country's rational strategic perspective on the structure of power in the world today.

Brazil's new role on the world stage has much to do with the country's success in addressing its own domestic challenges under a succession of democratically elected presidents. Over the past three decades, Brazil has left behind its history of economic disarray, established a robust democracy, and begun to address its record-setting inequality. It has found paths past the hyperinflation and financial crises of the 1980s and 1990s, undertaken substantial institutional reforms to overhaul the gargantuan and inefficient public sector, and implemented highly regarded social policies. Even its recent stumbles can be seen in the positive light of democratic progress: the demonstrations that took hold in many Brazilian cities in 2013 and 2014 can largely be attributed to a growing middle class impatient with the pace of change and increasingly conscious of its political rights, a direct consequence of the important successes of the past generation. After the economic boom of the 2000s, the lackluster growth of recent years does not appear to have led to any significant diminution in national capabilities. Although the country continues to face dissatisfaction with the domestic status quo and a number of domestic challenges such as inequality, criminal violence, and corruption, the achievements of the past generation appear to have fostered an enduring intent to play a role on the world stage.

Under Fernando Henrique Cardoso's presidency (1995–2002), the country began to cautiously look abroad to build a role as a pro-democracy actor in Latin America, with an emphasis on building relations with a host of governments in South America in ways that neither directly contested US dominance in the region, nor trespassed on Latin American partners' sensitivities about their large lusophone neighbor. In the past twenty years, Brazil has played a crucial part in negotiating conflicts between its neighbors (e.g., Ecuador and Peru in 1995 and Colombia, Ecuador, and Venezuela in 2008), as well as addressing political instability in the region (e.g., Bolivia

1995, 2000, 2006; Venezuela 2003–2004 and 2014; Paraguay 1996, 1999, 2000, 2012; Spanakos and Marques, 2014). In this quest for "consensual hegemony" in the region (Burges, 2009), Brazil has sought to preserve its legitimacy as a regional leader by appealing to notions of consensus and inclusion.

As Amitav Acharya (2013) has noted, Brazil is an "accomodationist" rather than a domineering regional power, but its power is nonetheless highly contested in the region, even as it seeks to use regional power as a launching pad for its global aspirations (Malamud, 2011). In its quest for "consensual hegemony," especially within South America, it has faced tensions that are natural for a nation whose economic reach is expanding: the favored role of Brazilian companies in regional development initiatives has been questioned, the goals of its national development bank have been criticized, and Brazilian corporate assets in South America have been seized and, in some cases, nationalized (Friedman-Rudovsky, 2012). Meanwhile, Brazil faces a conundrum well-understood by longer-established powers: it is criticized when it fails to intervene or intervenes only tepidly in neighboring countries' disputes (e.g., Venezuela's internal crisis in 2013–2014), but also lambasted when it does take a stance (e.g., in diplomatic crises with Ecuador over Odebrecht's work on a dam project in 2008; with Bolivia over the asylum given to an opposition senator in 2013). Its role as the predominant economy in the Mercosur (Common Market of the South) bloc, and the considerable effort it has put into preserving this customs union, has also forced it into often complex contortions. Mercosur has served, variously, as a way of resolving historical bilateral tensions with Argentina in the wake of authoritarian rule, as an instrument for promoting economic liberalization and integration when the four original member states were undertaking domestic economic reforms, as a foil to US-led efforts at a hemispheric free trade agreement, as a means of broadening Brazilian negotiating power in global trade negotiations, and most recently, as a means of constraining Bolivarian Venezuela's most extreme aspirations for South America. These various instrumental uses of Mercosur mean that Brazil's objectives are not always transparently obvious to the outside world, even when they have clear foreign policy motivations.

Particularly since Luis Inácio Lula da Silva's presidency began in 2003, Brazil has also simultaneously engaged in strategic construction of a more robust international role that goes beyond South American regional initiatives and gives great pride of place to global South–South relations. Despite announced plans to build a nuclear submarine and an aircraft carrier, Brazil has largely eschewed military projection and instead relied largely on instruments of soft power to gain influence in world affairs (Saraiva, 2014, p. 64).

Within the hemisphere, Brazil was joined by other Latin American nations in creating new institutions and groupings that meet some of the challenges posed by the increasingly antiquated system centered around the Organization of American States (OAS), which has been long-perceived by Latin Americans as predominantly focused on Washington's hemispheric security concerns (Soares de Lima, 2013; Vigevani et al., 2013). Without seeking to abolish the OAS, or supplant it directly with a competing institution, Brazil has focused considerable effort on organizing South America as a region, most importantly through the creation of the Union of South American Nations (UNASUR), an effort aimed at reducing the role of the United States in regional affairs and in regional negotiations with other global actors (Spanakos and Marques, 2013).

Notably, Brazil also began to engage in areas outside of the country's regional sphere of influence. In 2010, President Lula took the initiative with Turkey's prime minister Erdogan to attempt to negotiate a nuclear deal with Iran. In 2011, Brazil took a lead role in the global debate about humanitarian intervention when it launched the concept of the "Responsibility while Protecting" (RwP). More recently, President Rousseff placed Brazil in the center of the discussion about Internet governance by hosting a major international conference on the issue in April 2014. Brazil has also sought a bigger role in Africa and its trade with that continent has quintupled since the turn of the century, leading presidents Lula and Rousseff to assert Africa's strategic importance to Brazil, to forgive nearly $1 billion in old debt, and to seek to export Brazilian agricultural know-how to the other side of the Atlantic.

Brazil has been able to play roles that leading powers cannot or do not wish to fulfill, obtaining support from both established powers and more peripheral nations based on its history of non-interventionism and perceived cultural openness, combined with its economic and demographic clout. Brazil has simultaneously gained international exposure in a variety of ways: as the host of world events like the 2014 Football World Cup and 2016 Olympics, selection of a Brazilian diplomat as director of the World Trade Organization (WTO) (Armijo and Katada, 2014), and a successful push for a shift in voting rights and quotas within the International Monetary Fund (IMF). Brazil has seen success as a global leader on issues ranging from the Open Government Initiative (the transparency initiative Brazil codirects with the United States) to brokering backroom talks in the Colombian–Ecuadoran dispute of 2008 and leading the United Nations (UN) military force in Haiti for over a decade.

The past decade has also seen the nation's designation as one of a group of rising powers, in a series of "emerging powers" initiatives with IBSA (India, Brazil, and South Africa), BASIC (Brazil, South Africa, India, and China),

BRIC (Brazil, Russia, India, and China), and BRICS (Brazil, Russia, India, China, and South Africa). In July 2014, Brazil hosted the Sixth BRICS Summit, which saw the creation of a new development bank and a BRICS contingency reserve agreement (CRA), which represent an important institutional manifestation of emerging powers' desire to reform the global order. While it is too early to say what role these new institutions will play, they symbolize Brazil's desire to reach beyond established US-led structures, but without resorting to the stale third-worldism that marked the Non-Aligned Movement (NAM) during the Cold War (Daudelin, 2013, p. 214). The BRICS and associated initiatives with large middle powers are frequently criticized for the absence of a common vision or coherent strategy, yet the rise of the BRICS forum in the midst of the 2008 global economic crisis opened a window of opportunity for reform, particularly within global financial institutions, and the grouping has found meaningful ways to challenge extant institutional structures that previously provided little room for the developing countries. Indeed, despite deeply differing interests and affinities among its members, and the natural limitations these impose on cooperation, over the past decade, the BRICS grouping has helped Brazil to elevate its international position and gain more political space and influence in multilateral forums (Sotero, 2013).

Of course, this is not to suggest that Brazil's rise has been frictionless. Relations with the other big power in its hemisphere, the United States, have been tested in areas as varied as trade policy and intellectual property rights, in forums as diverse as the WTO and the UN, and in policies toward nations as different as Libya and Honduras. In 2013, Brazil became embroiled in a major diplomatic spat over US espionage against its government, companies, and citizens, driving bilateral relations to a low point. A scheduled state visit by Dilma Rousseff to Washington, the first by a Brazilian president in nearly two decades, was cancelled. One of the principal architects of a deliberate US policy of closer approximation to Brazil, Ambassador Thomas Shannon, returned from his posting in Brasília after enduring a series of seemingly calculated slights by his hosts. Late in 2013, after more than a decade of deliberation, the Brazilian government finally came to a decision on the $5 billion purchase of fighter jets for its air force, and it was widely believed in Washington, and gleefully circulated in Brasília, that Boeing fell from frontrunner status as a consequence of the US National Security Agency's (NSA) alleged spying. The NSA's espionage efforts, alongside other tensions in the bilateral relationship, meanwhile, suggested that Brazil's new influence as a leading middle power has not gone unnoticed by the great powers.

Meanwhile, Brazil's rising prominence has led many international observers, including many beyond Washington, to question its ability to play a constructive role on the international stage, both when it acts and when it fails to do so. Brazil's silence on Russian intervention in Crimea and the Ukraine was criticized at home and abroad, demonstrating the tough choices that will confront a more internationally prominent Brazil. Similarly, as noted earlier, Brazil was criticized for being slow to act when demonstrations and conflict resurged in 2014 between Venezuelan president Nicolas Maduro and the opposition, leading the Brazilian government to justify its inaction by arguing that it needed to preserve its neutrality so as to maintain its role as a potential interlocutor. But passivity is not the only source of criticism: proactive stances also have their downsides. This was exemplified in the wake of the 2014 conflagration in Gaza, when Brazil became the first nation to withdraw its ambassador in Israel for consultations, followed by President Rousseff's labeling of the conflict a "massacre." In response, a spokesman of the Israeli foreign ministry was quick to label Brazil a "diplomatic dwarf" and note that its stance was full of "moral relativism" (comments that later led to an apology from Israel's president to Rousseff).

Such complaints are new for Brazil, and will require some getting accustomed to, both for Brazilian policymakers and the Brazilian public at large, which has long been used to watching international affairs from a comfortable distance. Meanwhile, there is considerable variation in foreign policy across Brazilian presidencies. Despite their considerable policy differences, presidents Cardoso and Lula both actively sought and personally relished Brazil's rising prominence on the global stage. President Rousseff has demonstrated less interest in foreign policy, despite important accomplishments. Notwithstanding these differences in personal and ideological stances in Brazilian foreign policy, however, the past thirty years of Brazilian democracy has brought important gains that mean that Brazil is an increasingly relevant player on the world stage, as a result of economic stabilization and inequality reductions; the blossoming of democracy and a normal, mundane politics with clear institutional rules; and a conscientious diplomatic offensive waged by Itamaraty, Brazil's foreign ministry (Almeida and Diaz, 2009, pp. 229–235). Together, these factors contributed to Brazil's emergence as one of the largest middle powers at a time when traditional powers face important challenges to their continued dominance.

This volume, which brings together scholars from institutions in both Brazil and the United States, explores the implications of Brazil's rising international profile for global norms, and in particular, for the dominant global liberal order. The liberal international order is defined by open markets, international institutions, cooperative security, democratic community, collective problem solving, shared sovereignty over some issues, and the rule of law (Ikenberry, 2009). How do rising powers like Brazil, a country located on the periphery of both international institutions and the global distribution of power, seek to change their position in the present context of the internationalization of authority? How do they behave, react, and construct a discourse (Herz, 2010)? The authors in this volume argue from a variety of perspectives that as Brazil seeks greater integration and recognition within the prevailing global liberal order, it is emblematic of the challenges posed by a number of middle powers in an increasingly multipolar world system.

There is a systemic liberal institutionalist argument about why rising powers such as Brazil are likely to integrate into the global liberal order: they face a Western-centered system that, as Ikenberry stresses, is "open . . . and rule-based, with wide and deep political foundations, a force that will enmesh and entrap even the most powerful" (2008). The Western order, which Roosevelt had conceived to "ensure the end of beginning of wars," (Rubenfeld, 2003) is "hard to overturn and easy to join" (Ikenberry, 2008). Emerging actors encounter an environment in which they will be able to continue to rise, without enduring large costs of establishing global public goods. Unprecedented economic interdependence through trade, investment, and commercial flows leads non-established rising powers to seek to strengthen global governance to maintain the stability of this economic system (Friedman, 2000).

And yet, there is a counter-argument, premised in realism, that understands the system according to the distribution of power and predicts that the rising powers will not "play by the West's rules" (Stephens, 2010). Scholarship in this vein generally expects rising powers to use their "newfound status to pursue alternative visions of world order" (Narlikar, 2008) and challenge the status quo, for example, by joining forces with other rising powers and mounting a counter-hegemonic coalition.[1] Rising powers could create a parallel system with "its own distinctive set of rules, institutions, and currencies of power, rejecting key tenets of liberal internationalism and particularly any notion of global civil society justifying political or military intervention" (Barma et al., 2007). Krasner (1985) has argued in this vein that once the balance of power moves against the West, emerging powers will create different principles, for example, by introducing countervailing power against the US-led Bretton Woods institutions.

Where does Brazil fall on the continuum between these two possibilities of seamless integration and countervailing contestation? Brazilian policymakers have questioned the foundations that underlie the global liberal order, expressing differences of opinion on the scope of cooperation, the location of rules, and the allocation of authority. In so doing, Brazil has posited fundamental disagreements over substantive policies of the postwar liberal consensus. At the extreme, liberal internationalism has been interpreted by

Brazilians as a form of liberal imperialism, and the power of the hegemon at the center of the liberal order has been portrayed by Brazilians as a menace at least as threatening as anarchy within the international system. The result has been a critical challenge to the liberal internationalist project, in substantive areas such as trade, human rights, and nuclear non-proliferation. And yet, Brazil appears to be in agreement with the broad precepts of the contemporary international order, and the system-wide benefits this order produces for Brazil are far too significant for the country to seek to significantly upset that order. Brazil has little to gain from profound changes to the liberal order, and US hegemonic power fails to pose an existential threat that might trigger outright opposition or abandonment of the international order.[2]

In this sense, Brazil is a prominent representative of a new subset of important emerging players on the global stage—including other middle powers such as Indonesia, Mexico, Nigeria, Turkey, and South Africa—that share Brasília's ambiguous relationship with current international governance structures, but lack the traditional hard capabilities that mark Chinese or Russian foreign policy.[3] Implications drawn from this analysis of Brazil can therefore also be useful to assessing the impact that this subset of middle powers may have on the global order, as well as to understanding their sometimes seemingly ambivalent positions, which lack the clarity of China or Russia's more transparent strategic approaches. There is considerable uncertainty about the ideas and perspectives that inform these middle powers' agendas as they seek greater visibility and the capacity to influence the global order (Schweller and Pu, 2011). But recognition of these ideas and perspectives is needed if we are to understand how middle powers will seek to integrate into today's global structures and which aspects of global order they will seek to overhaul (Rubenfeld, 2003; Hurrell, 2006; Ikenberry, 2008).

Another difference between these middle powers and the more traditionally strategically oriented rising powers, such as China, lies in the tools that they will likely employ. These tools seem likely to differ from the traditional hard power military, political, and economic instruments that have usually accompanied the emergence of global players in the past. Brazil's depiction of itself as a bridge between the Global South and the wealthy North has been a very useful instrument in this regard. It has helped place it at the head of this community of middle powers, a tactic that is both deeply embedded in the country's views of its role, as well as in national self-interest. As Burges points out, the strategy of appropriating the role of de facto spokesman for the Global South—in WTO negotiations, as a leading light in the IBSA, BRICS, and UNASUR groupings, and as a mediator of conflicts in South America, among others—has helped Brazil gain a reputation as a coalition-builder, control flows between North and South, and become indispensable as a broker between old and new powers. While this diplomatic approach is deeply embedded in beliefs about Brazil's position as a developing nation, it also serves as a useful instrumental tool for a nation that has limited power projection capabilities. Brazilian diplomats have proven masterful at using their pan-southern leadership position to advance the national interest and turn global norms "slightly" in their own favor (Burges, 2013).

Brazil's limited hard power resources, and its strategic use of soft power, give great pride of place to the ideas that lie behind foreign policy. Throughout this volume, a recurring and central theme is the importance of deeply held Brazilian convictions about the world order, and the manner by which these ideas about the world shape this important middle power's approach to liberal international norms and institutions. The overarching objective is to understand the perspectives that underpin Brazil's foreign policy and how they have evolved over time, approaching the ideational foundations of policy from a variety of different angles by contributors with diverse perspectives. We are centrally concerned with three questions: First, what are the ideas and debates that have shaped Brazilian perceptions about the country's role in world affairs? Second, how have these ideas shaped policymakers' conceptions of the country's international interests, challenges, and threats? And finally, in what ways do these ideas push the definition and design of foreign policy in directions that may be orthogonal to the dominant international liberal order?

The volume begins broadly, with a general evaluation of Brazil's stance in the global order, an assessment of the ideational traditions that influence Brazil's foreign policy positions, and a discussion of the security relationship between Brazil and the dominant global power, the United States. Subsequent chapters address Brazilian postures on specific aspects of the global order, including foreign intervention, environmental norms, economic policy, trade, and nuclear policy. The foreword by Eric Hershberg has already placed the Brazilian case within the Latin American context, and the afterword by James Goldgeier highlights the role of Brazil as one of the middle powers that are gradually reshaping the global arena.

In the next chapter, David Bosco and Oliver Stuenkel (Chapter 2) explore the specific critiques of the prevailing global order that have guided contemporary Brazilian foreign policy. They seek to identify and critically assess key attributes of Brazil's recent multilateral diplomacy and the challenges it poses to the global liberal order. They identify several recurring rhetorical themes in Brazil's approach, including a focus on increased voice for the developing world, calls for greater accountability in multilateral institutions, and a desire to reduce the prevailing emphasis on the use of coercion. Drawing on several cases, including the UN Security Council, the WTO, and the Bretton Woods institutions, the chapter evaluates the gaps between the rhetoric and the reality of Brazilian foreign policy, and analyzes Brazil's contestation of fundamental aspects of the liberal order, such as international institutions, cooperative security, democratic community, collective problem solving, shared sovereignty, and the rule of law.

In the realm of peace and security, for example, Brazil has often expressed skepticism about Western policies and raised concerns about double standards regarding the use of force that resonate powerfully with developing-world positions (a theme that also reappears in Tourinho's chapter [Chapter 5]). And yet, in several surprising ways, Brazil has turned into an important provider of global public goods, for example, by sending peacekeeping troops to Haiti. While Brazil has insisted that the peacekeeping force remains fundamentally consensual, the shift toward more assertive policing may foreshadow a broader reckoning with the dilemmas of modern peacekeeping. Bosco and Stuenkel's assessment makes clear that the tension between Brazil's rhetorical commitments and its actual policies toward multilateral institutions is likely to increase as the country takes a more prominent place in global affairs.

João M. E. Maia and Matthew M. Taylor, for their part (Chapter 3), describe the broad ideational foundations that have historically shaped Brazil's foreign policy. Reflecting the discussion in Bosco and Stuenkel's chapter, they argue that Brazil does not seek to replace the global liberal order, and has found much to be gained from participating in it. Yet the country's participation is tempered by a historically conditioned approach to liberalism that is at odds with hegemonic conceptions of the global liberal order. The chapter draws on classical debates in Brazilian intellectual life about economic and political liberalism to evaluate the notion that liberalism is an "out of place" idea in Brazil. It also analyzes how dominant conceptions of economic and political liberalism present in Brazilian intellectual life condition and influence Brazil's preferences, strategies, and participation in the international system.

Their analysis provides crucial insights into the origins of Brazilian postures that are little understood outside of Brazil, yet that have a foundational influence on the way Brazil projects itself abroad. Democratization and democracy in Brazil may be changing the "attitudinal prism" through which foreign policy is generated and evaluated, as Belém Lopes (2013) has eloquently demonstrated, pointing to new forms of policy legitimation at home and abroad, the pluralization of actors involved in policy, and the tensions imposed on foreign policy by electoral politics and new, more open forms of public debate. Yet in the hierarchy of foreign policy objectives, Maia and Taylor note that Brazil often still gives sovereignty and development higher status than democracy or rights protection, in part as a consequence of its history of foreign intervention, weak territorial control, and delayed modernization. Further, they argue, the weakness of the liberal tradition in Brazil may not be the most important explanation for Brazil's weak allegiance to some aspects of the global liberal order, or its disagreements with the way that order is implemented. Rather, the central problem is the weakness of Brazilian democracy itself, and the fact that the so-called national question has so often proven more important than the "democratic question," which explains the sometimes baffling tendency of leaders such as Lula to praise authoritarian figures such as Getulio Vargas and Ernesto Geisel at home, or Fidel Castro and Hugo Chávez abroad. Maia and Taylor agree that Brazil does not seek to replace or fundamentally challenge the rules and norms that undergird the global order, but they emphasize the fact that foundational national values are weighted quite differently than in the United States and Europe, with significant consequences for foreign policy.

In the following chapter (Chapter 4), Ralph Espach analyzes security relations between the two largest powers in the Western Hemisphere, Brazil and the United States. He shows that bilateral security ties between the United States and Brazil are often depicted as unnecessarily conflict-ridden, even though few other Latin American nations can claim to have a closer security partnership with the United States. Even so, it is evident that the US–Brazilian relationship has been marked by increasing divergence since World War II.[4] The chapter argues that a critical factor behind the "thorniness" in the bilateral relationship is the lack of an underpinning in a common security threat and persistent differences in perspective regarding the appropriateness and purpose of military power. Brazil's policies and investments for defense have little to do with warfare, an aspect of foreign relations with which it has little experience and remains uncomfortable. For the United States, conflict and deterrence (for its own interests and those of its partners) have been central components of its rise to power and self-definition as a leader. Espach explores these perspectives, especially for Brazil, and the ambiguities they entail, for example, in Brazil's desires for advanced military equipment (to include nuclear submarines and aircraft carriers) and capabilities, without clear rationale for their use around the world. The author argues that Brazil, over time, has used its security sector and capabilities pragmatically as instruments of foreign policy, a practice well-suited to a stable, liberal international order but less useful during episodes of crisis or conflict. Despite enduring differences in their strategic perspectives, security relations between the United States and Brazil are relatively strong at the operational level, and could—if both governments see fit to allow them—develop further in areas of mutual interest such as peacekeeping, disaster response, and regional security cooperation. It is at the level of actual operations, Espach argues, that the potential for cooperation between Brazil and the United States is highest, and where such cooperation offers the most promise as a channel for realignment in bilateral relations.

Marcos Tourinho's thought-provoking analysis (Chapter 5) investigates Brazil's approach to norms about foreign intervention. In particular, his chapter seeks to specify and locate more precisely the disagreements Brazil has historically voiced regarding the enforcement of liberal norms about intervention in an international context. Tourinho argues that Brazil's primary concern with the emergence of liberal norms in international society has less to do with the substance of those norms and liberal values themselves, but rather is the product of a genuine concern with the hegemonic process by which such norms have been created, implemented, and enforced. Brazil's resistance to embracing key aspects of today's liberal order has less to do with the content of that order, in other words, than it does with the manner by which those rules have been interpreted and applied.

Tourinho argues that Brazil is not and has not been a revisionist state when it comes to the fundamental liberal norms. He cites former Brazilian foreign minister Antonio Patriota, who, in reflecting on these ideas and projecting his own vision for international order, noted: "What do we want? A multilateral system in which everyone is subject to the same rules."[5] While most liberal norms are largely welcomed by Brazil's government and society, the hegemonic manner of norms enforcement has produced substantial Brazilian dissent in international political debates. In this context, the best summary of the Brazilian position was offered by Celso Amorim, one of the most influential Brazilian foreign policy voices of recent decades, who stated: "We want neither multipolarity without the ballast of international law, nor multilateralism placed in the service of unipolarity. Strictly, what we seek is increased multipolarity with the juridical-parliamentary support of multilateralism. In other words, we want to preserve the UN framework, adapting it without disfiguring it to the new demands of contemporary reality."[6] This perspective has major implications for Western policymakers intent on integrating emerging democracies such as Brazil into the so-called liberal order, showing that categorizations of states according to whether they should be seen as supporters or enemies of the liberal order are too simplistic. Brazil has approached the liberal order with a nuanced stance, recognizing the attractiveness of this order, yet disagreeing with how leading actors within it, notably the United States, have used the liberal order as a tool to promote their own interests.

Eve Bratman's case study (Chapter 6) of Brazil's posture on global environmental norms provides a compelling perspective on the assumed rationality of Brazilian foreign policy, arguing that Brazil's engagement on environmental issues in the global arena is marked by unplanned and home-grown ambiguity. At first glance, Brazil looks like a global environmental leader, hosting major summits on environmental issues and taking a symbolic leadership position among less-developed nations on environmental issues. Yet Brazil has also adopted non-committal positions on climate change, increased its energy production goals in ways that are threatening to sustainability, and watered down domestic environmental laws to meet political and developmental goals. Ironically, Brazil generally adheres to the global liberal environmental order, yet this is largely because this order is weak and lacks rigor, rather than because Brazil is deeply committed to environmental objectives. Echoing Maia and Taylor, Bratman notes that domestic objectives such as development and national sovereignty have frequently trumped environmental priorities. Bratman's chapter also provides an important service by noting the influence that actors other than the federal government have exerted over Brazilian environmental politics. In an era when Itamaraty seems to be increasingly ceding space in the foreign policy agenda to other actors within the federal government (e.g., Cason and Power, 2009), Bratman demonstrates that the federal government itself is also increasingly forced to recognize the influence of subnational governments, the private sector, and national and international non-governmental organizations in the realm of environmental governance. The result is a confusing tapestry of positions and contradictions with regard to major environmental issues.

Togzhan Kassenova's (Chapter 7) discussion delves into another important yet often overlooked element of Brazil's foreign and domestic policy: its choices in the nuclear field. Brazil stands out among BRICS countries as the only country to have never developed nuclear weapons. At the same time, Brazil is the only non-nuclear weapons state to be working on a nuclear submarine, and it is one of only few countries in the world to have access to sensitive uranium enrichment technology. Brazil's ambitious nuclear program at home translates into growing assertiveness on the international nuclear scene. Brasília refuses to grant the International Atomic Energy Agency (IAEA) rights for more intrusive inspection of its nuclear facilities (by not signing the IAEA Additional Protocol).

Kassenova concludes that while there are no reasons to assume that Brazil will retreat from its Nuclear Non-Proliferation Treaty (NPT) commitments, the consensus position within the Brazilian government is one of caution in the face of the expansion and intrusiveness of non-proliferation norms. The analysis of Brazil's nuclear policy reveals interesting dynamics. Brazil's rhetoric on global nuclear issues emphasizes the values of justice and fairness—Brasília strongly criticizes the lopsided global nuclear order that promotes the interests of a "select few" countries with advanced nuclear programs. At the same time Brasília works toward being one of those "select few," and in pursuing this objective, it shrewdly picks and chooses which liberal international rules to adhere to.

One of the most important reasons for Brazil's rise in global prominence over the past two decades has to do with the steps the country has taken to address historically troubling economic challenges, such as hyperinflation, fiscal profligacy, and income inequality. Yet the lackluster growth of the past half-decade has called into question the sustainability of these policies, and indeed, has even led to questions about the sustainability of Brazil's rise on the global stage. The final two chapters of the volume tackle the economic challenges that Brazil faces, and the ideas that constrain policymakers as they consider economic policy alternatives both at home and in world affairs. Arturo Porzecanski (Chapter 8) provides a provocative account of Brazil's contemporary role in the global economy, noting that the scale and self-sufficiency of Brazil's economy has enabled it to develop internally, following a long-standing inclination toward state capitalism, expressed either as the old structuralist variant of the 1950s and 1960s, or in the "neodevelopmentalism" of the current century. As a consequence, however, relative to the size of its economy, Brazil has underperformed in other emerging markets, with comparatively small shares of global trade, low integration into global financial markets, and a small share of global outward foreign direct investment (FDI). Detailing the fact that Brazil punches below its weight in economic affairs, Porzecanski calls into question Brazil's capacity to sustain its current foreign economic policies over the long haul.

On the world stage, since the 1980s, Brazilian foreign economic policy has been premised on the belief that the country should build its global profile through the construction of alliances with supporters in the Global South. Brazil has taken a leadership role in groupings ranging from Mercosur and UNASUR in the Americas, the Community of Lusophone Countries (CPLP, largely in Africa),[7] and the Group of Twenty (G-20) on the global stage. These groupings were seen by Brazil as a means of increasing its credibility and bargaining power in various international forums. But the simultaneous strategy of committing to multilateralism in some forums, such as the WTO, and parallel efforts to sustain regional associations, has placed Brazil in an increasingly untenable position. In a world in which multilateral organizations such as the WTO seem likely to be increasingly sidelined by regional "super-blocs," Brazil is increasingly constrained both by the exigencies of short-term domestic economic policies and by its longer-standing Mercosur commitments. Powerful interest groups that benefitted in the past from developmentalist policies, such as the National Industrial Confederation

(CNI) and the São Paulo Industrial Federation (FIESP), have become increasingly restive, calling for a shift in Brazil's global economic policy stance. Together these tensions and pressures may become an important source of change in Brazilian foreign policy in coming years.

André Villela's (Chapter 9) chapter segues naturally from this insight about Brazil's strategic economic choices. He provides a comprehensive analysis of Brazil's trade policy from Bretton Woods to the G-20, seeking to explain the origins of Brazil's reluctance to fully embrace the liberal international economic order from its inception after World War II through the present. During the early wave of globalization at the turn of the twentieth century and throughout the subsequent de-globalization that took place between 1930 and 1945, Brazil was relatively convergent with the liberal consensus. It was only after World War II that Brazil would choose a form of engagement with the international liberal order that was often at odds with the central tenets of American-led multilateralism. In explaining the historical drivers of this shift, Villela's chapter focuses on the most significant economic aspect of this order: foreign trade relations. Villela demonstrates that anti-liberal and anti-market ideas in Brazil remain strong. Interestingly, he points out that both among policymakers and among citizens, the notion that imports are to be avoided in general is quite common, as is the view that a trade surplus must be achieved at all costs. This deeply ingrained mercantilist view of trade policy shows little sign of losing its attractiveness to Brazilian society, which dims the prospect of significant domestic support for a shift toward greater engagement in the international trade order.

The contributions to this volume help to explain the stances of the Brazilian foreign policy establishment, which are not infrequently depicted as enigmatic outside Brazil. This has led in the past to the view that Brazil is not a responsible global player, nor even—and this may be the more damning critique in foreign policy circles—a particularly consistent and predictable one. There is little question that there are occasional moments of inconsistency in Brazil's foreign policy, derived from some of the same factors of changing leadership, shifting fortune, limited policymaker bandwidth, and changing political calculations that drive the inconstancy of policymaking elsewhere in the world. But together, the chapters presented here help to demonstrate a great deal of coherence in Brazilian foreign policy, deeply embedded in firm beliefs about the national interest and about the nation's place in the world. These beliefs are similar enough to those of the global liberal order to suggest that Brazil will be a productive collaborator in that order. But Brazilian history and Brazilian thought also lead the country to prioritize its key objectives in ways that are different from those of the dominant powers, contributing to inevitable tensions as the country emerges as one of the key middle powers and perhaps assumes what many Brazilians firmly believe is its rightful place as one of the central players on the world stage.

Together, the essays in this volume suggest that Brazil will not be a passive actor in international affairs, and will make important contributions to debates on global norms, global institutions, and global order. It is our hope that the volume will help policymakers and scholars outside of Brazil to better understand the lasting sources and likely consequences of Brazilian foreign policy positions. But we also hope that it may allow Brazilians to reflect on how their country's postures are perceived abroad, and the constraints these perceptions place on the country's ability to play a constructive role in international affairs. Both objectives are salutary, for there can be little doubt that democratic Brazil has a rightful claim to a powerful voice on the world stage, and that its arrival on that stage has led to increased recourse to the institutions of the existing international order, as well as to rising demands for their reform.

Notes

1. For a broader discussion of where middle powers such as Brazil and India lie between the two perspectives described here, see Stuenkel (2010).
2. Layne (2006, pp. 16–17) points out that the United States does not threaten emerging powers' sovereignty and calls it a "liberal hegemon."
3. Brazil has more than 300,000 active military, which places it ahead of all of its neighbors except Colombia in absolute terms. But the country lacks the capacity to project this power beyond the region, and the armed forces are only the sixteenth largest in the world.
4. Echoing a point empirically demonstrated via an analysis of UN General Assembly votes in Amorim Neto (2011).
5. See Patriota, 2013; Patriota served as foreign minister from 2011 to 2013.
6. See Amorim, 1999; Amorim served as foreign minister from 1993 to 1995, and again from 2003 to 2011.
7. The Comunidade dos Países de Língua Portuguesa (CPLP), founded in 1996, includes Angola, Brazil, Cape Verde, East Timor, Guinea-Buissau, Mozambique, Portugal, and São Tomé and Príncipe.

CHAPTER 2

The Rhetoric and Reality of Brazil's Multilateralism

David Bosco and Oliver Stuenkel

I t has been widely noted that Brazilian foreign policy has become more ambitious since the early 1990s. As with several other emerging powers, Brazil appears to have taken a broader view of the country's foreign policy interests as its economic clout has increased. As it has done so, Brazilian policymakers have often identified multilateralism as a key tool of Brazil's more assertive and global foreign policy. "We see multilateralism as the primary means of solving conflicts and making decisions internationally," said former foreign minister Celso Amorim (2010a).

This chapter seeks to identify and critically assess certain key attributes of Brazil's recent multilateral diplomacy. To do so, it focuses on Brazilian policy toward global multilateral organizations. This focus leaves aside Brazil's very active diplomacy in regional forums such as the Organization of American States (OAS), the Union of South American Countries (UNASUR), and Mercosur. This choice does not reflect a judgment on the relative importance of regional versus universal organizations for Brazilian foreign policy but seeks to narrow the focus to institutions with global reach and mandates.

To help identify and assess the key aspects of Brazilian engagement with multilateral organizations, this chapter identifies several recurring rhetorical themes in Brazil's approach, including an emphasis on an increased voice for the developing world, calls for greater accountability in multilateral institutions, and a desire to reduce emphasis on coercive means. In important respects, Brazilian policy in key multilateral forums is consistent with these rhetorical elements. Yet we argue that there is also a significant gap between the rhetoric and the reality of Brazilian multilateralism and that this gap may become more pronounced in the future. Much of Brazilian rhetoric about existing multilateral institutions derives from its perceived status as an outsider and as a voice for other countries with limited influence. With increasing influence, however, that stance will be more difficult to maintain. We argue in particular that there is a latent tension between Brazil's institutional aspirations and its desire for south–south cooperation.

Rising Powers and Multilateral Institutions

Brazil's approach to multilateral institutions has often been addressed as a subset of a broader theme: how emerging powers interact with a multilateral order they have never historically led and played little role in creating.[1] Scholars and policy specialists have asked, in particular, whether emerging powers are integrating into the existing multilateral order or seeking to develop alternative structures and approaches. Some observers have concluded that these countries have mostly accepted the existing architecture. G. John Ikenberry has written, "China and other emerging great powers do not want to contest the basic rules and principles of the liberal international order; they wish to gain more authority and leadership within it" (2008, p. 23). From this perspective, the key global challenge is to gradually and sensibly transfer certain authority to these emerging powers and, in so doing, broaden and update the existing architecture.

Others are more skeptical that these states accept the basic premises of the existing multilateral order. "Emerging powers may be clamoring for greater global influence," Stewart Patrick has written, "but they often oppose the political and economic ground rules of the inherited Western liberal order, seek to transform existing multilateral arrangements, and shy away from assuming significant global responsibilities" (2010, p. 44). Jorge Castañeda has argued along similar lines that the BRICS countries (Brazil, Russia, India, China, and South Africa), in particular, share a worldview that places them at odds with the existing multilateral architecture:

> Brazil, India, and South Africa are representative democracies that basically respect human rights at home, but when it comes to defending democracy and human rights outside their borders, there is not much difference between them and authoritarian China. On those questions, all four states remain attached to the rallying cries of their independence or national liberation struggles: sovereignty, self-determination, nonintervention, autonomous economic development. And today, these notions often contradict the values enshrined in the international order. (Castañeda, 2010, p. 109)

Those who see emerging powers integrating into the existing multilateral order and those who do not disagree mostly about how divergent the values and interests of emerging powers are from those who are "enshrined" in the multilateral order. Answering that question requires an examination of what principles underlie multilateral institutions, which is not a simple exercise. Castañeda and other skeptics of the integration model tend to downplay the degree to which sovereignty and nonintervention are themselves key principles of the international order. Once this is recognized, the emerging-power perspective can be seen less as a rebuff of the multilateral order than as a shift in emphasis between different goals already recognized by the system.

There are limits to the utility of discussing an "emerging power" approach to the multilateral architecture. The emerging powers have themselves encouraged this approach by championing forums like BRICS and IBSA (India, Brazil, and South Africa), which emphasize their shared goals. But their embrace of these mechanisms does not absolve analysts and scholars of the responsibility to assess the individual approaches of these states. However one defines the set of emerging powers, they are a diverse group with quite different domestic pressures, foreign policy traditions, and diplomatic approaches. This chapter seeks to consider Brazil's approach on its own merits, rather than as a subset of a broader group strategy. The chapter turns first to an examination of Brazil's substantive and rhetorical engagement with key global institutions. The next section provides a broad overview of Brazil's global multilateral engagement. The chapter concludes by assessing that record in the context of three recurring rhetorical themes.

Brazil's Multilateral Record

Brazil participates in the full range of multilateral institutions at the global level. Therefore, a comprehensive examination of all aspects of its engagement is beyond the scope of this chapter. However, this section briefly outlines some of the salient points in Brazil's recent participation and engagement with both formal and informal multilateral forums. While formal organizations like the United Nations (UN) and World Bank and informal groupings like the Group of Twenty (G20) cannot be analyzed through the same lens, they interact in important ways, and both types of institutions speak to Brazil's multilateral engagement.

The UN system remains the cornerstone of the multilateral architecture, and Brazil is a consequential participant in multiple elements of the UN system, including in the General Assembly and the multiple specialized agencies. In broad terms, Brazilian officials have insisted that the organization should be the focal point for world politics. "Multilateralism is the international face of democracy," Celso Amorim, Brazil's then foreign minister, told the General Assembly in 2010. "The UN must be the main center of decision-making in international politics" (Amorim, 2010, p. 3).

Amorim's linkage of democracy with multilateralism underlines the depth of Brazil's recent rhetorical commitment to multilateralism. But moving beyond this broad but abstract support for the UN requires a more specific examination of that institution's components. Brazil's performance in the UN Security Council and the Human Rights Council, in particular, has required it to take public positions on contentious international issues and therefore has thrown into sharper relief its view of the proper role and place of the organization.

UN Security Council

Brazil has a long and rich history of participation on the UN Security Council; it even came close to being one of the Council's permanent members. During the 1944 Dumbarton Oaks negotiations that produced the first draft of the UN Charter, the United States sought to include a Latin American country on the Council and proposed a seat for Brazil. Soviet and British representatives resisted, however, largely on the grounds that a Brazilian seat would de facto become another vote for the United States. Their skepticism eventually prevailed (Bosco, 2009).

Even without a permanent seat, Brazil has been a frequent presence on the Security Council. Along with Japan, Brazil has been elected to the Security Council more than any other UN member. In the post–Cold War period, Brazil has won a Council seat more frequently than any other major emerging power, including India and Turkey.

Its multiple stints on the Security Council have afforded Brazil the opportunity to engage substantively on a range of issues, particularly peacekeeping operations and sanctions regimes (Table 2.1). Brazilian diplomats have served on the multiple sanctions committees and other working groups that the Security Council has created in recent years. Brazil has been a consistent participant in Council-authorized peacekeeping missions. In financial terms, Brazil's contribution to peacekeeping is relatively modest: the UN scale of assessments makes Brazil the 28th largest contributor. In personnel terms, Brazil has been a more significant player: in 2012, Brazil had approximately 1,700 troops in UN operations and was the 17th largest contributor to UN peacekeeping. Most Brazilian peacekeepers have served in the UN mission to Haiti, and a Brazilian general has served as force commander of that mission since 2004. Brazil's leadership role in the Haiti operation has forced it to face one of the most difficult questions for modern peacekeepers: whether and when to use force.

In a few cases, Brazil's presence on the Council has afforded it a platform for independent diplomatic initiatives. The most notable example occurred during 2010, when Brazil and Turkey (then also serving as a nonpermanent

Table 2.1 Frequently Elected Members of the UN Security Council[a]

Country	Times elected	Times elected since 1990	Most recent term
Brazil	10	4	2010–2011
Japan	10	4	2009–2010
Argentina	9	4	2013–2014
India	7	2	2011–2012
Pakistan	7	3	2012–2013
Canada	6	1	1999–2000
Turkey	4	1	2009–2010
South Africa	2	2	2011–2012

[a] United Nations, available online at http://www.un.org/en/sc/members/elected.shtml

member) negotiated with Iran regarding its nuclear program. Brazilian president Lula da Silva invested considerably in the diplomatic endeavor and ultimately traveled to Iran for final face-to-face negotiations. The joint initiative was viewed skeptically by several of the Council's permanent members, however, and the agreement ultimately foundered. The Council as a whole imposed new sanctions on Iran just days after Brazil and Turkey announced their agreement (Brazil voted against those new measures, the first time the country opposed a successful Council resolution).

Brazil also played a significant role during and after the 2011 Libya intervention. When the Council authorized the use of force to protect civilians during the conflict between Muammar Gaddafi's government and rebel forces, Brazil and several other members abstained.[2] During the debate, Brazil's ambassador insisted that the abstention did not signify support for the Gaddafi government, but expressed concern that coercive measures "may have the unintended effect of exacerbating tensions on the ground and causing more harm than good to the very same civilians we are committed to protecting."[3] As the NATO-led military campaign developed, Brazilian officials criticized NATO's conduct of the air campaign. And in the wake of the intervention, Brazilian policymakers advanced the concept of "responsibility while protecting" as a corollary to the more established "responsibility to protect" doctrine. Foreign Minister Antonio Patriota framed the initiative as being essentially about the accountability of the Security Council:

> [T]he use of force must produce as little violence and instability as possible. Under no circumstances can it generate more harm than it was authorized to prevent; in the event the use of force is contemplated, action must be judicious, proportionate and limited to the objectives established by the Security Council;

enhanced Council procedures are needed to monitor and assess the manner in which resolutions are interpreted and implemented to ensure responsibility while protecting. (Patriota, 2012)

Why, Brazilian policymakers asked privately, did Libya qualify as a case of (Responsibility to Protect) R2P, but not Gaza, Afghanistan, or Iraq? They joined other observers in suggesting that the West cares most about protecting civilians when doing so aligns with other economic or strategic interests. As Bellamy observes, "While there is growing consensus about the R2P in principle, in practice R2P is applied selectively and inconsistently and its use is often contested" (2011, p. 71).

The Libya episode also produced another example of the Brazilian emphasis on accountability at the multilateral level. Security Council Resolution 1970, which imposed an initial round of targeted sanctions on Libya, also referred the situation to the International Criminal Court (ICC). As a member of the court, Brazil expressed "deep reservations" about the language in the resolution exempting non-ICC member states from the court's jurisdiction. Even as she voted for the referral, Brazil's ambassador insisted that "initiatives aimed at establishing exemptions of certain categories of individuals from the jurisdiction of the International Criminal Court are not helpful to advancing the cause of justice and accountability and will not contribute to strengthening the role of the Court."[4]

Even as Brazil has emphasized Security Council accountability, it has continued its efforts to reform the Council's membership. Brazilian officials have argued consistently that the Council cannot operate as designed without membership reform. "With a composition that reflects the realities in the aftermath of the [Second] World War, the UN Security Council is out of touch with today's world," Brazil's UN ambassador argued. "The Security Council must be brought to the 21st Century, in order to preserve and enhance its legitimacy and effectiveness" (Viotti, 2010). Through the Group of Four (G4) grouping, Brazil has collaborated with Germany, India, and Japan to promote membership reform and to advance their candidacies for permanent Council membership. All of these states have insisted that the existing Council membership structure is outdated and that reform is essential to preserve the Council's legitimacy and relevance. While there is near unanimity in the abstract about the need for Council reform, there is little agreement about the appropriate approach to reform. In their advocacy efforts, the G4 states have often collided with another group of states—the "Uniting for Consensus" bloc—which opposes new Security Council permanent seats. Mexico, Argentina, Italy, and Pakistan have been key players in this group, and they have insisted that new permanent Council seats would merely perpetuate an international order that privileges major powers.

UN Human Rights Council

Brazil has been a frequent member of the UN's Human Rights Council, a subsidiary body of the General Assembly charged with monitoring compliance with established rights. Brazil has been elected to the Council multiple times and most recently during a three-year term ending in 2015. Brazil has participated in the Council's new Universal Periodic Review process and has welcomed several UN special rapporteurs, including one who examined prison conditions in the country. Brazilian scholar Paulo Sérgio Pinheiro, a former UN special rapporteur for Myanmar, has also served as the chair of the Human Rights Council's panel of experts on Syria.[5] In that capacity, he has often served as a notable voice in the UN response to the crisis.

On the Human Rights Council, Brazil has developed an extensive voting record on proposed resolutions. While many of these resolutions are adopted by consensus, others are contentious. In many of these contested votes, the Council breaks down along north-south lines, with the United States and European Union on one side and Non Aligned Movement (NAM) countries on the other. Brazil has often voted with the NAM countries. As one observer has noted critically:

> [I]n the recent cases of Cuba, Iran, Venezuela, and most recently Syria, Brazil has taken a more ideological or "soft-balancing" approach, siding against the United States and Europe by avoiding criticism of human-rights abuses and ducking behind the defense of noninterventionism favored by diplomats in the foreign ministry. (Piccone, 2011)

However, there is evidence that Brazil's approach has been significantly more complex than is often portrayed. Brazilian officials have advocated a gradual international abolition of the death penalty through the work of the Council despite the use of that practice in countries such as China.[6] There is also evidence that Brazil has shifted its approach to condemnation of individual governments. In 2011, Brazilian diplomats reportedly met with Iranian opposition figures and then voted to condemn some aspects of the regime's behavior in the Council.[7] On some accounts, these choices marked a notable shift from the policy followed during the Lula da Silva administration and an acknowledgement that international condemnation can be appropriate.

World Trade Organization

Brazil was an early member of the General Agreement on Trade and Tariffs (GATT) and joined the World Trade Organization (WTO) when it was created in 1995. One of the key institutional innovations of the WTO framework was its more formal and binding dispute resolution mechanism. This system is often described as the world's most advanced dispute resolution initiative and a critical test for the ability of states to resolve differences through international law. The degree to which states affirmatively employ the WTO system is one important metric for assessing participation in the organization. In recent years, Brazil has emerged as one of the most frequent and consequential litigants. It has affirmatively used the dispute resolution system more than many emerging and established powers (Table 2.2).

Brazil's WTO has not only been a frequent user of the dispute resolution system, it has done so in high-profile ways. In particular, Brazil has brought cases against the United States and the European Union over what Brazil claims are subsidies for their agriculture sectors. These cases attracted significant attention and have appreciably altered the landscape of international trade law, particularly on questions of subsidies. In the cotton case against the United States, Brazil has sought to follow up its legal victories with broad WTO-authorized trade sanctions to compel full US compliance with the ruling. While Brazil has brought cases against several developing countries, the European Union and the United States have been the focus of its litigation efforts. Of the 26 cases it has brought, 17 have been against either the United States or the European Union. Brazil has also sued Argentina, Canada, Mexico, Peru, South Africa, and Turkey.

In addition to being an active litigant, Brazil has been a lead participant in the Doha Round of global trade talks taking place under the WTO's auspices. During the 2003 negotiations in Cancun, Brazil helped form the G20, which comprised many of the largest developing countries.[8] "[P]oor countries are the greatest victims of the narrow and selfish view that still prevails in international trade," insisted Amorim. The G20 played a critical role in the negotiations and served as a counterweight to the United States and the

Table 2.2 Brazil as WTO Litigant[a]

Member	Cases as WTO complainant	Cases as WTO respondent
United States	105	119
European Union	89	74
Canada	33	17
Brazil	26	14
Mexico	23	14
India	21	22
Japan	18	15

[a] World Trade Organization, available online at http://www.wto.org/english/tratop_e/dispu_e/dispu_by_country_e.htm

European Union. Several scholars have argued that Brazil's diplomatic role was critical in shaping the current WTO negotiating dynamic. Several policymakers from the Global South have argued that 2003 marked a fundamental change in the overall dynamics of multilateralism. Vieira and Alden even asserted that "the unified stance of resistance shown in Cancun by major players in the developing world marked the beginning of a new era in the international relations of the third world" (Vieira and Alden, 2011, pp. 507–528).

Brazil's engagement with the WTO may have entered a different phase now with the selection of veteran diplomat Roberto Azevedo as the organization's director general. It appears that Brazil expended significant diplomatic effort to secure Azevedo's selection. In the final round of the selection process, Azevedo prevailed over Mexican candidate Hermínio Blanco largely because of strong support from developing nations, who perceived the Brazilian as more sympathetic to their perspective on trade issues (*Inside U.S. Trade*, 2013). China publicly welcomed the selection of a BRICS member, citing it as further evidence of emerging-power influence. For her part, Brazilian president Rousseff sought to downplay this aspect of the process. His selection, she said, "is not a victory for Brazil, nor for a group of countries, but a victory for the World Trade Organization" (Agence-France Presse, 2013).

The Bretton Woods Institutions

At the International Monetary Fund (IMF), Brazil is in the process of gradually transitioning from a borrower state to a lending state. In 2002, Brazil received an IMF loan of approximately US$40 billion as investor fears about the country's solvency mounted. That loan was paid back in full in late 2005, two years early. There has been no discussion of further loan packages. In 2010, Brazil moved to a creditor relationship with the IMF when it purchased US$10 billion in IMF-backed notes. Then managing director Dominique Strauss-Kahn at the time lauded the country for demonstrating "strong support to the international economic and financial system."[9]

Brazil has, however, remained a major recipient of World Bank loans. These loans have come through the International Bank for Reconstruction and Development (IBRD), the World Bank arm that lends to middle-income countries. Brazil has consistently ranked as one of the IBRD's top borrowers (Table 2.3).

A World Bank country partnership strategy for FY 2012–2015, finalized in September 2011, serves as the current basis for the Bank's lending.[10] The strategy document broadly endorses Brazil's economic policies for having lifted millions out of poverty but notes that income inequality and environmental

Table 2.3 Top Borrowers, International Bank for Reconstruction and Development, FY 2011

Country	IBRD loans outstanding
China	13.0
Turkey	12.9
Mexico	12.2
India	11.4
Brazil	10.4
Indonesia	8.9
Colombia	7.5

sustainability remain pressing challenges for the government. Given the size of Brazil's economy, the World Bank acknowledges that its lending will have limited impact and should aim to be catalytic in nature.

Brazil is no longer eligible for loans through the International Development Association (IDA), the Bank's concessional-lending arm. While not an IDA recipient, Brazil has also not yet become a significant contributor to IDA: in the latest replenishment round, Brazil contributed only 0.3 percent of IDA's capital stock.[11] This placed Brazil significantly below almost all European countries and several other emerging powers.

Brazil's approach to the governance of the World Bank and the IMF has often mirrored its broad complaint that developed states have excessive influence. It has consistently criticized the custom that a US citizen serves as World Bank president while a European official serves as IMF managing director and has instead advocated an "open and transparent process, without restricting candidacy to one nationality" (Deutsche Presse-Agentur, 2007). It has strongly backed reform of voting shares in the Bank and the IMF. In 2010, the Bank approved reforms that increased Brazil's voting share to 2.24 percent from 2 percent. The IMF hailed these steps as "historic" and pointed out that they represented "a major realignment in the ranking of quota shares that better reflects global economic realities, and a strengthening in the IMF's legitimacy and effectiveness." However, the reforms have so far not been implemented due to resistance in the US Congress.

On more specific issues, Brazil has only occasionally voiced public differences with other key shareholders in these institutions. In part, this relatively muted approach is a function of the unique formal governance structure at the Bank and the IMF and their strong informal consensus culture. On the executive boards of the two institutions, Brazil is represented through an executive director that it appoints. However, this executive director also represents five other countries. Moreover, the decision-making processes at the Bank and the IMF are normally based on informal consensus and tend to be opaque.

However, it is apparent that Brazil has diverged from other board members on a few issues. With China and Russia, Brazil has expressed concern about one of the World Bank's flagship publications, the annual *Doing Business Report*. Alongside other large emerging economies, Brazil criticized the report's methodology and its system of ranking countries in terms of their openness to business activity (the World Bank president appointed a special panel to consider the concerns of these states and a final decision is pending). More recently, Brazil's representative at the IMF also publicly distanced himself from the IMF's lending policies toward the Eurozone countries. But even that discontent was quite restrained; Brazil's director abstained on the Board vote approving the loan rather than opposing it. Confusingly, Brazil also recalled its IMF director after the episode for consultations, leaving some uncertainty as to whether this stance represented considered government policy.

G20

Since the creation of the G20 in 1999, Brazil has been an active member of its consultative group. During the 2008 financial crisis, the G20 began meeting at the level of heads of state, and the group has now declared itself "the premier forum for our economic cooperation."[12] Brazilian officials have welcomed this displacement of the Group of Seven (G7) and Group of Eight (G8) by the G20 as a move toward more effective and representative multilateralism. "No one asks anymore: 'What are you doing here?'" a Brazilian diplomat said in advance of the 2010 G20 summit. "Because it's obvious what Brazil is doing there. It has the weight" (Aly, 2010). While the United States and Europe have emphasized economic and financial coordination, Brazilian officials have often framed participation in the G20 as a means of achieving even more fundamental reform in the world's institutional structure.

BRICS and IBSA

Brazil has expended significant diplomatic effort in the BRICS and IBSA consultative groups. Former foreign minister Amorim has described the BRICS as a "new heavyweight of international relations" (Amorim, 2010). In a recent high point of engagement, Brazil hosted consecutive summit meetings of the BRICS and IBSA groups in April 2010, and again in July 2014. The overlapping membership of BRICS and IBSA has produced questions about duplication. Officially, Brazil maintains that they both serve valuable and distinct purposes, with IBSA having a particular competence in democracy promotion for which BRICS is ill-suited. However it is apparent that the investment of time and resources necessary to keep these groupings active may not always be available. For example, there are recent signs that Brazil may be de-emphasizing IBSA and focusing its efforts on the BRICS grouping (Kasturi, 2013).

While President Lula seemed intent on turning the groups into a centerpiece of Brazilian foreign policy, it is not clear that the Rousseff administration is as committed to seeing the groups becoming operational or serving as the genesis of new multilateral architecture. The political interventions of these groupings have been ad hoc and short-lived. A delegation from IBSA attempted briefly to play a mediating role in the Syria conflict, traveling to the country in August 2011 to encourage a political dialogue (Kasturi, 2013), but it left without having achieved significant gains. IBSA launched a fund for the least-developed countries in 2004 that became operational in 2006. The three countries describe the fund as a "remarkable example of cooperation among three developing countries and [it] constitutes a pioneering initiative to implement South-South cooperation (SSC) for the benefit of other Southern countries in partnership with the UN system."[13]

The 6th BRICS Summit saw the creation of the BRICS Development Bank and the BRICS Contingency Reserve Agreement (CRA), which markedly increase the BRICS grouping's degree of institutionalization. Yet the creation of the new institutions will not destabilize or challenge the global financial architecture for now. The new bank is notable, but does not represent a direct challenge to the World Bank at this point, given the relatively small level of investment to date. Arrangements similar to the BRICS CRA already exist and have not undermined the IMF; indeed, the BRICS CRA is closely modeled on the Chiang Mai Initiative—created in May 2000 between the Association of Southeast Asian Nations (ASEAN) countries as well as China, Japan, and South Korea—which did little to alter global financial order.

Perhaps more notable was that in March 2014, the BRICS countries, in a joint declaration, expressed "concern" over Australian foreign minister Julie Bishop's comment that Russian president Vladimir Putin could be barred from attending the G20 Summit in November. "The custodianship of the G-20 belongs to all member-states equally and no one member-state can unilaterally determine its nature and character," the BRICS said in a statement. The final document also stated that "the escalation of hostile language, sanctions and counter-sanctions, and force does not contribute to a sustainable and peaceful solution, according to international law, including the principles and purposes of the United Nations Charter."[14] Criticism of Australia's threat to exclude

Russia from the G20 served as a clear sign of dissent against Western efforts to enlist the international community in its attempt to isolate Russia.

The Rhetoric of Brazilian Multilateralism

Unsurprisingly, Brazilian leaders have presented an array of different justifications and interpretations for their policy choices at the multilateral level. However, several key rhetorical themes recur in Brazil's recent approach to multilateral institutions. This section outlines these themes and seeks to assess the degree to which they match the reality of Brazilian policy.

Equity for the Developing World

Perhaps the most consistent theme is a stated desire to increase the participation of the developing world at the multilateral level. Policymakers have frequently portrayed Brazil as a champion for the developing world on the global stage and have explicitly linked increasing representation and voice for developing countries with more effective global governance.

> At the crossroads of all the main guidelines of Brazilian foreign policy is the effort to establish closer relations with other developing countries. Building coalitions with developing countries is also a way of engaging in the reform of global governance in order to make international institutions fairer and more democratic. (Amorim, 2010, p. 231)

There are several ways in which this rhetoric meshes with the reality of Brazil's multilateral policy. Brazil's litigation strategy at the WTO has featured prominent cases against the leading developed states, designed to remedy agriculture policies that most observers see as detrimental to the developing world. More broadly, Brazil has insisted in global trade negotiations that the most developed states make significant concessions. In the realm of peace and security, Brazil has often expressed skepticism about Western policies and concerns about double standards regarding the use of force that resonate powerfully with developing-world positions.

There are several points of tension in this aspect of Brazil's multilateralism, however. In its bid to reform the UN Security Council, for example, Brazil has linked its candidacy to those of highly developed Germany and Japan. The G4 initiative is therefore difficult to frame as one designed to boost the influence of the developing world. More broadly, the phenomenon of special privileges for the world's largest states—via permanent Security Council seats or membership in groupings like the G20—sits uneasily with the emphasis of many developing states on greater equality in multilateral forums.

Emphasis on Noncoercive Means

A second key theme in Brazilian multilateralism has been skepticism of coercion as a tool of multilateral diplomacy. This theme became most pronounced in the context of Brazil's diplomatic initiative toward Iran in 2010. In that context, President Lula emphasized the distinction between Brazil's approach and that of the Western powers. "I will try to use the power of persuasion in this dialogue," he said. Brazilian foreign minister Amorim insisted that Brazil would not "bow down" to a consensus that additional sanctions were required. As he prepared to visit Tehran in 2010, President Lula presented the Brazilian–Turkish initiative as fundamentally distinct from the Council's punitive approach. "People aren't talking," he said. "I'm going there to talk." When the Council imposed a new round of sanctions on Iran shortly thereafter, both Brazil and Turkey opposed it. Brazil's UN ambassador insisted that "[w]e do not see sanctions as an effective instrument in this case" (Macfarquhar, 2010).

In discussing Brazil's participation in the Haiti peacekeeping mission, President Lula also emphasized the mission's noncoercive nature, often pointing out that peacekeeping forces no longer merely played the role of police, but that they should build confidence. In even broader terms, senior Brazilian diplomats have insisted that the use of multilateral instruments to isolate and condemn states is counterproductive. Amorim made this point in the context of human rights. "The exercise of human rights is more effectively ensured by dialogue and cooperation than by arrogant attitudes derived from self-declared moral superiority. A harsh condemnation of this or that country in Geneva or New York, based on a self-ascribed position of moral high ground, does little to ameliorate the situation of those perishing in the field" (Amorim, 2010).

Brazil's insistence on noncoercive means clearly has roots in Brazil's own restrained military posture and strategic situation. At times, Brazilian officials have linked their preference for noncoercive means explicitly to Brazil's own practices. In the midst of the Iran diplomacy, for example, Lula presented Brazil as "a country with the smallest number of weapons." In this sense, Brazilian officials have suggested that the country's lack of global military ambitions gives it a different profile and enhanced credibility as a global actor. As the statements above indicate, however, the emphasis on noncoercive means also draws on a deep belief that coercion is unlikely to succeed.

It can be asked whether Brazil maintains this position consistently and will be able to do so in the future. Two quite distinct experiences have recently strained this principle. In its Haiti peacekeeping role, Brazil faced significant criticism for not more actively confronting gangs and criminals. Eventually, with Brazilian acquiescence if not enthusiasm, the peacekeeping force adopted a more assertive posture that produced several clashes between peacekeepers and armed members of Haitian society. While Brazil has insisted that the peacekeeping force remains fundamentally consensual, the shift toward more assertive policing may foreshadow a broader reckoning with the dilemmas of modern peacekeeping. In a very different multilateral context, Brazil has also found itself moving toward coercive measures. At the WTO, Brazil has sought stiff penalties against the United States in order to compel compliance with WTO rulings on agriculture subsidies. While this kind of penalty is provided for in the WTO agreements, it is in tension with the frequent Brazilian refrain that sanctions and other forms of economic coercion are an ineffective means of achieving policy change.

Accountability and Consistency

In several contexts, Brazilian officials have argued in favor of greater consistency and accountability in the multilateral arena. They have criticized double standards and what they portray as abuse of multilateral instruments by the most powerful states. Prominent examples of this theme include the "responsibility while protecting (RwP)" initiative and Brazil's criticism of exceptions to ICC jurisdiction for certain states.

This emphasis has been pursued unevenly, however. In the context of the UN's role in Haiti—the peacekeeping mission in which Brazil has invested the most energy and resources—Brazilian officials have been largely silent on the question of the UN's role in fomenting the nation's devastating cholera epidemic (poor sanitation practices by the Brazilian-led United Nations Stabilization Mission in Haiti [MINUSTAH] are believed to have led to the outbreak). In other contexts as well, Brazil's policy has been significantly more restrained than its rhetoric. While Brazilian officials have often criticized the World Bank and IMF, they continue to draw on Bank loans and contributed additional funds to the IMF recently. Brazil's effort to omit rankings from the Bank's *Doing Business Report*, moreover, suggests a willingness to encourage less transparency rather than more in certain circumstances (Bosco, 2011). If Brazil acquires greater influence in multilateral forums, it may find itself the recipient of calls for accountability as often as it dispenses them.

Conclusion

It has been argued that Brazil's distinctive approach to multilateralism may come under strain as the country's powers and responsibilities in the international system evolve. The ultimate resolution of that tension will likely involve some combination of shifts in Brazil's approach and changes to the international architecture itself. How much change Brazil is able to accomplish will, in turn, depend on whether it can maintain meaningful linkages with other emerging powers and whether it can persuade established Western powers of the merits of its approach. Those two strategies—working as an emerging power bloc and swaying the established powers—may not be entirely compatible. If Brazil works mostly in conjunction with countries like China, India, and South Africa, it can amplify its influence, but there is a danger that the joint approach may generate antagonism or suspicion among the more established powers. Deft diplomacy will be required if Brazil is to reshape the multilateral architecture.

Notes

1. There is no consensus on what constitutes an emerging power or a rising power. While China is at times called a "rising power" (see, e.g., Florini, 2011; Ikenberry, 2011a), others argue that it is well established within today's institutions such as the UN Security Council (Johnston, 2003). Brazil and India are at times called "middle powers" (e.g., Alden and Vieira, 2005), "rising powers" (e.g., Hurrell, 2008) or "emerging powers" (e.g., Cohen, 2002). The latter two terms will be used interchangeably here, as is common in the literature (see, e.g., Schweller, 2011).
2. UN Security Council Resolution 1973 (March 17, 2011).
3. Provisional Records of the Security Council, S/PV.6498 (March 17, 2011).
4. Provisional Records of the Security Council, S/PV.6491 (February 26, 2011).
5. See "UN rights council appoints international Syria inquiry panel," Reuters, September 12, 2011.
6. See, for example, Council of the European Union, "Factsheet: EU-Brazil Summit, 24 February 2014" (noting that "the EU and Brazil are like-minded on many issues such as death penalty . . . and have agreed to join forces to advance them at the UN"), available at http://www.consilium.europa.eu/uedocs/cms_data/docs/pressdata/EN/foraff/141088.pdf
7. See "Brazil's UN vote on Iran marks first great difference between Dilma and Lula da Silva," Merco Press, March 26, 2011.
8. This G20 should not be confused with the G20 which has served as a broad consultative group on global financial and economic matters.
9. IMF Press Release No. 09/207 (June 10, 2009).

10. World Bank, Country Partnership Strategy for FY 2012–2015, available online athttp://documents.worldbank.org/curated/en/2011/09/15273914/brazil-country-partnership-strategy-cps-period-fy2012-2015

11. World Bank, "Contributions to IDA Replenishment 16," available online at http://www.worldbank.org/ida/papers/IDA16_Donor_Contributions_Table_1.pdf

12. G20 Leaders' Statement, The Pittsburgh Summit (September 24–25, 2009).

13. See the IBSA mission statement, available online at http://tcdc2.undp.org/IBSA/

14. Chairperson's Statement on the BRICS Foreign Ministers Meeting held on March 24, 2014 in The Hague, Netherlands http://www.dfa.gov.za/docs/2014/brics0324.html

CHAPTER 3

The Brazilian Liberal Tradition and the Global Liberal Order

João M. E. Maia and Matthew M. Taylor

A famous Brazilian Marxist once wrote that liberalism was a "misplaced idea" in nineteenth-century Brazil (Schwarz, 1973).[1] After all, how could one speak of liberalism in a society marked by slavery, patronage, and other forms of personal domination? Liberals in contemporary Brazil, meanwhile, argue that the failures and shortcomings of the Brazilian economy stem from the lack of "real" liberalism in a society where corporatism and populism flourish (e.g., Pinheiro and Giambiagi, 2006). Observers across the political spectrum largely agree: liberalism and Brazil are two words that do not go together.

This chapter challenges this conventional wisdom by recognizing that there is a lengthy liberal tradition in Brazil, although this liberalism has been accompanied by a uniquely Brazilian critique. The central argument is that the challenges that liberalism faced throughout Brazil's efforts to achieve democracy, and the existence of influential intellectual currents critical of liberalism-as-practiced, contribute to a revisionist, idiosyncratic Brazilian approach to the globally dominant Anglo-Saxon notions of liberalism. The history of the Brazilian liberal tradition helps to explain the contemporary beliefs held by the country's elite, which differ in significant ways from mainstream liberalism elsewhere in the world. Further, these beliefs about liberalism in domestic politics carry over into Brazilian beliefs about liberalism on the international stage.

As a consequence, although Brazil accepts the "high returns" provided by the global institutions present in the liberal international order, it nonetheless rejects key remnants of hierarchy present in a world order characterized by "institutionalized constitutionalism" (Ikenberry, 2011a, p. 268) and actively seeks reforms to the global order championed by Washington.

These intellectual traditions have not infrequently caused Brazilian foreign policy to proceed in a direction that diverges not only from the dominant American liberal paradigm, but also from the positions of the other BRIC nations (Brazil, Russia, India, and China) and from those of social democracies such as Canada and the European Union.

The Brazilian case is thus a powerful example of "norm localization," a process by which local actors evaluate outside ideas about the world order and reconstitute them based on their own past experience (Acharya, 2009). It is also a case of norms-moderation, rather than passive norm-acceptance, on the part of emerging powers. Brazilian elites and policymakers do not accept the global liberal order unquestioningly, and in evaluating the explicit and implicit rules of behavior of actors within that order, frequently emphasize slightly different norms and prioritize norms differently than the dominant powers. Brazilian ideas about liberalism thus help to explain the foundations of this large emerging nation's preferences and strategies, and their effects on Brazil's potential roles in the international system, whether as "challenger," "new influential," "reformer," "free rider," or "responsible stakeholder" (Kahler, 2013).

Critics have noted several potential problems with using ideas to explain foreign policy positions. Ideas, defined as the beliefs held by individuals (Goldstein and Keohane, 1993, p. 3), can be difficult to pin down, and broad stereotypes are always subject to exceptions. Furthermore, national self-interest plays a highly relevant role in Brazil's foreign policy postures (Burges, 2013), and ideas may therefore serve only to provide a veneer of legitimacy to what is cold, self-interested calculation. Complicating matters is the vast ideological spread apparent in Brazil's multiparty system, which makes it difficult to speak of a broad ideational consensus that might have explanatory power. Further, ideas are not solely determinative: the structure of the international system, current events, agency, leadership, institutions, and capabilities all play an important role in determining how nations behave.

These issues pose some limits on the argument presented here. Yet there is an inherent value to exploring competing ideas about liberalism, if only because there is increasing recognition in the field of international relations that ideas can have a causal effect on policy by dint of their function as road maps, as tools for strategy choice, and as embedded guides that forge a sense of common purpose within institutions.[2] By discussing the broad political and intellectual debates that have developed concerning the liberal tradition in Brazil, this chapter aims to offer insights into a variety of Brazilian postures on the world stage. A "tradition" presupposes a sense of continuity that is consciously evoked and recreated by different generations that resort to political languages in order to act meaningfully and to justify their actions. The chapter turns first to liberalism as one of many intellectual currents in the

Brazilian political tradition, before addressing the dominant critique of economic liberalism in twentieth-century Brazil (a subject further developed in Porzecanski and Villela's contributions to this volume [Chapters 8 and 9]) and the economic ideas of "development" and "dependency" that dominated Brazilian debates between the 1950s and 1980s. The chapter concludes with an assessment of the effects of these ideas on Brazilian foreign policy postures.

Liberalism within the Brazilian Political Tradition

A variety of historical currents have shaped Brazilian political thinking with regard to liberalism. Influences include the legacies of colonialism; the clan-based, patrimonial distribution of regional power during both the Empire and the First Republic; the tenuous territorial integrity of the nation well into the early 1900s; and the very recent incorporation of the broader citizenry into a national project. From the early 1800s through the present, Brazilian liberals have been buffeted between the distinct priorities of the liberal project—seeking to achieve individual rights, equal citizenship, political freedom, economic liberty, and local autonomy while checking state power—and the opposition to liberalism found in often dominant political viewpoints, including the conservative dominance of the mid-nineteenth century, the positivist groups of the early twentieth century, and the developmentalist project of the second half of the twentieth century. Under challenging conditions, liberalism has survived, but it has done so frequently by prioritizing one or another component of the liberal project over others, or simply by remaining a passive, critical voice on the sidelines of the dominant political debate.

After declaring independence, Brazil maintained a constitutional monarchy. The 1824 Constitution, which was imposed by Emperor Pedro I, provided a check on representative politics by granting the Emperor the so-called *Poder Moderador* (moderating power). This *Poder Moderador* was in essence the power to act as the final arbiter on politics, enabling the Emperor to nominate the prime minister of his own choosing, as well as to dissolve the Chamber of Deputies. The Constitution also concentrated power in the hands of the central state, a fact that generated bitter resentment among the provinces of the north, where support for federalism and liberalism was far greater (Machado and Mello, 2004).

From 1824 onward, the debate over constitutional interpretation became central to understanding the dynamics of the Brazilian political system. Liberals argued for an English model of constitutional monarchy, supporting different measures that checked the power of the Emperor and favoring policies that granted more rights to the provinces. Conservatives and even some moderate liberals, however, supported the thesis that the Emperor's *Poder Moderador* was essential to preserving stability, and would prevent Brazil from following the path of its Spanish American neighbors, whose wars of independence were followed by lengthy processes of political fragmentation (Lynch, 2009). The Brazilian conservative elite regarded these bloody civil wars as examples of the dangers of republicanism and radical federalism, and they successfully impeded the liberal federalist project until the resignation of the first emperor, Pedro I, in 1831.

Pedro I's resignation heralded the nineteenth-century apogee of radical liberalism, and during the 1830s, liberal groups fostered political reforms seeking greater local autonomy and decentralization of political power to provincial elites. A sequence of crises and revolts, however, prompted a conservative reaction known as the *Regresso*. In 1840, the son of Pedro I was declared mature enough to reign (becoming Pedro II) and the conservative factions seized power once again. This period is known in historical research as the *Saquarema* period, and it was marked by the consolidation of the central state and some degree of political stability (Mattos, 1987).

Classical Brazilian historiography interprets this period as the key moment for Brazilian nation-building (Carvalho, 1975; Holanda, 1985), but it was also a low point for liberals. The main leaders of this process were conservative politicians who sought centralization and moderate reform. The state was regarded as the main political actor, with the mission of bringing civilization to Brazil's hinterland. This project was buttressed by the writings of conservatives such as Paulino José Soares de Souza (1807–1866) and Bernardo Pereira de Vasconcelos (1795–1850), two key figures who wrote in support of the *Poder Moderador*. Meanwhile, elsewhere in South America, liberals largely set aside their concern with individual rights to focus on nation-building, depleting any sense of common cause that might have offered succor to Brazilian liberals.

Brazilian liberals could have found other problems to address: the Brazilian Empire was based on slavery and on a very unequal concentration of land, for example. Meanwhile, the 1824 Constitution granted civil rights to all Brazilian citizens (except slaves), but restricted political rights to those who had been born free and held a certain amount of property. During the following decades, race would be a regular source of social tension as non-whites had to constantly prove that they were not current or runaway slaves (Mattos, 2000). The Liberal Party,[3] however, shied away from these issues until the 1870s, and the most important reforms regarding either slavery or the slave trade were passed under Conservative cabinets.[4] Rather than focus on these social issues, however, liberals during the nineteenth century primarily concerned themselves with changing *political* institutions, via electoral and judicial reforms, separation of powers, and decentralization (Carvalho, 2009; Werneck Vianna, 1997). They did not address social issues such as slavery and rural property that might have expanded their appeal to a broader swathe of the population.

It is no small irony, then, that the end of slavery would lead to the dissolution of the Empire and the subsequent rise of liberal government in 1889. Following a lengthy period of anti-slavery mobilization,[5] the Emperor gradually imposed the abolition of slavery on the landowners, carrying out incremental advances between the first speech from the throne in 1868 and the partial reforms of the *Lei dos Sexagenarios* and the *Lei do Ventre Livre* two decades later. In the wake of the gradual dissolution of the Empire and transition to republicanism, liberal dominance seemed assured, guaranteed by the institutional structure designed by jurist and statesman Rui Barbosa and his colleagues, and the complete breakdown of the conservative coalition. The Republican Constitution of 1891 was modeled after the US Constitution: Brazil was renamed "The United States of Brazil" and the local states were granted several powers that were once held by the Imperial state.

But the question of how to incorporate the populace remained unresolved (Santos, 1992, p. 19). The promise of the First Republic (1889–1930) was undermined by deals that preserved the dominance of southeastern states, leading to an elitist regime with highly restricted suffrage. Early political turmoil led ruling elites to enforce political order through an arrangement that restricted political participation and guaranteed the power of local elites in their own provinces (Lessa, 1988). At the national level, power-sharing between elites from the dominant states of Minas Gerais and São Paulo greatly restricted the progressive character of the new republic. The failure of the liberal First Republic to find a satisfactory solution to this elite *Café com Leite* pact for political alternation, combined with rising regional disparities and the obvious failure to modernize, generated widespread dissatisfaction.

Meanwhile, throughout the First Republic (1889–1930) political turbulence never ceased to threaten the political system. As disappointment with the Republic grew, a group of intellectuals argued that liberalism and particularly the ingenuous acceptance of liberal ideals without reflection on their practical application within Brazil's unique social and political context were partly to blame. This group was formed by a generation that came of age in the 1920s, as distaste with republicanism reached its apogee. Many of them drew on the ideas of Alberto Torres (1865–1917), a former politician and a respected social thinker. In their view, liberalism was to be blamed for the lack of progress in Brazil. Oliveira Vianna (1883–1951) and Vicente Licínio

Cardoso (1889–1931) criticized the liberal Constitution of 1891 for its federalism, faulting the Constitution for granting local elites too much power, leaving the central state weak and incapacitated. They argued that the liberal American model did not reflect Brazilian reality, turning the Constitution into a "fiction" with no organic ties to society.

Critics from both right and left discredited Rui Barbosa and his so-called "lawyerly liberalism" (*bachalerismo liberal*) for reifying institutions and failing to consider the power of deeper social forces in the functioning of political institutions. Arguing against institutional fetishism, they noted that it was not sufficient to simply adopt good laws and good institutions—such as an independent court, federalism, or an active Parliament—to produce a good society (Brandão, 2001, p. 33; Santos, 1978a, 1978b). A strong central state would be essential to modernization, in their view. Long before Schwarz labeled it an "out of place idea," then, liberalism was being criticized as unsuited to Brazilian reality, imported by elites with little recognition of liberalism's incompatibility to a former colony with a long history of slavery and local strongmen. Liberalism-as-practiced was derided for its debasement of the central tenets of liberal theory: failing to achieve its universal pretensions, overcome patrimonialism, and achieve the promised ends of liberty and representation.

Meanwhile, a deep-seated sense of fragility and vulnerability took hold of Brazil by the 1920s, fomenting a nationalist, modernizing, centralizing push with support from across the ideological spectrum. This push reached its zenith by the centenary of Independence in 1922, during which the first *Semana de Arte Moderna* was held, celebrating modernist design and art; the Brazilian Communist Party was founded, heralding the rise of an urban proletariat; and the *Movimento Tenentista* (Lieutenants' Movement) consolidated its rebellion, seeking profound reforms and the development of the interior (Comparato, 2001, p. 97). These challengers, in disparate ways, were pushing for modernization, greater incorporation, and broader territorial penetration by the central state.

Conservatives found common cause with these demands, a move that is perhaps best encapsulated in the work of Oliveira Vianna, whose *Populações Meridionais* (1918) expressed concern at the possibility of democratic revolution, in part because it threatened the one great legacy of the Empire: the construction of a national state, however weak (Werneck Vianna, 2001, p. 38). In Oliveira Vianna's view, a strong state was essential to overcome the power of local elites and reduce regional fragmentation. Such a state could not develop "organically," but would need to be created by a strong hand: Oliveira Vianna argued that the only place in the country where the populace had acquired political consciousness was Rio Grande do Sul, where the *gauchos* had been forced to organize to resist the ongoing threat from Argentina (Brandão, 2007, pp. 21–67). Many, if not most, of these modernizers saw liberal democracy as a dangerous illusion, which would be vulnerable to exploitation by regional *coronéis* and elites, and thus fail to protect citizens against powerful local actors. Unlike Europe and the United States, where the state was seen as the primary threat to civil liberties, in Brazil, the state was the only possible guarantor of civil liberties (Brandão, 2007, p. 47). In a nation governed by local power brokers, only a strong central government would be able to protect individual rights. This state-centric consensus was both a reaction to, and a negation of, the liberalism practiced during the First Republic.

This growing anti-liberal consensus set the stage for the so-called *Revolução de 1930*, which began an era of political centralization and economic interventionism. Getulio Vargas harnessed the modernizers' reformist impetus to win office and hold it in increasingly authoritarian ways between 1930 and 1945. He was able to coopt the military, which had little difficulty in recognizing that it stood to gain from Vargas' modernizing efforts and from the accompanying centralization of government and increasing industrialization, which together resulted in a larger cut of the budget flowing to the military, and the elimination of the national military's territorial rivals such as the state *Guarda Nacional* (Santos, 1992, p. 25). In 1937, Vargas and the armed forces instituted an authoritarian regime known as the *Estado Novo* that lasted until Vargas' ouster in 1945.[6] During the *Estado Novo*, a wide spectrum of political groups supported the idea that the state must play a central role in the political process. The intellectuals that wrote against liberalism in the 1920s were now in power, and some of them took up their pen to support the new order. Oliveira Vianna, for instance, became chief legal consultant to the Ministry of Labor (Gomes, 1993).

A corollary of political centralization, on both right and left, was administrative modernization: the creation of a strong central bureaucracy, with the capacity to impose the central government's will at the local level. Especially under Vargas' government, the state bureaucracy grew significantly in scale and capacity. This pattern of development in many ways reversed the European model of state formation and citizenship. In Brazil, the state and the armed forces "acquired their collective identities before the liberal ideology achieved hegemony in the universe of values in dispute for purposes of political socialization" (Santos, 1992, pp. 31–32). Political parties did not mobilize to create or empower the bureaucracy or the military, and these state actors in many ways preceded popular participation in politics, in the process weakening subsequent partisan politics and patterns of popular incorporation. The result, as Santos emphasizes, is that social policy was used—in an uneven and top-down manner that favored urban workers—to resolve the crisis of popular incorporation; as a consequence, politics remains bifurcated to this day between the autonomous technocratic bureaucracy and the democratic political process.

Development on the Periphery

Brazilian economic thought has reinforced the anti-liberal ideas present in the political sphere, especially from the 1950s onward. Brazilians have found much to disagree with in classical liberal economic thought, ranging from Ricardian theory to contemporary orthodox economics. Many of these critiques evolved out of the nation's unique position as a developing nation, which led its community of economists and bureaucrats to develop a unique view of state-led development in the wake of the Great Depression and World War II. It is no coincidence that two important currents of critical economic theory—structuralism and developmentalism—were heavily influenced by the Brazilian experience. As responses to the empirical realities of Brazil's reaction to the Depression and War, these ideas then became full-blown theories in their own right by the early 1950s. They would also trigger the development of dependency theory, an influential depiction of the *political* repercussions of *economic* underdevelopment at the periphery of the world order.

Structuralism argued that underdeveloped economies such as Brazil's faced substantively different constraints than those faced by developed economies, and that capitalism on the "periphery" of the global order was historically unique, rather than merely being an early stage of capitalist development. It argued, too, that economic relations with the developed world would not always yield the same economic gains for underdeveloped nations that they yielded for developed nations. Working in dialogue—if not always in complete sync[7]—with Raul Prebisch and (UN Economic Commission for Latin America and the Caribbean) CEPAL, Brazilian economists such as Celso Furtado argued that peripheral development was a unique phenomenon, marked by syndromes of low productivity and excessive consumption (largely by elites), which in turn triggered unemployment, chronic deterioration in terms of trade, structural imbalances in the balance of payments, and structural inflation. Peripheral nations that specialized in commodity exports, such as Brazil, would be particularly vulnerable to deteriorating terms of trade, given that industrial products were consistently advancing technologically, contributing to improving worker productivity in the wealthy countries, while commodities showed negligible productivity gains. At home, Latin American structuralists sought a strong government role in the allocation of scarce savings within the domestic market to rationally plan and carry out investments and policies—including trade protections—that would help develop nascent industry.

The second—and highly inter-twined—school of thought was developmentalism, "the ideology of overcoming underdevelopment through capitalist industrialization, planned and supported by the state" (Bielschowsky, 1988, p. 431). Although it had origins in the writings of Alberto Torres in the 1910s, developmentalism arose as a practical response both to the shortages of the post-war era and to structural theories of savings allocation. At its broadest, it incorporated the notion that economic modernization was needed to permit social development, which would then facilitate the implementation of a stable democracy (Comparato, 2001, p. 100). This broad focus on development as an instrument to resolve political instability, social inclusion, and economic well-being has been central to the goals of the developmental state, regardless of ideological stripe, throughout much of the past sixty years. But even at its narrowest, *desenvolvimentismo* is both theoretically and technically ambitious: beginning from the structuralist argument that spontaneous market forces will never achieve efficient and rational industrialization on their own, developmentalists argued that state planning was needed to define the strategy for development, prioritize sectors for expansion, and allocate resources effectively to them (Bielschowsky, 1988, p. 7).

While important distinctions emerged among Brazilian economists with regard to structural and developmentalist theories and policy prescriptions, there was a high degree of consensus around their central tenets. As Bielschowsky's magisterial treatment of the economic thought of the postwar period demonstrates, developmentalists of varying stripes such as Ary Torres, Lucas Lopes, Celso Furtado, and Roberto Simonsen found common ground with more left-leaning or idiosyncratic thinkers such as Caio Prado, Nelson Sodré, and Ignacio Rangel in their commitment to resolving underdevelopment through state action. Their influence dominated thinking both within government bodies, such as the Brazilian development bank (BNDE), as well as outside it, as in industrial associations such as National Industrial Confederation (CNI) and São Paulo State Federation of Industry (FIESP). Even the so-called "monetarists"—such as Eugenio Gudin and Roberto Campos—were still very much Keynesian in their thinking and committed to state action; they were labeled "monetarists" primarily because they opposed the structuralist theory of inflation,[8] rather than because they were anti-developmentalist.

A third important stream of thinking built upon structuralism was the concept of dependency. Like the structuralists, *dependentistas* were concerned with the "alleged properties of unequal exchange embedded in the international economic system and perpetuated by economic orthodoxy" (Taylor, 1998, p. 6), including but not limited to the tendency of the global trading system to systematically marginalize lesser-developed nations in what Prebisch termed the "periphery." Dependency theory built not only on these economic arguments, but also on many strands of national political thought, to argue that underdevelopment was largely an outcome of a subaltern position in the global order. Influential thinkers such as Caio Prado had noted that the history of the colonial era was in many ways a reflection of the global expansion of capitalism, while Florestan Fernandes argued that democracy faced special problems because of Brazil's position on the capitalist periphery. At its core, then, dependency authors emphasized the political implications of this capitalist system, especially how economic relations with the "center" impacted class formation, economic structure, political coalitions, and institutions in the "periphery" (Cardoso and Faletto, 1968; Coatsworth, 2004, p. 134). The diffusion of dependency theory gained stimulus from the political events of the 1960s and 1970s, which provided a gripping illustration of the close "confluence of interests between Latin American bourgeoisies, foreign capital, the U.S. government, and Latin American militaries" (Haber, 1997, p. 10).

Developmentalism and structuralist thought hit their stride in the 1960s, but underwent a period of crisis during the 1970s. Rising world trade, a changing geopolitical scenario, the increasing hegemony of orthodox economics in leading universities, and the glaring counterfactual example of the Asian tigers' growth all cast a shadow over the Latin American prescription for development. These trends would reach critical levels with the debt crisis of the early 1980s.

Yet despite these challenges, Brazil remained averse to liberal or neoliberal prescriptions. Even as it negotiated its debt obligations under the Brady Plan, undertook several increasingly radical anti-inflation plans, and subjected itself to International Monetary Fund (IMF) conditionalities in the late 1980s and 1990s, economists within the Brazilian government argued against adopting the most stringent tenets of the Washington Consensus. It is worth recalling that the heterodox *Real* Plan—Brazil's final, successful effort to tackle hyperinflation—never received the blessing of the IMF, and even as the Cardoso administration moved to privatize and modernize the economy during the "neoliberal" 1990s, many of the institutions created under developmentalism remained in place. This is not to say that the "neoliberal" 1990s did not change Brazil. But the changes may have even reinforced some of the previous pragmatism and heterodoxy in Brazilian economic thought. And in any case, the neoliberal experience did little to change hearts, especially because the reforms in Latin America coincided with the worst twenty-five years of growth in a century (Coatsworth, 2005, p. 137).

As a consequence, over the past decade, a "new developmentalism" has emerged in practice and, increasingly, in theory. As a strategy, it emphasizes Keynesian macroeconomics, structuralist development macroeconomics, and suspicion of conventional economic orthodoxy (Bresser-Pereira, 2009, pp. 7, 16). One of its strengths is unintended but fortuitous: because it coincides with democratic consolidation in Brazil, this new developmentalist approach has been marked by pragmatic responses to voter demands for a stable currency and a more effective state, preserving the currency against external shocks and pressures from protected sectors, without falling prey to populism. In this sense, it has avoided many of the most perverse consequences of the old model, particularly the production of inter-regional and inter-group income inequalities (Arbix and Martin, 2010, p. 8), as well as the inflation trap. The nation was helped in this regard by the commodities boom and prudent macroeconomic policies: during the crisis of 2008, Brazil could draw on its strong foreign currency reserves to glide through the crisis, with Lula even praising his country's resilience to this crisis made by "white people with blue eyes."

The state-led project continues, albeit with changes. Many aspects of the old developmentalism were jettisoned, and the new developmentalism is not simply a revival of the old variant, although many of the central driving ideas remain (Arbix and Martin, 2010, p. 6). The past two decades have brought the abandonment of some of the most egregious institutional manifestations of state inefficiencies, such as corruption-ridden regional development agencies like the Superintendency for Amazon Development (SUDAM), inefficiency-generating trade control boards, and sky-high tariff protections. At the level of ideas, structuralist theories of inflation and a closed economy were also shed, as was import-substituting industrialization. But the past twenty years did not bring an end to the predominant view that the state is the essential player in development and that markets are unable to provide development if left to their own devices. Likewise, very much alive is the notion that the development of peripheral economies is a historically unique process that cannot be accomplished without guided state action.

The state remains a crucial actor, providing credit, tax breaks, export financing, and training to a select group of champions. Indeed, many agencies—such as the BNDES[9]—were remade in new clothes and retasked to new priorities, while remaining attuned to the legislated mandate of promoting "national development" (Hochstetler and Montero, Forthcoming; Armijo, Forthcoming). The BNDES' cross-shareholdings, through BNDESpar, provide it considerable leverage over large private companies and former state-owned enterprises (Lazzarini, 2010; Lazzarini et al., 2011; Musacchio and Lazzarini, 2014). State banks continue to provide the bulk of credit, nudging the private sector to the technocracy's policy priorities. While Lula was forced by financial markets to sign on to fiscal responsibility and to uphold his predecessor's commitment to the policies that had overcome inflation, this "conversion to neoliberalism" (Hochstetler, 2011, p. 6) was limited, in part because even under Cardoso's reformist administration, Brazil had made only a very partial and hesitant conversion.

To sum up: the dominant actors in Brazilian politics for much of the past century have expressed ample support for a strong central state which can protect individual rights against powerful patrimonial elites, promote the broader public good, and carry out the national project, however defined. This consensus lies behind perhaps the most influential trend in twentieth-century Brazilian political history: the growing autonomy of the state bureaucracy, and the central state's dominant role in most important social, structural, and economic transformations, under both authoritarian and democratic regimes. The autonomy of the bureaucracy was a key conditioning factor both during the guided transition to democracy in the 1980s, as well as in the extension of social policies to the poor during the drafting of the 1988 Constitution. The bureaucracy has never been fully free from external pressures of politicization and interest group pressures, but presidents since Getulio Vargas have been able to count on "pockets of excellence" that have enabled them to carry forward autonomous policy projects (e.g., Abrucio et al., 2010; Andrews and Bariani, 2010; Bersch et al., Forthcoming; Geddes, 1994; Nunes, 1997). The central conceit that guided all of these efforts was the justification of state action based on the state's purported ability to represent the "national interest," above the petty disputes of individual political actors (Werneck Vianna, 2001, p. 40).

Under these conditions, the intellectual tradition of political liberalism has struggled mightily. Liberals in Brazil still regard themselves as "lonely warriors" who are condemned to start from scratch under each new political regime. The challenges liberals face, though, go beyond the faults of liberalism-as-practiced, reflecting the historical weakness of the democratic tradition in Brazil. The dominance of positivist-inspired modernizing objectives on both Left and Right meant that for much of the twentieth century, the "national question" was considered more important than the preservation of individual rights and political democracy. Under these conditions, the classical defense of individual rights inherent to liberalism could not be realized, and liberalism was seen either as dangerously ingenuous, lacking discernment of real-world conditions, or as willfully deceitful, allied to the worst impulses of retrograde elites.

Foreign Policy Thought

These dominant political and economic worldviews have provided the foreign ministry (Itamaraty) with considerable autonomy that it has sought to use to overcome the nation's founding fragility and vulnerability, as well as to engage in a defensive effort that reflected the prevailing suspicion of the most simplistic expressions of liberal institutionalism both at home and abroad. Brazil's early period of independence, in which it was often in a position of subservience toward great powers, did a great deal to shape dominant Brazilian foreign policy postures. In the pursuit of state sovereignty and territorial integrity against the great powers, Brazilian diplomats developed a significant commitment to modernization, the instrumental use of multilateral treaties, and the construction of international prestige.

Many facets of Brazil's foreign policy thinking originated in the traumatic first century after independence. Independence did not bring rapid recognition from Europe, and in fact, the conditions under which the major powers agreed to recognize Brazilian sovereignty were harsh: an indemnity paid to Portugal, most favored nation status for Great Britain, and special concessions to Britain and France, including extraterritorial rights for their citizens and special tariff protections, between 1822 and 1845 (Rodrigues, 1962). In 1844, Brazil declared that its 1827 treaty with Britain, which included a commitment to halt the slave trade, had lapsed. The British responded with the Aberdeen Bill of 1845, which permitted British Navy ships to board and seize Brazilian merchant vessels suspected of participating in the slave trade. While the Brazilian government favored the end of the slave trade, it had been too weak to actually halt it as agreed by the treaty. The Aberdeen Bill triggered Brazilian resentment, yet Brazil was also too weak to resist the British policy, and suffered from aggressive British naval actions throughout much of the subsequent two decades, including the blockade of Rio in 1861. The Brazilian State Council complained bitterly of the Aberdeen Bill as an abuse of power that "threatens the rights and privileges of all free and independent peoples" (Feldman, 2009, p. 550).

During the second half of the nineteenth century and the first quarter of the twentieth, a recurring concern was the vulnerability of Brazil to foreign intervention and threats to its territorial integrity. These were substantiated by loss of the Cisplantine Province soon after independence; international pressures to open the Amazon to international shipping, which Brazil acceded to in 1867; and the War of the Triple Alliance (1864–1870), a conflict that was driven in part by Brazil's fear that Paraguay's increasing militarization threatened the integrity of its western Mato Grosso province. Rio Branco, the leading diplomatic statesman between 1893 and 1912, built his formidable reputation by resolving most of the country's pending border controversies, as well as purchasing the Acre territory, with an area larger than France (Burns, 1970, p. 234). But there was still considerable concern with the country's small population and its inability to populate the interior. Partly as a result, Brazilian policymakers sought throughout the twentieth century to use treaties to peacefully establish the country's boundaries in international law. A leading diplomatic historian of this period argued that "as a country potentially subject to attack on account of her small population and her rich but unexploited resources, Brazil adopted, vis-à-vis Europe and the United States, a pacifist ideology, favoring international arbitration. Brazilian foreign policy has always preferred juridical to political solutions" (Rodrigues, 1962, p. 325). Brazilian foreign policymakers have also been strong defenders of state sovereignty as a principle, decrying foreign interventions that threaten territorial integrity elsewhere. The fear of foreign designs on Brazilian territory is one of the lasting traits of Brazilian foreign policy discourse, ranging across governments of all ideological stripes. Even today, a strong majority of Brazilians believe that it is likely or extremely likely that a foreign power will invade to seize the nation's Amazon resources (67%) or its pre-salt reserves (63%; IPEA, 2011).

Accompanying the focus on sovereignty and territorial integrity has been the vital emphasis on modernization as a safeguard against foreign encroachment. Examples can be found across much of Brazilian history, whether it was in Visconde de Uruguai's suggestion that the best way to address the British threat would be through modernizing production, the *tenentista* movement's desire to incorporate the *sertão* into the modern nation during the 1920s, or the military regime's push to colonize the Amazon in the 1960s and 1970s.

The first century of Brazilian independence also contributed to a healthy skepticism toward international treaties and conventions. There has been a recurring tension about the role of international treaties in Brazilian foreign policy circles, pitting those who saw treaties as the only available way to bind stronger powers against critics who blasted the inherent injustice of international treaties. For example, in response to a US proposal for a trade agreement in the 1860s, the Viscount of Abaeté argued internally that trade agreements are promoted with "caustic perseverance" by the wealthiest nations, and should be cautiously evaluated, since they tend to amplify the inequalities of the international arena (Feldman, 2009, p. 541). Abaeté was ultimately overruled, however, and Brazil adopted the treaty.

In this case and many others, the debate has been resolved through an implicit compromise: Brazil would sign on to international law as a shield against the great powers, using international law as weapon of weak state realism. But it would temper this belief in the rule-based order with a close eye to the biases and inequalities perpetuated by international institutions. While the Brazilians were forced by their relative weakness to use multilateralism to constrain the worst impulses of the great powers, they nonetheless sensed that the agreements pushed upon weaker states by the wealthy powers of Europe and North America not uncommonly privileged those powers and cemented their dominance. Even as Brazil signed the treaties, it would do so with a revisionist attitude and the intent of preventing international law from "freezing" into place unacceptable inequalities.

The upshot is that although Brazil is skeptical of the instrumental purposes to which rich countries put international treaties and institutions, the country has a long history of soft balancing through multilateralism, which makes Brazil perhaps more dependent on formal international institutions than most other emerging powers (Hurrell, 2010, p. 65). The country has sought to use these treaties to build autonomy from the great powers (Vigevani and Cepaluni, 2009), and within international institutions, Brazil has long relied on coalitional strategies and appeals to legitimacy to curb the larger powers. Brazil has used these strategies to great effect in the World Trade Organization (WTO), the Bretton Woods institutions, the United Nations (UN), and other venues. Perhaps more importantly, it has been able to use coalition-building to reform these institutions from within.

South–South Strategies

Soft balancing and autonomy-seeking have contributed to Brazil's most important foreign policy stance of the past half century: building south–south relations. Although this effort has been more emphatic in some periods than others, and has been exceedingly pragmatic (eschewing, for example, participation in the Non-Aligned Movement [NAM] during the 1970s for fear that it would be unnecessarily constraining; Spektor, 2004), Brazil has prioritized south–south relations with an eye to building prestige and, consequently, support on the world stage. Whether as cause or consequence, the rhetoric of presidents from the 1960s to the present has emphasized the need to form "a single front in the battle against underdevelopment . . . and oppression" (Quadros, 1961, p. 22) and to dedicate resources to the "eradication of asymmetries and injustices" on the world stage (Lula, cited in Hurrell, 2008, p. 52). The combination of south–south alliances and a convincing rhetorical position has enabled Brazil's influence in global institutions to frequently outweigh its material military and economic resources, and permitted the country to challenge the legitimacy of the global order that emerged from the Cold War (Hurrell, 2010, p. 61).

The south–south strategy has led, however, to an incipient tension in contemporary Brazilian foreign policy: whether from a sincere commitment to global justice or an instrumental effort to harness votes in multilateral institutions, Brazil has privileged representation and justice for developing nations in its diplomacy, while frequently taking an agnostic approach to the nondemocratic and repressive nature of the developing nations' governments. In its pursuit of global justice, more equality, and expanded representation within international organizations, then, Brazil has often ignored domestic rights and representation. Still, despite its inconsistencies, the efficacy of this posture should not be discounted. Over the past quarter century, this strategy has been effective in moving Brazil into globally influential positions, as seen in the creation of the Group of Twenty (G20) and the BRICS grouping; Brazilian effectiveness against dominant powers, as in the Doha Round; and the success of Brazilian diplomats who have won election to leading international organizations.

Regional Politics and the Search for Autonomy

Brazilian pursuit of autonomy against great powers is another major theme in the country's foreign policy tradition. If Brazil were in a different hemisphere, perhaps US concerns would matter less and Brasília would adopt a stance toward the United States more akin to its somewhat more cordial links with the EU. But Brazilian foreign policy aims do not map neatly onto US designs, for reasons that have much to do with the beliefs explored here. Indeed, there is considerable ambivalence: a recent government survey found that Brazilians simultaneously see the United States as the best potential ally for the country, as well as its most likely antagonist in case of conflict (32% versus 37% of respondents; IPEA, 2011). This ambivalence reflects a long history of US intervention in Latin America, as well as the very different approaches to economic and political liberalism in the two countries. At a strategic level, too close an embrace is seen as constraining Brazil's possibilities on the world stage, rather than opening new opportunities (Hurrell, 2010, p. 61). As a result, Itamaraty has frequently sought to bind the United States—and especially US efforts in Latin America— within a web of regional organizations and norms, especially the norm of non-intervention.

In this context, relations with Latin America have become especially important in the last half century. Prior to the 1970s, Brazil had either little interest in the Spanish-speaking portions of the region, or was openly hostile to their territorial claims. The only significant regional objective of Brazilian foreign policy during the early twentieth century was to preserve the border peace that had reigned since the bloody War of the Triple Alliance ended in 1870. The notion of Latin America was foreign to most Brazilians, who felt culturally separate and distinct from the smaller Spanish-speaking republics and looked north and east instead. During much of the early twentieth century, furthermore, there was a perception among policymakers that Brazil's greatest antagonist, Argentina, could turn the Latin American states against it, by virtue of their shared cultural heritage and, especially in the cases of Bolivia, Paraguay, and Uruguay, historical subordination.

This approach toward its neighbors began to change by the early 1970s, as Brazil sought to simultaneously build autonomy from the United States while forging new partnerships in the region (Spektor, 2004). This shift was facilitated by theories such as dependency or structuralism, changes in the Cold War arena, including US weakness in Vietnam, and Brazil's "economic miracle" of the late 1960s and early 1970s. Furthermore, the military regime's desire to shift the focus away from domestic politics encouraged Brazil to strike out in a forceful manner on the international stage. In Latin American relations, this contributed to an increasingly aggressive stance toward Argentina and an effort to realign the smaller satellite nations bordering Argentina and Brazil with Brasília.

With the return to democracy, much of the most hostile rhetoric—often calculated to distract domestic audiences weary of military rule—was shelved, and democratic presidents in both Argentina and Brazil sought to bind each other through regional accords. In fairly rapid succession, Brazil built regional ties through Mercosur in 1994, with expansion into broader South American cooperation via the Union of South American Nations (UNASUR) by 2008. In keeping with the broader objective of "non-hegemonic leadership" in South America, it has proved willing to tolerate slights from a number of actors in Argentina, Bolivia, and Venezuela. Yet as Shifter (2012, p. 59) notes, these organizations have few goals for implementing regional governance and are instead calculated merely to increase cooperation and dialogue, with no effort at deeper integration that would cede sovereignty.

Brazil's distrust of the international liberal order also includes skepticism about liberalism's appropriateness for peripheral economies. In policy terms, this leads to the active use of (WTO-permissible) selective trade protections, sectoral investment regimes, national production incentives, and a web of state support for national industrial champions such as mining behemoth Vale, building companies Odebrecht and Camargo Corrêa, meatpacker JBS, aircraft manufacturer Embraer, and less successful ventures such as Eike Batista's crumbled petroleum and shipping empire. Alongside these runs a healthy dose of skepticism toward orthodox liberal economic prescriptions, whether in the adoption of Washington Consensus reform recommendations in the 1990s or the rigid IMF position on capital controls in the 2000s. Brazil has also held a jaundiced view of wealthy nations' own hypocrisy on trade protections, becoming—as Bosco and Stuenkel noted in their chapter—one of the most active employers of WTO trade dispute mechanisms, with increasing success in challenging US and European subsidies and protections.

In sum, Brazil's foreign policy approach to the global liberal order has been shaped by domestic suspicion of classical liberalism, a history of vulnerability to great power aggression; the fragility and vulnerability of a small population and weak borders; and a skepticism of dominant powers and the opportunities offered by liberal globalization. The result has been a belief in domestic modernization as an essential component of foreign policy success; a commitment to state sovereignty and non-intervention in international affairs; a skeptical and revisionist approach toward international treaties; limited interest in regional political integration; and soft balancing through prestige building, regionally and in south–south relations.

Historical Beliefs and Contemporary Postures

By now it should be evident that Brazilian strategic beliefs have deep roots in the country's political and economic thinking. They also have important implications for Brazil's contemporary postures on the global stage. Unlike many European nations, Brazil has few security interests that are furthered by the security order led by the United States (e.g., NATO), and it does not see its economic or political interests furthered by many of the global or regional institutions suggested by the United States (e.g., FTAA). More importantly, though, the US post–Cold War effort to employ "institutions to lock in other states to desired policy orientations" (Ikenberry, 2001, p. 235) faces challenges from Brazil that are deeply rooted not in interests but in ideas, including the importance of state sovereignty, skepticism about the allocation of the benefits of international organization, and multilateralism as a response to unipolarity.

Brazil's fundamental concern with state sovereignty plays out both within South America and further abroad. Perhaps the most salient recent example of the fundamental anxiety caused by great powers operating close to home was the Brazilian reaction to the United States–Colombia basing deal, but other examples abound: for example, criticism of US intervention in Iraq, Libya, and Syria, the reaction to the reactivation of the US Fourth Fleet in 2008 and the strategic emphasis on the Amazon and the blue Amazon, reiterated most recently in the 2008 National Security Strategy. The decision by Dilma Rousseff to cancel her 2013 state visit to Washington in response to

National Security Agency spying confirms the strong domestic political constraints against relaxation of this norm. The sovereignty concern—oftentimes magnified by ideological affinity, especially under the Workers' Party government—has led to support for Venezuela and Cuba in international forums. At least part of the motivation for the last minute Brazilian–Turkish intervention to preserve the Ahmadinejad regime against sanctions can also be credited to this concern with non-interventionism.

A second major current has been skepticism of the constraints imposed by international treaties, accompanied by active efforts to revise these agreements from within. Brazil does not propose a competing global order, but it seeks to use the extant order to more tightly bind the leading powers while avoiding unnecessary restraints on its own action. One of the most relevant contemporary examples of this phenomenon has been Brazil's refusal to adhere to the *International Atomic Energy Agency* Additional Protocol's rules governing access to nuclear sites, for fear that this would hamper both commercial nuclear development and place additional financial burdens on developing states (Kassenova, Chapter 7 this volume; Vieira de Jesus, 2012, p. 378). Another was Brazil's reaction to the emergence of the "right to protect" (R2P) doctrine at the UN in the mid-2000s: "[a]lthough Lula's Brazil was officially supportive of the idea, in practice it saw the doctrine as 'a ploy of the strong to secure the legal right to intervene at will across the developing world' to suit their interests" (Christensen, 2013, p. 282), and responded with a proposal of its own for "responsibility while protecting" (RwP; Tourinho, Chapter 5 this volume).

Alongside this skepticism about the "real" intentions of international treaties comes an eagerness to point to the hypocrisy of great powers, and their own non-compliance. Most recently this has been evident in the Brazilian pushback against agricultural subsidies at Doha, Brazil's strict adherence to global trade strictures, and its use of the WTO to threaten cross-retaliation against the United States for its abuses in cotton, as well as its willingness to initiate actions against the United States and Europe on a range of subjects.

Multilateralism has been a constant of Brazilian foreign policy for much of the past half century. In the past decade, Brazil has been an active participant in a range of new multilateral efforts, including the BRIC forum, founded in 2007, with an emphasis on reforming global economic governance, especially the IMF. Going beyond its two-decade long efforts within the Community of Portuguese-language Countries (CPLP), Brazil has greatly expanded its presence in Africa as part of its South Atlantic strategy (laid out in the 2008 and 2012 white papers), using a web of development agencies to expand its influence.[10] The creation of the Group of 20, in part to supplant the Group of 8, is yet another example of an effort to use multilateralism to change the terms of the debate. Closer to home, Brazil in the past decade has emphasized the Community of Latin American and Caribbean States (CELAC) and the Union of South American Nations (UNASUL), institutions that—not coincidentally—exclude the United States.

Like all countries, Brazil's positioning on the world stage is strongly conditioned by its beliefs about how that stage serves its interests. Brazil does not seek to replace the global liberal order and has found much to be gained from participating in it. Yet the country's acceptance of that order is tempered in perceptible ways by the ideas and traditions described here, which are likely to continue to have substantive effects on the manner by which Brazil operates on the global stage, and the moderating lens through which it views the leading powers' objectives on that stage.

Notes

1. Translated in Schwarz (1992b).
2. The first three are from Goldstein and Keohane (1993), the fourth from Hall (1989, p. 389). Causal beliefs, in Goldstein and Keohane's construction, are the narrowest category of ideas, by comparison with two other categories: worldviews (e.g., religions or conceptions of sovereignty) or principled beliefs (e.g., normative choices about abortion, slavery, human rights).
3. The Liberal Party was created in 1837. In 1860 it was transformed into the *Liga Progressista* (Progressive League), but in 1870 radical liberals would recreate a new Liberal Party, more connected with the social agenda of those times.
4. The most striking examples are the Eusébio de Queirós Law in 1850 (Monte Alegre Cabinet 1849–1852) and the Law of Free Birth in 1871 (Rio Branco Cabinet 1871–1875). The former abolished slave trade while the latter granted freedom to all newborn children of slaves. Both were passed under Conservative cabinets.
5. Slavery was abolished in 1888, following almost a decade of great political mobilization. However, social movements were more important to this outcome than political parties, including the new Liberal Party. Even when it was in power (Sinimbu Cabinet 1878/1880), the Liberal Party was unable to promote a liberal agenda that tackled slavery (Alonso, 2012). Two prominent exceptions to this trend were Joaquim Nabuco, a major figure in the political establishment (Alonso, 2010) and one of the main leaders of the new Liberal Party, which recruited many "radical" liberals, and André Rebouças, an engineer of African descent who championed social reforms and was a close friend of Emperor Pedro II (Carvalho, 1998).
6. He returned to power in 1951 through free elections, but committed suicide in 1954.

7. Indeed, Brazilian economists frequently went further than *cepalinos* in their advocacy of an activist state effort for the development of infant industry and the improvement of agricultural productivity (Bielschowsky, 1988, p. 13).

8. Namely, that inflation was caused by structural bottlenecks, such as a backward agricultural sector, which led to inelastic supply in the face of rapidly rising urban demand (Love, 1996, pp. 238–239).

9. The BNDES loaned three times as much as the World Bank in 2010 (Hochstetler, 2011, p. 28).

10. Marques (2013) notes the web of Brazilian institutions operating in Africa includes Embrapa, the Fundação Oswaldo Cruz (Fiocruz), National Service for Industrial Training (SENAI), Brazilian Service for Support of Micro and Small Entreprises (SEBRAE) , BNDES, and ABC. There is a fascinating debate underway about the ultimate objective of these agencies in Africa, which Itamaraty has been eager not to term "foreign aid," perhaps for fear of being seen as instrumental, realist, or exploitative of poorer members of the Global South.

CHAPTER 4

The Risks of Pragmatism: Brazil's Relations with the United States and the International Security Order

Ralph Espach[1]

This volume explores Brazil's relationship with the liberal global system within which it seeks greater autonomy and influence. This chapter contributes to that effort with a focus on security capabilities and relations. These involve a nation's ability to defend its citizens and those of its allies, and to promote its interests abroad, through the real or threatened application of force. Security affairs and military relations receive relatively little attention in South America, a region virtually free of international armed aggression. However, as South American nations expand their relations in other regions and increase their global presence, security affairs will assume greater relevance. For many countries security affairs and defense are essential elements of their politics. For powers like the United States, China, and Russia, security relationships and capabilities, and their occasional use, are important not only for defense but as elements of their foreign policy. Trade, finance, and diplomacy are the everyday stuff of foreign relations, but when contention leads to crisis it is often the use or threat of force that determines outcomes.

Similar to the global political economy, the international security system consists of a patchwork of formal and informal agreements and arrangements. The most developed of these are between and among industrialized democracies, including most of those of North America and Europe. At the center of this network of security partners, which includes not only the NATO alliance but also Australia, Japan, and South Korea, sits the United States, which since the end of the Cold War stands alone in its willingness to dedicate vast resources and efforts to sustain a military capable of operating virtually worldwide. Since the two world wars the US military—its ability to provide credible protection and partnership to its allies and friends—has been a major component of its foreign policy. Maintaining these capabilities demands not only ships, aircraft, and other weaponry, and a highly trained fighting force, but critically also intelligence, specialized training, and additional skills for which the United States relies on cooperation with its security partners.

Over the last decade Brazil has invested a significant amount of money and effort to modernize and strengthen its armed forces. The government has defined missions and policies for its military that improve national defense and, in addition, help the nation act in the international arena in support of its interests and partnerships abroad. As discussed throughout this volume, central features of Brazil's foreign policy are its drive for autonomy and the promotion of "multipolarity" in international politics. In politics and economics Brazil operates in a sophisticated manner, both participating in—and reaping the benefits from—liberal systems of rules and practice, while also exploring avenues of resistance and reform. In its security policies and affairs, Brazil's leaders also seek an appropriate degree of military cooperation with the dominant international security coalition, which purports to act in defense of the liberal order, as well as other initiatives and security relations outside of that coalition.

Brazil's bilateral relationship with the United States is central to those considerations. Despite common interests in hemispheric stability and prosperity, shared democratic and liberal values, and the lack of any history of conflict, the US–Brazilian relationship is hindered by mutual distrust, frustration, and contrasting worldviews (Spektor, 2011; Frechette and Samolis, 2012; Brown, 2013). Among the many factors that contribute to this problem, an essential one is the lack of any common security threat or vision.

The two nations' different historical experiences and threat perceptions generate distinct perspectives on national security, military affairs, and the international use of force. One core component of modern US foreign policy—since the two world wars—has been its self-regard as an active proponent of freedom and democracy around the world, including when the use of force is required to promote those values. The experience of winning two terrible, global wars instilled in Americans an appreciation for their military and a national narrative about valor and greatness proved through armed conflict. Fifty years of a Cold War against a formidable enemy reinforced these ideas.

In contrast, modern Brazil has had minimal experience with warfare and has never suffered, nor been seriously threatened by, attack. Unlike the United States, Brazil was not pulled into the great wars among the European powers, but chose to play modest roles in those conflicts. Brazilians tend to see neutrality and pacificism as national virtues and to treat military affairs with disinterest or distrust (a legacy, in part, of their experience with military dictatorship). For the majority of Brazilians, expeditionary military actions (those taken in a foreign country) are perceived to be imperialistic and unjustifiable, except perhaps in the most extreme circumstances. These differences in perspective toward the exercise of military power pose an enduring, essential dilemma for the US–Brazilian partnership.

This chapter seeks a greater understanding of this dilemma through a historical review of the relationship and considers its implications for Brazil's current strategic and security affairs. The central argument is that for Brazil national defense and military affairs, because they are not essentially driven by perceptions of threat, are subordinated to more compelling objectives related to economic development and foreign policy. Lacking an overriding mission in its foreign security relations, it tends to act pragmatically, seeking benefits from cooperation but limiting its commitments. Also, because of its core adherence to the principles of national autonomy and sovereignty, it is fundamentally opposed to the use of force in foreign affairs. Despite some exceptions to these policies (for example, its abiding interest in acquiring and presumably deploying expeditionary assets such as nuclear submarines and aircraft carriers, and its calculated cultivation of the capacity to develop nuclear weapons), it has for decades adhered to these strategic principles. This pragmatic strategy of carefully proscribed international security cooperation can reap benefits for Brazil at low cost within a stable, liberal global order, one in which major conflicts are avoided. If conflict erupts, however, and the order is destabilized, Brazil's fence-sitting and modest security capabilities could marginalize it from the coalitions which will determine the outcome of those conflicts. More relevant to Brazil's actual circumstances is the problem that this strategy complicates its efforts to improve indigenous security cooperation with its neighbors in South America. The US–Brazil security relationship will likely continue as a productive but limited one, given enduring differences in strategic vision. This is unfortunate, because deeper cooperation in areas of shared interests such as peacekeeping, regional security cooperation in South America and across the South Atlantic, and disaster response could help both nations improve regional and global security and stability.

A History of the US–Brazil Security Relationship

The following survey of the history of the bilateral security relationship highlights the divergence between the two nations' strategic interests and perspectives since the 1940s, punctuated by episodes of cooperation when short-term interests overlapped. It also emphasizes several historic continuities in the relationship which serve as the themes for the section that follows on the future of Brazil's security relations with the United States and other foreign partners.

1898–1945: The Era of a "Special Relationship"

The idea of a "special relationship" between the two giants of the Western Hemisphere dates back to the early years of the twentieth century. At that time the Baron of Rio Branco, Brazil's preeminent foreign policy statesman, defined the two critical objectives of Brazil's foreign policy to be: maintaining good relations with the colossus in the north, and keeping it from interfering in Brazil's South American neighborhood while preserving peace with its neighbors, in part by securing clear border agreements (Zaluar, 2010).

Like the US national sentiment of "manifest destiny," Brazilians had a general sense of *grandeza*, that by virtue of its resources the nation was destined to become a power on the international stage. Brazil's leadership in that period generally accepted the logic of seeking good relations, including security relations, with the United States in a subordinate role, as a strategy for ascendance on the global stage. For example, Brazil's naval cooperation with the United States in the First World War gave it a hand in victory, and a seat at the table at the Versailles conference.

Throughout this period and into the 1930s, Washington was alarmed by the efforts of Germany and Japan to build strategic relations with nations of Latin America, including significant military and intelligence cooperation. As the United States prepared to enter the Second World War, Brazil became a focus of intense US efforts to build a strong security relationship, given Brazil's vast resources and its geographical location dominating the southern Atlantic Ocean and proximate to north Africa.

Brazilian president Getúlio Vargas welcomed such treatment in the early 1940s because it aligned with his vision and plans for national development. But he was not committed, ideologically or otherwise, to the Allies. While he could, Vargas acted pragmatically to maintain Brazil's relations with the United States and the Axis powers, reaping benefits from both sides. Ultimately, however, Japan's shocking attack on Pearl Harbor, German attacks on Brazilian shipping, and the rising insistence of US demands made neutrality impossible. In May 1942 Vargas signed a military alliance with the United States.

During the war the United States and Brazil established a cooperative and effective military partnership. Thousands of US military personnel worked in Brazil, and US aircraft and Navy vessels operated out of Brazilian air and sea bases. US money and expertise helped build and expand Brazilian infrastructure for the war effort. The two navies formed a joint naval fleet that together hunted and sank several German U-boats (McCann, 1973; Roth, 2009). When the Brazilian Expeditionary Force (BEF) fought in Italy in 1944 its training, weapons, and equipment came almost entirely from the United States. The BEF, in fact, fought as a unit of the United States Fifth Army Division (Tollefson, 1998).

Brazil's leaders assumed that such cooperation and interoperability would translate, after the war, into an enduring strategic relationship. They believed fighting side-by-side ensured special US considerations for military and economic development, which would help elevate Brazil's stature in international affairs (Davis, 1996).

1950s: Diverging Strategic Objectives and Visions

The end of the conflict and the onset of the Cold War led to disillusionment in Brazil. Washington immediately faced a Soviet effort to install and support communist regimes in Eastern Europe and Asia, countering which became the overriding focus of its strategic planning. Now the preeminent global power, the United States faced more threats and problems than ever and had little attention or resources to give to its neighbors to the south.

US policymakers generally did not share the view of their Brazilian counterparts that the close wartime relationship, and bilateral military commissions that administered the operations, should be enduring institutions. For American leaders, they were wartime necessities which now lacked a rationale. US strategic interests in South America centered on keeping Soviet influence at bay, largely through improving US relations and promoting security cooperation in the region. US policy shifted away from favoring Brazil, toward emphasizing unity and equality among nations, a stance Brazil resisted but which underpinned the Rio Treaty for mutual defense signed in 1948. The shift in US policy even included the cultivation of relations with Brazil's traditional rival Argentina, which had refused to join the Allies in the war until their triumph was assured. From the perspective of US strategists, Argentina's controlling position over the Straits of Magellan made good relations a top priority.

Still, the US armed forces maintained strong relations with their Brazilian counterparts. In the 1950s the United States maintained around 200 military officers and 100 enlisted personnel in Brazil, and officers' training and exchange programs remained the most robust in South America (Weis, 1993, p. 20). The US Navy, in particular, fought off various economizing efforts that would have cut staff for joint commissions and other engagement activities. Even so, as the years passed, it was clear that the postwar benefits that the "special relationship" was to have brought to Brazil would not materialize. Brazil's leaders and strategists had learned a troubling lesson.

In the 1950s, the strategic interests of the two nations diverged as different perspectives on world affairs began to permeate their politics. The drive to contain Soviet influence and the spread of communism consumed Washington. In Brazil, a growing number of voices began to espouse the strategic wisdom of an independent foreign policy that would situate Brazil between the East and West. After the US-led overthrow of Guatemala's reformist president Arbenz in 1954, and the attempted invasion of Castro's Cuba at the Bay of Pigs, many Brazilian intellectuals—including President Jânio Quadros—called for an anti-imperialist foreign policy and the positioning of Brazil as a friend and leader of the underdeveloped countries of the Third World.

This slide in the bilateral security relationship was halted, for a time, when Washington supported the military coup of 1964 and the resulting administration of Castello Branco. Itself concerned about the spread of Cuban and Soviet influence through the region, Brazil supported the US-led, Organization of American States (OAS)-sanctioned invasion of the Dominican Republic in 1965. Afterward, however, the trend of disagreement and disengagement resumed. Brazil's decision not to send troops to fight in Vietnam reflected the long-term direction of the bilateral relationship.

Another important factor behind the weakening of US–Brazilian security relations was that the attention of Brazil's military leadership largely focused on its positioning and veto role within domestic politics. The Cold War wrought change within Brazilian society, and many of Brazil's security leaders began to view Leftist domestic insurgency as the nation's principal threat. Brazil's military leadership fractured internally. While many leaders continued to argue in favor of a traditional defense role for the armed forces, a growing majority of officers began to endorse military missions to suppress insurgency and defend the nation's political stability. Their training in the sciences of public administration and economics within the *Escola Superior de Guerra* (ESG) inculcated this vision and prepared Brazil's top officers for the mission of replacing, if necessary, incompetent or corrupt civilian administrators (Stepan, 1971).

1960s and 1970s: Growing Turbulence

Relations grew turbulent during the 1960s. Though the militaries remained cooperative, the two governments' positions on strategic and security affairs diverged. Washington's support for an international regime to limit the transfer of nuclear weaponry and technology became an issue of contention.

As Togzhan Kassanova's chapter (Chapter 7) describes, the international nuclear non-proliferation regime that developed at this time has become an enduring, significant point of contention between Brazil and the United States. Within Brazil, civilian and military strategists debated two contrasting strategic visions. The longstanding idea that an alliance with the United States offered Brazil its best path to development and global prominence lost ground to a more Realist-informed strategy of improving autonomy through balanced, diverse relations within an increasingly multipolar international system. General Golbery do Couto e Silva at the ESG was an enormously influential advocate of the latter, and under the nationalist military presidents of Costa e Silva (1967–1969) and Médici (1969–1974) it became the dominant view within the government and among most elites (Stepan, 1971). This shift in the strategic vision of leaders on the Right—who stressed national prestige and autonomy—was in effect a convergence with the traditional, anti-capitalist, and anti-US views of the Left. This created a near-consensus national perspective, one that remains highly influential today.

Nevertheless, many still saw great promise in the relationship. Brazil was a key component of Secretary of State Henry Kissinger's plan for sustaining global influence for the United States through partnerships, and despite much resistance on both sides he and Foreign Minister Antonio Azeredo da Silveira successfully achieved the signing of a strategic agreement in 1976 (Spektor, 2009). Relations again soured, however, when the Carter administration took office and first showed determination in blocking the transfer of nuclear technology between West Germany and Brazil and then directly criticized Brazil's military government for its record of human rights violations. This treatment shocked Brazil's military government and provided further evidence in support of the spreading theory, espoused by military strategists, that the United States was not a reliable partner, but rather a rival and antagonist whose national interest was served by keeping Brazil in a subordinate position. In 1977 the bilateral relationship reached its nadir when Brazil canceled its twenty-five-year-old security agreement with the United States.

1980s: Democratic Transition and Fading Relevance

With the end of the security accord, US service posts and training programs within Brazil were slashed. Brazil turned to other nations, including France and Russia, to replace US defense equipment and training. Personnel and military training exchanges with the United States continued, but at a smaller scale than before. The attention of US security leaders shifted to other Latin American partners where they perceived more communist penetration and more US national interests at stake, mostly in the Caribbean and Central America.

During the 1980s Brazil specifically and South America in general remained marginal to US strategic and security concerns. For Brazil, the 1980s was a decade of economic duress and political transformation. With the transition back to democracy, military budgets were cut and the defense sector was valued primarily for its capacity to generate revenues by exporting defense equipment, mostly to the Middle East.[2] As relations warmed between Brazil and its neighbors, especially its traditional rival Argentina, national security faded as a compelling issue. The military began to experience what would be almost twenty years of budget cuts and marginalization from national public affairs.

1990–2002: New Post–Cold War Missions and Security Reforms in Brazil

The fall of the Berlin Wall recast the global security environment and stripped both the United States and Brazilian militaries of their primary mission— countering the global spread of communism. Both armed forces searched for new roles, as their budgets were cut. In Brazil, civilian leaders seeking to modernize the armed forces and reign in their leadership under a new, more cooperative and liberal foreign policy, instituted reforms to reduce their independence. President Collor de Mello (1990–1992) cut defense spending down to approximately 0.3 percent of GDP, replaced the military-dominated National Information Service (SNI) with the civilian-led Strategic Affairs Secretariat (SAE), privatized the Brazilian Aeronautics Company Embraer, and revealed the army's secret nuclear bomb project as he established an agreement with Argentina for cooperative oversight over nuclear materials.

Regional security relations were transformed in the early 1990s. Democratic governments across South America signed a series of bilateral, and then multilateral, economic and security cooperation agreements. Intrahemispheric foreign relations centered on negotiations for trade accords such as NAFTA, Mercosur, and the Free Trade Area of the Americas. National defense and military matters were not of high public or political interest.

Also, the US military's mission and operations in Latin America narrowed during the 1990s to a focus on building regional capabilities and partnerships to curb the production and trans-shipment of illegal narcotics. Since most Latin American governments, to one degree or another, viewed this activity as a problem fueled by US drug consumers and weapons sellers and traffickers, this security cooperation was limited and often controversial. This difference of perspectives on the causes and nature of the illegal narcotics problem became an enduring wedge in the security relations between the United States and many Latin American partners, especially in South America and including Brazil.

Under President Fernando Henrique Cardoso, Brazil began a process of reform and modernization of its armed forces to improve their coherence within a consolidated democracy. The most important of these reforms was the creation, in 1999, of a civilian Ministry of Defense and a Joint Chiefs of Staff (*Estado-Maior Conjunto das Forças Armadas*). The government modestly increased the military's budget and capabilities within traditional lines of operation: in support of UN peacekeeping missions, and improved surveillance and presence across Brazil's Amazon region (via the *Calha Norte* and Amazon Surveillance System [SIVAM] projects).

These initiatives provided several opportunities for US–Brazilian security dialogue and cooperation. Because the United States and its defense sector had technological, operational, and administrative expertise relevant to these types of reforms and programs, there was much to offer Brazilian partners. Pragmatic leadership in Brasília and within the armed forces began cautiously to explore areas of possible cooperation. Similar alignment and cooperation began to take shape in economic and political matters, as well, though major disagreements remained (especially regarding trade policies and preferences in the hemisphere). Figures in Washington once again began to speak of Brazil as a leader in the region, despite Brazilian resistance to several key US diplomatic projects, especially the Free Trade Area of the Americas (FTAA). In 1996, Brazil's clear opposition to a coup attempt in Paraguay was lauded within US foreign policy circles as an important step toward the regional defense of democracy. In terms of security, it was significant that the United States allowed Brazilian officers to command US aviation units as part of the four-party Ecuador-Peru Military Observer Mission (MOPEP) following the Peru–Ecuador conflict in 1995 (Weidner, 1996).

Differences remained, however, especially when Brazilians perceived US actions as excessively unilateral and dismissive of international laws. For example, Brazil refused to sign an Article 98 agreement, which would have given US military personnel bilateral immunity from the Rome Statute and the International Criminal Court. This, in turn, led the United States to cut funding and other support for Brazilian military training at US centers and universities. Over the years this proved a serious blow to the security relationship because a generation of officers, scientists, and engineers in both countries lost opportunities to train and learn together.

The 2000s: New Attention and Investment for Brazil's Military

The Lula da Silva government presided over a period of economic growth and a resurgence in the institutional coherence and capabilities of Brazil's military. After years of shrinking military budgets and scant attention, the government increased budgets and salaries for defense and took several measures to help modernize the defense sector and provide it direction. In 2008 Brazil published a National Defense Strategy which provided new guidance for the development and use of the armed forces. The Strategy is guided by three overarching objectives:

1. The need to rebuild and reorganize Brazil's armed forces to improve mobility, nationwide presence, and joint command capabilities, with special attention to strengthening state control along Brazil's borders, in the Amazon, and over Brazil's waters and maritime resources. The most prominent developments in this regard have been reforms and new guidance to allow the military to support federal police in counter-gang and counter-trafficking operations, and significant new investment in naval surveillance, monitoring, patrolling, and sea control capabilities to protect the nation's maritime resources, its Blue Amazon, or "Amazonia Azul."

2. To build and support the nation's defense equipment and technological industries in order to attain self-sufficiency and to serve the country's broader industrial development, with special focus on nuclear, space, and cyber technology. This objective supports massive state investments in and subsidies for related research and technical projects, including the design and manufacturing of advanced aircraft and ships, including a nuclear-propelled submarine.

3. Integrate the military into national life and the nation's broader development programs.

The Strategy is consistent with Brazil's traditional view that the nation's defense and security and its industrial development are interrelated. The investments it envisioned and propagated, from the state outward, contributed rationally to numerous industrial, scientific, and trade-related interests, for example, the promotion of higher value exports and support for the exploitation of the country's (maritime) resources. Beyond objectives relevant to national defense, the Strategy highlights other goals for the nation's security forces:

- More engagement in South American collective security initiatives;
- Assumption of leadership in multinational peacekeeping missions;
- Stronger presence and closer security relations across the Atlantic, including with African nations.

One remarkable element of the Strategy is the emphasis it places on naval investments and capabilities. There are at least two reasons for this: (a) because so many of Brazil's newly discovered resources lie under its seabed, and defense and control over those resources is a national priority from both the developmental and security perspective, and (b) because naval capabilities are essential for the projection of power and/or the sustainment of presence abroad. For centuries the great powers have been naval powers, able to defend and promote their interests (chiefly commercial) in the markets upon which their economies depended.

The Strategy, and its implementation, reflects Brazil's strategic ambiguity and ambivalence toward relations with the superpower to its north. It was formulated at a time when Brazilians and their government held Washington and the G. W. Bush administration in exceptionally low regard. The use of false intelligence to justify the Iraq war, the Abu Ghraib scandal, and US human rights violations against civilians it deemed "terrorists," evinced Washington's imperialism and hypocrisy for a new generation of Brazilians. In regional affairs, cynicism about US commitment to democracy grew following Washington's support for a coup attempt against Venezuelan president Chávez in 2002, and its later ambivalence in response to a coup against Honduran president Zelaya in 2008. In 2008 when the United States and its European allies suffered major financial and economic crises from which South America escaped largely unscathed, thanks in large part to sustained Chinese demand for their exports, it deepened the sense that the days of looking to the United States and Europe for public policy models were over.

Within the Lula government, these events reinforced the perspectives of several of Lula's closest foreign policy and strategic advisors that the world order was increasingly multipolar. Shifting back toward the Realist and nationalist perspective as espoused by the ESG in the 1970s, they argued that Brazil's best strategy was not, as Cardoso's government was inclined to do, to seek ascendance by involving itself more actively with the global, US-centered, "liberal" political, economic, and security coalition. Instead, they advocated resistance against US-led initiatives in the region and globally, and the balancing of Brazil's relations across the North and South, East and West. Moreover, for Lula and his advisors Brazil had a special role to play as an emerging power in affairs in the Middle East and Africa, and should develop special prominence within a region of geo-economic and cultural influence that spread across South America and the South Atlantic, to include Western Africa. A key goal was to rollback, and limit, US influence in these regions and to encourage the growing presence of other powers, most notably China, as a source of counter-balance in partnership with Brazil.

Remarkably, for all its emphasis on modernization, Brazil's National Defense Strategy did not abandon a long-held doctrinal belief that great powers pose an armed threat to Brazil's natural resources, particularly in the

Amazonian region. This notion of potential foreign territorial incursions, explored in greater detail in Maia and Taylor's chapter (Chapter 3) in this volume, has historically served as a central rationale for building nuclear and other deterrent capabilities (Amorim, 2012). The contrast between the basic assumptions behind Brazil's strategic thinking, and that of the United States, casts significant light on the distrust and misunderstanding at the core of bilateral security relations. Brazilian strategists believe it is obvious that what it perceives as precious natural resources—including fresh water—will be the target of foreign conspiracy and armed actions (Granovsky, 2013). To Americans this seems ridiculous. The United States has plenty of forest and water of its own and can buy more if it needs to without resorting to an anachronistic idea of invasion. Furthermore, no rational military would ever contemplate invading the Amazon basin, a region so vast and inhospitable that for over four hundred years the Brazilians and others who own it have never succeeded at developing or even populating it. For Brazilians such dismissals can seem disingenuous. This doctrinal logjam encapsulates the challenge of reaching a deeper, more comfortable level of bilateral confidence.

Improving Bilateral Security Relations

Despite these serious and persistent differences in strategic vision, recent years have seen significant improvements in the bilateral security relationship. This assessment may surprise readers familiar with the well-publicized crises between the two governments: Washington's frustration and dismissal of Lula's attempt in 2010 to broker, along with Turkey, a deal in which Iran could sustain its nuclear program; and in 2013 President Rousseff's angry response—and cancellation of a state visit to Washington—at the discovery (via the Edward Snowden leaks) that the US National Security Agency (NSA) had been secretly recording her phone calls. Certainly those events severely undercut the bilateral relationship. Following the Snowden leaks, Brazil effectively froze all senior-level engagements and talks, including high-level defense talks.[3] Below the level of visible, senior-level engagements, however, at the level of service-to-service relations and technical and operational cooperation—where most actual military work is done and relations are built—bilateral security relations continue to develop and deepen in several areas.

The two countries' security relations are buoyed by pragmatic thinking and mutual needs. Brazil's Strategy and its 2012 White Paper (*Livro Branco de Defesa Nacional*) define several objectives and desired capabilities for its military which require foreign technical and operational cooperation to achieve. For the US Department of Defense the realities of enduring budget constraints and of national security threats that are worldwide and insidious (i.e., terrorist and criminal networks) have led it to truly recognize its growing dependence on foreign partners. Key US strategic guidance documents, especially those relating to security relations in the Western Hemisphere, stress the fundamental importance of cooperation and the need for partners to provide their own national and regional security more effectively. For Brazil's military, the US defense sector and military are the world's most highly capable and advanced in many areas where it seeks to learn and gain new techniques and technologies. For the United States, Brazil's dominance in South America and its rising global presence make it a critical partner. These mutual, complementary incentives for cooperation continue to drive relations even if their full expression remains limited by resistance at the top level.

In recent years security cooperation has advanced in particular in the following areas.

- *The broadening and institutionalization of the security dialogue at the ministerial and bureaucratic levels, as well as between the various services.* This "Defense Cooperation Dialogue" is one of several strategic dialogues created by presidents Rousseff and Obama in 2010 under the rubric of the Global Partnership Dialogue. However, since the summer of 2013 the Defense Cooperation Dialogue has been postponed, by Brazil, in response to the Snowden leaks about NSA spying within Brazil.
- *The progression within regional and bilateral military exercises, planning games, and other engagements toward more complexity, interoperability, and regional leadership.* This includes joint training exercises and conferences that develop and exercise collaborative processes and systems for Brazil and other nations to assume leadership roles in future regional task forces. Through these exercises Southern Command is helping Brazil and other regional partners develop architecture and processes for cooperative security missions developed and led within the region—one of Brazil's principal strategic objectives.
- *The growth of scientific, technological, and industrial cooperation.* In the last few years, relations in these areas have flourished. Examples range from high-profile investments such as the US purchase of Embraer Tucanos and Brazil's purchase of Sikorsky helicopters and US-designed submarine operations and weapons systems, to new areas of cooperation in aircraft design and production (including unmanned aircraft systems). This cooperation involves the highly sensitive issue of technology transfer restrictions, which—like strategic views on the Amazon and conflicts over resources—pose a thorny challenge to strategic relations. An opportunity for significant, long-term collaboration was

missed when in December 2013 Brazil decided to purchase the SAAB Gripen rather than Boeing F-18s for its next-generation fighter jet (widely believed to be another item of fall-out from the Snowden episode). Still, several major cooperative efforts are underway and in development.

- *Operational cooperation on missions that serve shared interests.* These include defense and law enforcement capacity-building in African nations, support for UN peacekeeping missions, emergency response, and countering trans-national organized crime. Brazil's longstanding participation in such operations and its growing capabilities have enhanced its leadership and autonomy in conducting them. Brazil's effective leadership of the United Nations Stabilization Mission in Haiti (MINUSTAH) peacekeeping mission in Haiti demonstrated its military's capacity for taking on greater roles in multinational missions (Einaudi, 2011). Brazil's strong participation in the US-orchestrated response to Haiti's 2010 earthquake, which killed numerous Brazilians, helped build bilateral confidence. Also, the recognition in Brazil that drug trafficking and traffickers pose a serious security problem has led to regional cooperation on intelligence, border surveillance, and patrols, including with the United States. In recent years Brazil has increased its security cooperation on its borders with Bolivia, Paraguay, Peru, and Colombia (Muggah and Diniz, 2013).[4]

It is worth pointing out that Brazil's interests, more than those of the United States, seem to set the parameters of this cooperation. If it were up to the US Department of Defense, the bilateral security agenda would include cooperation with training and assistance in gang-plagued Central American countries, joint counter-narcotics operations, and the contribution of Brazilian forces and assets to more multilateral task forces, for example, in Afghanistan.

The fact that this is not the case suggests that the United States' desire for a more robust relationship is stronger than Brazil's—a pattern borne out historically. The effectiveness of the United States as a leader of the global liberal order depends on cooperation with nations that share with the United States a preference for the principles and practices of democracy under the rule of law. Its security alliances, arrangements, and cooperation are an important element of this strategy. In contrast, Brazil's objectives for security cooperation are less defined, especially beyond its borders and jurisdictional waters. Brazil faces no clear security threat and tends to view strong, externally capable or expeditionary security forces as optional, rather than critical, to the national interest. While Washington sees security cooperation as critical to the success of its global strategy and potentially its survival, Brazil views security relations as largely a question of costs and benefits, echoing the era when Getulio Vargas played the Axis powers off the Allies for national advantage as long as he could.

Implications for Brazil's Relations with the International Security Order

In the history of the US–Brazil security relationship we can discern some trends that are likely to endure and have implications for the future scope and trajectory of that relationship. The health of that relationship will in turn shape Brazil's disposition toward the prevailing international security coalition, a key component of the "liberal" international order.

First, for both nations security relations are a low-priority element of the US–Brazil relationship. Presidents and ministers almost never mention security cooperation in their speeches about the relationship, and presidential and ministerial visits bring entourages of diplomats and business leaders, not generals. US defense leaders are focused on threats and missions in other parts of the world to which Brazil's armed forces, with their limited capacity for expeditionary operations, matter little. Looking to the years to come, the implication is that in the absence of a security threat or crisis that directly affects both nations, security and military relations will continue to take a back seat to economic and political affairs. In Brazil in particular, they will likely remain subjected to political interference, roll-back, and symbolic gestures and as items for negotiations.[5]

A second trend is the enduring differences between the two governments' perspectives on foreign policy goals and priorities. Most of the elites and broader public opinion in both countries tend to regard their countries as Western and as willing participants in the global liberal order, desirous of a world in which democratic governments and free people coexist peacefully. However, many Brazilians tend to view the United States as a unilateralist, aggressive actor whose actions in pursuit of its self-interest threaten that liberal order, as much as or more than it is a cooperative partner in its realization. Most Americans, in turn, look to a history of warfare against fascist, autocratic, and communist regimes and believe that the end-state of a global liberal order will come about only if it is promoted and defended against forces that oppose it. Informed by different historic experiences, strategists in the two countries disagree fundamentally over the appropriate international use of coercion, not only outright military power but also the promotion of democracy, economic sanctions, and covert operations. This divergence is unlikely to change in the years to come. As a result, security cooperation is likely to persist and develop mostly at the operational level, chiefly between functional elements of the armed forces in support of limited missions that clearly fit the interests of both nations. A deeper strategic partnership remains unlikely.

The record of the US–Brazilian partnership shows that the strength of security cooperation has fluctuated over the decades as threat perceptions change or as one party—in most cases, Brazil—sees opportunities to obtain other benefits from cooperation, such as a better trade deal or new loans or infrastructure. Free from existential threats, Brazil has the luxury to follow a pragmatic course. This gives it an advantage over nations like the United States, Russia, or China, whose foreign policies can be susceptible to bouts of adventurism in the name of abstract values like freedom or national greatness, or for whom nationalism has a militaristic aspect. In the coming years nothing is likely to compel Brazil to enter into binding commitments with the United States and its security coalition partners, nor with China, Russia, India, Argentina, or anyone else. Brazil can be patient, dedicate its resources to other national priorities, develop its military capabilities deliberately, and choose among opportunities for action as they arise.

In the future as in the recent past, Brazil will most likely continue to look for opportunities in specific regions or countries, and serving particular functions (e.g., peacekeeping, basic law enforcement and military training, disaster response) which best fit its policy objectives, have limited risks, and reflect the nation's self-perceptions as a soft power with special ties to less-developed nations. Regions like West Africa and the South Atlantic appeal to Brazil's leaders and strategists. They are areas where Brazil's presence is welcome, where risks and costs are relatively low, and where Brazil can operate as leader or among equals, rather than in a subordinate position. Brazil will likely forego opportunities to join coalitions that involve violations of sovereignty (e.g., UN-sanctioned operations in Libya in 2011), that give it a clearly subordinate role, or that risk the loss of lives. Brazil's leaders will be wary of overextending their military, and taking on undue costs, considering the public's limited interest in such operations.

These functions and missions for Brazil's military align with US Department of Defense aspirations for international security partnerships. With the Obama administration's shift toward Asia-Pacific as its key area of focus, and Washington's recognition that it cannot be the world's police, the US military recognizes the high value of security partners capable of cooperating to provide their own regional security. Ironically, however, US expressions of strategic support for such missions and initiatives on the part of Brazil do not necessarily help—and may hinder—their realization if they cause Brazilian senior leadership to rethink actions that the superpower endorses.

Brazil's Alternatives for Coalitions and Partnerships

Brazilian leaders tend to be cautious in their relations with the United States because in their view close relations may restrict, in various ways, Brazil's autonomy. For the same reason Brazil's leaders will likely be cautious in forming a strategic security partnership with any other power. First, Brazil's historic partners in Europe, such as France and Germany, have close security relations with the United States, not only between their militaries but also with their police and intelligence services. If Brazil were to strengthen its security cooperation with those nations, it would find itself pushed to accept the agreements, policies, and standard practices of NATO, through which they interoperate with US forces.[6] Thus a security partnership with other countries that are also partners of the United States does not mitigate altogether the risks of influence on Brazil's autonomy. Also, the benefits to Brazil of a security partnership with those countries would be limited, given their modest capabilities. Furthermore, it is debatable whether Brazil's strategic vision and interests are any more aligned with, or compatible with, those of France or Germany, than with the United States.

Other options for a strategic security relationship would appear to involve a high degree of risk for limited reward. Some degree of security cooperation with China or Russia can be beneficial for Brazil in terms of the transfer of technology and knowledge. However, if cooperation were to deepen and take on a strategic, military character it could generate significant risk due to the lack of alignment between those governments' core values and those of Brazil, and the rift such relations could cause with other important partners. Over the long term, Brazil must consider the possibility that China will emerge as the preeminent global power, but in the short or medium term any such alignment would be difficult for Brazil on various levels: politically, economically, culturally, as well as in terms of security.[7]

Brazil already has strategic agreements with other South American nations, particularly with Argentina, and engages in security cooperation with other South American nations. These nations clearly share an interest in preserving regional peace, stability, and autonomy. However, Brazil faces the dilemma that several of its most important regional partners share an affinity and partnership with the United States (one purpose of which has been, historically, to provide some balance and protection against regional rivals including Brazil). More importantly, the significance of regional agreements, associations, councils (as with the South American Defense Council), or blocs is compromised by the lack of any shared threat to compel their institutional development. Finally, while improved security cooperation within South America could be enormously beneficial, it would not contribute significantly to achieving Brazil's desire to raise its profile at the global level.

The Risk of a Regional Security Crisis

The greatest current risk facing Brazil's security leaders and strategists is that of a security crisis in South America of sufficient scale and violence to generate a demand for an international response. Over the last decade, Brazil has led efforts across South America to promote security dialogue and cooperation without any US, European, or even Canadian involvement. Most of the progress has come at the bilateral level, where Brazil has worked with various neighbors to improve border surveillance and patrol capabilities. Efforts at the multilateral level, including through the South American Defense Council, have been less productive (Muggah and Diniz, 2013, pp. 19–20).

The region is poorly prepared to act rapidly and in a coordinated fashion in response to a security crisis or conflict, such as a civil war. While regional dynamics and history suggest international conflict is unlikely, the deteriorating political and economic situation in Venezuela, and the rising influence and capacity for violence among regional drug trafficking networks in the region, present various frightening and not unrealistic scenarios of crisis. In such circumstances, the region's political and military leaders would need to overcome their political differences and find effective ways to cooperate, potentially in a matter of weeks. Gross differences in national capabilities and the lack of a functioning multilateral framework for security cooperation would complicate the efforts of Brazil and other countries to coordinate a regional response. Most likely, effective action would require setting aside the region's traditional adherence to the norm of consensus-based decision-making. This may put Brazil—if it assumes leadership—in the uncomfortable position of having to overrule or ignore the objectives of regional partners.

Further difficulties would arise from the limited capabilities of South American militaries for large-scale rapid response, sea- or air-lift, and minimal real-world training or preparations for mobilization and operations, potentially in a hostile environment. The details of such a challenge, and how various scenarios could play out, are beyond the scope of this chapter, but the region is poorly prepared logistically to respond to an urgent security crisis in its midst. In such an event, it is likely that today, as in the past, countries of the region would turn to the United States to lead the coordination and support for a multilateral response, perhaps via the United Nations (UN) or the OAS.[8] Even if managed with sensitivity, such a sequence of events could acutely worsen US relations in the region, and with Brazil.

An event of such scale and immediacy may be unlikely. Nevertheless, such a crisis would be costly enough to the region and to Brazil's aspirations as a regional and global leader to merit, from a strategic perspective, significant attention from Brazil. In this light, Brasília's cautious, pragmatic, low-level approach to institutionalizing security cooperation within South America seems insufficient. The effective development and institutionalization of security cooperation requires years of dialogue and collective decision-making among government and military offices at various levels, joint training, and significant investments by all parties in equipment and infrastructure that support joint operations. Member nations must reach numerous legal and technical agreements, determine the command and control structure and communications systems to be used, and allocate roles to their various forces. In South America, such efforts seem to be decades away at best.

Conclusion: What Does Brazil Really Want from Its Armed Forces?

Brazil's security policy and strategy include significant tensions: its antipathy toward the United States despite the core values and interests the two countries share; its desire for affinity with nations like China, Iran, Russia, and Cuba despite its differences with their systems and values; its limited efforts—despite the rhetoric—to implement South American economic integration and security cooperation; and its tendency to treat the military as a tool for industrial development and national prestige, with little interest in its actual capabilities or preparedness for conflict or contingency. These incongruities give shape to the country's complex relationship with its armed forces.

This complexity is reflected as well in its recent equipment purchases and investments. Many clearly support missions and objectives related to national defense, such as new border surveillance and control measures, operating bases spread throughout the country, ocean patrol vessels, and helicopters. Other projects (more expensive ones) have limited relevance to current or medium-term needs and missions, such as the acquisition of advanced fighter jets, nuclear submarines, amphibious-capable tanks, and more aircraft carriers. Those assets are useful for combat, and for the deployment of force across the seas, for example, as a member of a multinational joint task force operating off the shores of a conflict-ridden region like the Middle East. Yet Brazil's National Defense Strategy describes no such intentions, and such action would be antithetical to the principles Brazil espouses within the UN and other international forums.

Investments in nuclear submarines, aircraft carriers, shipbuilding facilities, and jet fighters also complicate Brazil's efforts to improve security cooperation with its South American and African partners, who have little capacity to interoperate with such vessels. Assets and capabilities that are useful for forward presence, that is, projecting force from the sea onto another country's territory, can be questionable from the perspective of foreign partners. These enormously expensive projects, undertaken at a time when many of Brazil's borders are virtually uncontrolled and neighbors seek help against urban gangs and rural terrorist groups, raise skepticism about Brazil's concept of and commitment to regional security cooperation. Does Brazil view security cooperation as the development, over time, of common military objectives, joint training, and interoperability, or instead as the increase of its defense exports? Are its resources sufficient to support both?

Such ambiguity and inconsistency between strategy and spending on security are common in military affairs and should be of no surprise to any US observer. What is unfortunate, however, is that this ambiguity combined with Brazil's tendency to keep its distance from Washington and US-supported security operations, hinder the advance of bilateral security cooperation in areas where it would be mutually beneficial (e.g., peacekeeping, disaster response, security capacity-building in Africa, counter-illicit trafficking). Of course the United States has also contributed to this problem by acting in ways that undermine trust and cooperation. The reparation of the strategic partnership seems far off, but security cooperation in these areas of mutual interest could help pave a path ahead if both governments would give it a chance.

Notes

1. I want to express my gratitude to Louis Goodman, Margaret Daly-Hayes, Joseph S. Tulchin, Thomaz G. da Costa, and Leonardo Day for their thoughtful comments on an earlier draft of this chapter.
2. Several companies that the Brazilian government had created and/or supported as part of their strategic industrial development program in the 1960s—manufacturers of rockets and missiles, planes, ships, and ammunition—grew profitable in the 1980s, in particular because of profitable sales to Iraq, and its partners, as it fought against Iran.
3. For example, the bilateral Defense Cooperation Agreement of 2010, which would allow and facilitate broader and deeper security cooperation, remains stuck within the president's office (Planalto). It appears to have few prospects of being sent to Congress for ratification anytime soon, at least under a Rousseff administration.
4. The case of Brazil's growing bilateral cooperation with Bolivia to improve counter-drug surveillance and interdiction operations is instructive in that it surged after Bolivia cancelled its longstanding cooperation with the US military and Drug

Enforcement Agency (DEA). In this example, Brazil effectively replaced the United States as a security partner of choice—but regional security cooperation may be improved as a result. Both Brazil and the United States achieved security objectives; however, from a strategic perspective Brazil seems to have gained at the expense of US presence and influence.

5. The difference in how much the two nations "value" security relations is also a function of the influence of the armed forces and defense sector within the political and policy-making system. In Washington this influence is significantly higher than in Brazil.

6. Security cooperation that does not directly involve interoperability, such as regarding science and research, the sales of materials, and doctrine or education, does not face such a limitation. Brazil could continue to develop such cooperation with partners around the world, with relatively few costs. My argument concerns cooperation that directly improves interoperability and training to improve joint operations, that is, the joint exercise of military power.

7. Proença Junior and Duarte (2010) provide a fascinating discussion of Brazil's strategic positioning, and options, from a "realist" perspective.

8. Incidentally, it is highly unlikely that China, Russia, or any European power would play a significant role.

CHAPTER 5

For Liberalism without Hegemony: Brazil and the Rule of Non-Intervention

Marcos Tourinho

This chapter investigates Brazil's approach to norms about foreign intervention in international society. It does so from the perspective of the relationship between the country's foreign policy and what has been frequently called the contemporary "liberal international order." In particular, it seeks to specify and locate more precisely the potential disagreements Brazil has had historically with the enforcement of liberal norms in an international context. In essence, it argues that Brazil's primary concern with the emergence of liberal norms in international society has not been about the substance of those norms and liberal values in themselves, but rather is the product of a genuine normative concern with the hegemonic way in which these norms have historically been enforced and implemented.

The position of Brazil relative to the so-called Western world is in many ways necessarily uncomfortable. While in the scholarly literature Brazil and other Latin American states are most often regarded simply as Western offshoots (Bull, 1984, pp. 229–230), the country's political self-identity in this regard has been subject to a far more complex debate. Brazil's international identity revolves around the principle that Brazil is positioned in the borders or frontiers of the West. In essence, Brazil can be clearly seen as "Western" if compared to China, India, or the Islamic World, but it is also evidently "non-Western" when considered in contrast with the "global" manifestations of the Anglo-Saxon empire such as Australia or Canada. Furthermore, the historical and cultural legacy of those who arrived in Brazil as slaves should not be underestimated: the long-standing and profound processes of racial miscegenation and religious syncretism were crucial to place Brazil in this position, in what has been called the "far West" (Spektor, 2014, p. 27).

In the study of international relations, contemporary international society is most often considered to be a product of Western design (Bull and Watson, 1984; Grewe, 2000; Ikenberry, 2001). In this view, the fundamental norms and institutions of international society result from the expansion of a previously existing European order through the parallel forces of colonialism and international law. Starting at the turn of the last century, the United States, a new centre of the Western core, refreshed this global politics and law by substituting the "old" European power politics with a new, liberal, international order based on self-determination, sovereign equality, and the rule of law. John Ikenberry, the most prominent raconteur of liberal internationalism, has described it as "open," "user friendly," and founded on hegemonic self-restraint (2001). In this narrative, the ownership and design of this order is indisputable: it is Western. The inevitable question then, is how do other countries relate, resist, and adjust to an international order that is not theirs (Barraclough, 1990; Bull, 1984)?

While a broader questioning of these narratives of "expansion" and of the establishment of a "liberal international order" is well deserved, it is not the subject of this chapter. In contrast, this chapter seeks, more modestly, to make a contribution to the understanding of Brazil's positions in relation to core international norms. A crucial aspect of this volume in general is precisely to locate where exactly Brazilian dissent from the contemporary international order lies. This chapter seeks to accomplish this with regard to the fundamental norm of non-intervention. The rule of non-intervention is crucial because it has historically determined the practical limits of sovereign autonomy and has been an important indicator of the boundaries of the rule of international law. Furthermore, because it is such a determining international norm, the rule of non-intervention also serves to indicate broader elements of Brazil's understanding of international order and international justice.

In essence, this chapter argues that Brazil's foreign policy has no existential quarrel with the fundamental principles of what has been called in the North American academic literature a "liberal international order,"[1] but rather that it has expressed strong disagreement with the hegemonic practices that have accompanied it. This is manifested, for instance, in the regular Brazilian complaints about the selective application of international norms and in their view of the fact that the United States has been historically reluctant to accept intrusive international norms applied to itself (Leigh, 2001, pp. 124–131). In Brazil's traditional foreign policy perspective, what has been euphemistically called "strategic restraint" (Ikenberry, 2001) can also be understood as a substantial and systematic effort to formalize hegemony and legalize power-based hierarchies (Simpson, 2004).

The argument unfolds in four steps. The first section investigates the relationship between liberalism and the rule of non-intervention, particularly in the context of the emergence of a global international society in the late nineteenth and early twentieth centuries. This is the starting point for the argument that hegemonic intervention and global liberalism emerged together in the late nineteenth century and already developed a relationship of political interdependence at that point. The second section briefly recounts Brazil's historical views about intervention norms from the late nineteenth century to the Cold War, emphasizing its relationship with the enforcement of liberal political and trade norms. The third section looks specifically at norms about humanitarian intervention in the post–Cold War setting, and explains how Brazil's initial reluctance to engage with these issues are associated with a reluctance to accept hegemonic practices in the field of international security. It also describes Brazil's transition toward a more constructive and engaged policy in relation to these norms. The chapter concludes with a discussion about the importance of more precisely locating dissent in the study of the global implementation and enforcement of liberal norms.

Global Liberalism and the Question of Intervention

In December 1902, the military forces of Great Britain, Germany, and Italy imposed a military blockade on Venezuela to force the settlement of a series of private financial claims with their nationals. Venezuela had refused to share legal authority over its territory and imposed local jurisdiction on the claims of some resident aliens who had suffered losses due to the country's political situation. As a result, and a standard practice at the time, the great powers intervened militarily in the country.

The case of Venezuela was no exception. Since the independence of states in the Americas, and until at least the US invasion of Nicaragua in 1928, political instability and the protection of citizens abroad have served as a justification for the use of military force in the region. Brazil, a large and relatively stable country for the standards of the region at the time, was more than once subject to intervention and displays of military force by great powers in that context. Serving as a normative justification for these actions were two distinctively liberal ideas: the defense of private property and a belief in the idea of civilizational progress.

The first justification was developed initially as a result of the increase in activities of European enterprises abroad. As Donald R. Shea explained, "In response to pressures brought to bear by the resident aliens and their associated business interests, the major investor powers sought to institutionalise procedures whereby their citizens would not suffer by being subjected to [what they saw as] inferior standards of law and justice" (1955, p. 4).

This instrument, broadly known as consular or extra-territorial jurisdiction, was hardly new. It had been developed for centuries, particularly in the coastal towns of the Indian Ocean, the Mediterranean, and Southeast Asia. According to Jörg Fisch, "Foreign merchants were granted the privilege of living under and of settling their disputes according to their own laws. This was not seen as an infringement of the sovereignty of the local ruler, but rather as means of attracting commerce without losing control over it . . . [it was a] basic institution for the accommodation of foreigners" (1992, p. 23).

The meaning of extra-territorial jurisdiction was significantly transformed, however, when throughout the nineteenth and twentieth centuries European and North American individuals and corporations significantly expanded the reach of their activities across the world. With the increase in the number of foreigners abroad and the greater formalization of international legal, diplomatic, and trade relations, great powers developed a consistent practice of political differentiation in the access to legal prerogatives. The gradually increasing power disparities between great powers and other actors meant that their extra-territorial legal privileges became a consolidated aspect of global international order.

The result was a comprehensive legal regime for the protection of citizens, property, and capital abroad. As Becker Lorca explained, "Military interpositions to protect foreign residents adopted the form of police actions to suppress riots and restore order. Reprisals included embargoes, blockade of ports, bombardment of coastal towns, punitive expeditions, and military occupation of alien territory, typically involving the seizure of the local custom office in order to take direct control of the satisfaction of pecuniary claims" (2011, p. 17). Borchard reinforced the normality of such practices: "Practically all the great powers have at different times resorted to a display of force to give moral support to a request for the protection of nationals in foreign countries or for the redress of injuries inflicted upon nationals" (1928, quoted in Becker Lorca, 2011, p. 447).

At that very same time, in Europe, the first military interventions with a humanitarian justification were taking place, particularly in the Ottoman Empire, and under the same legal framework of the protection of citizens abroad. These were also founded on a hierarchical outlook of the world: "The European 'most civilised' nations contrasted their 'superior' civilisation with that of a 'barbarous,' 'uncivilised' target state, prone to inhumanity, whose sovereignty and authority they contested. Since the early nineteenth century the rationale of interventions was saving fellow 'Christians' in the short term and exporting 'civilisation' (European civilisation) in the medium term" (Rodogno, 2012, p. 12).

While it is evident that military interventions conducted in that period are by no means equal or equivalent to contemporary ones, it is still important to consider the extent to which the emergence of liberal norms in international society is historically founded upon the acceptability of international hierarchy and in practices of global hegemony. Under classical international law, military actions taken by great powers to protect their citizens and property abroad were seen, above all, as a fundamental guarantor for liberal trade, international investment, and, more broadly, of the primacy of (Western) "civilization."

The idea of civilization and the promotion of civilizational progress have also, in themselves, served as a justification for military intervention and were foundational to the rise of liberal internationalism after the First World War. While Woodrow Wilson's rhetoric about self-determination was broad in promise and messianic in style, it certainly was not universal in application. Wilson's views on race, the progressive development of societies in hierarchical stages and the need for white tutoring of "backward" peoples are imperial in origin, domineering in implementation, and, thus, "illiberal" in a very practical sense.

According to Roger Louis, the Mandates System defended by Wilson "in effect defined three classifications of mankind: the 'A' peoples of the Middle East, who in a relatively short period of time would be able 'to stand alone'; the tribal 'B' peoples of tropical Africa, who would require an indefinite number of years or decades of economic and political advancement under European tutelage; and the 'C' 'primitive' peoples of the Pacific and the 'Hottentots' of South West Africa, who probably would remain European subjects at least for a period of centuries, if not forever" (1984, p. 201).

While it is true that European powers had a more blunt view of the mandates system (British prime minister Lloyd George explained that there was "no large difference between the mandatory principle and the principles laid down by the Berlin Conference [of 1884]"),[2] the logic of establishing colonial protectorates around the world to fulfill "the white man's burden" was by no means only an European one. Wilson himself, reflecting on the American colonial experience in the Philippines, argued that his country was a "trustee" of its overseas possessions, being there not for self-benefit, but to carry out a duty (Manela, 2007, pp. 24–28).

The hierarchical outlook that permeated Wilson's vision of international order did not go unnoticed by its targets in the Global South. In describing the disappointment of nationalist movements worldwide with their exclusion from the Versailles settlement, Manela explains: "The campaigns they led in 1919 did not set out to tear down the existing international order but rather to join it as members of equal status. When the quest to achieve self-determination through the peace conference failed, however, many anti-colonial activists, disillusioned with the results of Wilson's liberal internationalism began to seek alternative ideological models and sources of practical support in their struggles for self-determination" (2007, p. 224). The birth of liberal internationalism was observed from the South not as a new era of openness and opportunity but rather as the reaffirmation "in new clothes" of a fundamentally hierarchical vision of world order as well as of the standard political practices of hegemony.

The continuities between the imperial project of civilization and the "liberal" international order proposed by Wilson in the lead up to 1919 deserves a more careful consideration. As Wertheim has noted, "The prevailing historiographical paradigm depicts the development of international society as a progressive advance from power politics toward global community." This teleology, he argues, "Occludes alternatives within internationalism, in this case taking at face value the League's presentation of itself as a momentous first step from anarchy to order and from politics to law" (2012, p. 211).

Two elements are crucial to balance this historiographical account. First, much of what is often described as the core foundations of "Wilsonian" liberal internationalism (i.e., the ideas of free trade, sovereignty, sovereign equality, collective problem solving, the rule of law) were well established in the public political debates of the late nineteenth century (Ikenberry, 2009; Mazower, 2012). Already in that century, the diversity and scope of (liberal) internationalisms were broad, ranging from regular trans-governmental cooperation to informal networks and institutions created by technical experts (statisticians, jurists, etc.), scientists, and athletes. It was this internationalism that laid the most solid foundations for the global international society that would emerge in the century that followed (Geyer and Paulmann, 2001). In fact, some have persuasively argued that Wilsonianism was not really an advance, but in fact a retreat from more radical forms of liberal internationalist ambitions present at the turn of the last century (Mazower, 2012; Wertheim, 2012). Second, as described above, embedded in many of Wilson's ideas for the design of the League of Nations was a hierarchical view of world order that was imperial in origin. Beyond the mandates system and the racist limits of his views of self-determination, Wilson's global outlook clearly differentiated the institutional, political, and legal prerogatives of great and "small" powers, ultimately creating an international order that, in practice, was neither "open" nor "user-friendly."

In this sense, liberal internationalism and empire are not as entirely antagonistic as the literature and the traditional historiography of the period suggests. Starting in the late nineteenth century and continuing into the present, these two ideas engaged in an interdependent relationship: a liberal order is only acceptable if hierarchically implemented. Displays of military force were a fundamental tool for this enforcement. It was in this context that some of Brazil's most lasting views of the emergence of a liberal international order were developed and, as such, they can help explain why so much importance was given by Brazil to the rule of non-intervention throughout the last century.

Brazil and the Rule of Non-Intervention: A Brief History

Independent Brazil's first encounter with a rule of non-intervention took place almost immediately after its independence, and still in the context of American[3] regional efforts to affirm national autonomy from the European colonial powers. In this context, the doctrine proclaimed by US president James Monroe stated that any European "interposition for the purpose of oppressing [the American republics], or controlling in any other manner their destiny" would be understood as an unfriendly disposition toward the United States.[4]

Different from what is often presumed, Brazil and Hispanic America's views on the Monroe Doctrine at that point were largely favorable. As understood throughout the nineteenth century, the declaration simply reaffirmed the converging view in the region that keeping the Europeans away from the hemisphere was indispensable to the consolidation of the independence of the American republics.[5] At the Panama Conference of 1826 organized by Simón Bolívar, the doctrine was formally adopted as a part of the outcome declaration. Reflecting on this issue, Clovis Blevilaquia, a Brazilian jurist, stated: "From the American point of view, the Monroe Doctrine, like the Pan-American congresses which since 1826 have met in America, is an expression of the consciousness of American unity revealed by the continent, and the affirmation of the fact that the nations of this hemisphere should be considered as equally free and sovereign by the Powers of the Old World and that their territory can not be acquired by the latter under any pretext nor temporarily occupied" (Alvarez, 1924, p. 240). In 1824, Brazil and other states in the Americas sought to institutionalize the doctrine into a formal treaty of security alliance, a proposal that was rejected by the North Americans (Alvarez, 1924, pp. 10–11).

In that period, it is important to note, a distinct collective legal consciousness was being formed in Latin America on the basis of principles of sovereign equality, peaceful dispute of settlements, and the rule of non-intervention (Becker Lorca, 2006; Obregón, 2012). While Brazil was far from being a main proponent of these ideas (in fact, some Brazilian jurists and diplomats were critical of the idea of a distinctively Latin American international law at the time), they have had a lasting impact on the country's international political and legal consciousness (Becker Lorca, 2006; Vianna, 1912).

Following the proclamation of the Roosevelt Corollary in 1904, which effectively transformed the Monroe Doctrine into an instrument of US hegemony in the region (particularly Central America), significant international public debates about both hegemony and intervention took place in the Second Hague Conference, in 1907. In response to these policy changes in the United States, as well as to the Anglo-German-Italian intervention in Venezuela in 1902, Latin American republics strongly pushed for a revision of norms about intervention to collect debt. Based on the work of prominent jurist Carlos Calvo, Argentine foreign minister Luis Drago took this discussion first to the Pan-American conference in Rio de Janeiro (1906) and later to the Second Hague Conference (1907).

In The Hague, Brazil expressed the problem in terms of the conflict between a legal–moral question about the sovereign equality and autonomy of states and the more practical problem of trade. Brazil was determined to provide the necessary guarantees needed for foreign investors to remain interested in countries like Brazil. With a foreign policy that at that time was fundamentally dedicated to enhancing its trade volume, Brazil pushed for the establishment of arbitration mechanisms that could avoid intervention, but that at the same time sought to preserve the fundamental interests of creditors. This synthesis, known as the Drago-Porter compromise, was ultimately adopted by the Conference.

A fundamental turning point in Brazil's position regarding intervention was made during the Cold War, as Brazil gradually distanced its foreign policy from that of the United States. In his inauguration speech in 1961, Foreign Minister San Tiago Dantas stated his views on the underlying principles of the nation's foreign policy: "Our country, conscious of its responsibilities towards international order and perfectly clear about the national objectives it pursues, cannot avoid being always more than what it has been before: an independent nation, a nation loyal to the democratic principles based on which its internal order lies, loyal to its international commitments (. . .) loyal to the great cause – that of the emancipation and economic development of all peoples – that led us to be solidary to them and take (. . .) an attitude, a coherent and uniform line of conduct in defence of the emancipation of the peoples through the abolition of the residues of colonialism in the world. We cannot, also, avoid from being a nation that is decidedly engaged in the preservation and application of the principle of non-intervention in the lives of the peoples" (Dantas, 2007).

Under the military regime, which lasted for over twenty years, Brazil evidently de-emphasized democracy as an international value, but maintained emphasis on international cooperation, international institutions, and a firm consistency with regard to the norm of non-intervention. Foreign Minister Azeredo da Silveira stated: "[Brazil] observes with intransigent devotion the fundamental principles of the coexistence of nations: non-intervention, the right to self-determination, the juridical equality of states. It sees in these principles the necessary foundation for the duty of cooperation among countries, which should not be subordinated to the wills of some, but must be in practice and in spirit the convergence of the sovereign desires of all states. For Brazil, this is the concept that must permeate the interdependence of all peoples as an inescapable fact of international life."[6]

At that point, Brazil had started to take more seriously its rhetorical commitment to the process of decolonization and increased its ties with countries in the so-called Third World. This was crucial to determining the country's views on non-intervention and to increasing its sympathy toward the postcolonial cause more broadly. During the Cold War, Brazil took political steps to reaffirm its status as living on the "frontiers" of the Western world. While with the end of the Cold War these debates transformed significantly, Brazil's own positions on these issues remained largely unchanged, with the principles of self-determination, non-intervention, and the formal equality of states written into its constitution and composing the fundamental basis for its diplomats' self-image.

Humanitarian Intervention and the Responsibility to Protect

It is well known that the end of the Cold War brought about a series of profound normative transformations to the core of international society, and reform of the institutional framework of 1945 was high on the agenda. A crucial aspect of this transformation had to do with a changing political environment about the question of intervention in world politics. This can be noticed in the intense intellectual debate about intervention norms that took place starting in the 1980s. This discussion was promoted initially by the French non-governmental organization Médecins Sans Frontières (then led by Bernard Kouchner, who would later become the French Foreign Minister), which advocated for a "droit d'ingérence," or a right to intervention for humanitarian purposes, and lasted through the 1990s.

Evidently, this intellectual debate did not occur in isolation, and was in active dialogue with the concrete peace and security challenges of the time. In spite of that extensively debated "liberal moment," already at the beginning of that decade Brazil was reluctant to accept a more robust use of force by the

Security Council in the maintenance of international peace and security. Secretary General Boutros Boutros-Ghali's Agenda for Peace, the first substantial step the United Nations took in that direction, was later called by an influential Brazilian (and later foreign minister), Celso Amorim, an "intrusive and militarizing" proposal that was bound to create excessively high expectations and ultimately lead to frustration (1999, p. 2). Reflecting on the case of Haiti in 1994, Amorim argued that the military intervention authorized under Chapter VII sought to resolve a problem that was "of an obviously internal nature and without any clearly discernible international impact," and was institutionally inadequate.[7] Brazil ultimately abstained from the vote on that resolution.

In the case of Rwanda, Brazil's position reveals to some extent its views on the problem of hegemony and the then emerging norm on the acceptability of humanitarian intervention. As an elected member of the Security Council at the time, Brazil defended the strengthening of the capacity of United Nations Assistance Mission for Rwanda (UNAMIR) and its expansion as a Chapter VII peace enforcement mission. At the same time, it challenged the belated UN-authorized French Operation Turquoise on both normative and practical grounds. In a Security Council meeting discussing the issue, Brazil's permanent representative Ronaldo Sardenberg declared: "On the question before us, my Government, aside from problems of a political nature related to the implementation of the mission, has serious doubts as regards its likely impact on the [UNAMIR], considering the present political environment. As a principle, Brazil has repeatedly maintained that the Council should do its utmost to avoid invoking the extraordinary powers conferred upon it by Chapter VII of the United Nations Charter. In this connection, it strikes us that the Security Council has avoided placing the humanitarian mandate given to UNAMIR under that Chapter."[8]

Later in that decade, and particularly after the failure of the Security Council to avoid or stop the genocide in Rwanda, debates about a potential "just" cause for military intervention for humanitarian purposes accelerated. Two contributions are worth noting. The first was Francis Deng's proposed reconceptualization of the idea of inalienable sovereignty to one based on "sovereignty as responsibility." Then serving as the Secretary General's Special Representative for Internally Displaced Persons (IDPs), the respected Sudanese diplomat was trying to resolve a humanitarian problem, but also in the context of a longstanding normative political question. His fundamental starting point was that the primary responsibility to protect IDPs lay with the host government, and that only later, if they were unable or unwilling to do so, should they request international assistance (Bellamy, 2011, pp. 9–10).

This debate gained strength with the humanitarian, political, and institutional crisis of Kosovo. Responding to a request by the Secretary General, a commission set up by the Canadian government sought to address the most fundamental political question of that time: how to resolve the dilemma between inaction in the Council on the face of humanitarian disasters and the collapse of the global framework of international security through recurrent unauthorized military action. The result was the idea of a Responsibility to Protect (RtoP) (Bellamy, 2011, pp. 16–17). Kofi Annan also played an integral role in this process: while he certainly did not single-handedly reach a global agreement about humanitarian intervention, he did subtly impose the idea that international intervention for humanitarian purposes could not be completely excluded from consideration (Roberts, 2006).

As the idea of an RtoP started to emerge in the international arena, Brazil was reluctant to change its traditional discourse. While it should be noted that the country was not a major player in these early debates, its officials consistently highlighted their scepticism toward what they saw as a new doctrine of hegemonic intervention. Particularly in the aftermath of the unilateral interventions of Kosovo and Iraq, Brazil was fundamentally concerned with the weakening of the authority of the Security Council, which in the view of its diplomats posed the single greatest threat to international peace and security. In this context, then foreign minister Celso Amorim commented that "the most questionable section of the [ICISS[9]] report" refers to what may happen if the Council fails to act. The projection of the unilateral action of "concerned states," Amorim wrote, "leaves the door open for some countries to arrogate to themselves the right to intervene without the express authorisation of the Security Council or the follow up by a truly multilateral institution" (2004, p. 141). This is a clear manifestation of Brazil's longstanding concern with the hegemonic enforcement of international norms, and particularly those that are described as "liberal."

As Amorim's discourse suggests, an important aspect of Brazil's reluctance to accept RtoP as proposed by the ICISS, was the problem of authority in relation to the Security Council. Brazil's problem at that point was not really with the idea of a responsibility to protect, per se, but rather with the broader movement away from the centralized authority of the Security Council in relation to these issues. During the workings of the Secretary General's High-level Panel on Threats, Challenges and Change and in the lead up to the 2005 World Summit, Brazilian perspectives on the issue would become more refined. Essential to Brazil's acceptance of the new concept of humanitarian intervention was placing it under the collective security framework of the UN Security Council. At that point, avoiding unchecked hegemonic enforcement of that norm was a crucial priority. At the World Summit, Brazil pushed for two aspects that ultimately culminated in the final text about the RtoP: a clear statement of the four crimes that would trigger an RtoP and the firm placement of the responsibility to protect (and intervene) under the authority of the Security Council. This is in line with Brazil's traditional view that in the enforcement of collective security, "collective" is just as important as "security."

Nowhere were the practical consequences of these concerns clearer than in the Security Council debates over the case of Libya, in March 2011. As the issue reached the Council, it was evident that Libya's Muammar Gaddafi had clear intentions of crushing a popular rebellion without distinguishing civilians from armed combatants. At that point, Brazil's foreign ministry under Antonio Patriota decided to more actively engage with the principle and practice of the "Responsibility to Protect." By the time Resolution 1973 was voted upon, Brazil was in favor of the invocation of RtoP and, at that point, had no objections to the use of military means in its enforcement.

Brazil, however, did not ultimately vote in favor of that resolution. In its perspective, the resolution's terms of enforcement (particularly the last-minute addition of operational paragraph four)[10] were so broad that those intervening could do almost anything they pleased. The fear was that a broadly authorized no-fly zone with unclear terms of implementation would enable intervening powers to conduct a political intervention and essentially overthrow the Gaddafi regime. As the foreign ministry would later put it, Brazil worried that this would set a precedent, under which arguments for humanitarian intervention "might be misused for purposes other than protecting civilians, such as regime change."[11]

As the months passed, that concern proved reasonable. Despite criticism from the Arab League, the African Union, and others, shortly after the no-fly zone was put in place the leaders of the United States, United Kingdom, and France announced with fanfare in major papers that the mandate to protect civilians had become an outright intervention for the purposes of regime change (Cameron et al., 2011). Much to Brazil's normative concern, at that point there was not much the Security Council could do: its hands were tied to an operation the Brazilians believed was being distorted. In the view of Brazilian policy-makers, it was a clear example of how liberal international norms can be, and often are, implemented under terms characterized by unilateral action and hegemonic practices.

Echoing to some extent the country's position in relation to the crisis in Kosovo in 1999, Brazil's perspective on Libya gave as much weight to the recognition and implementation of a responsibility to protect, as it did to the consideration of how this should be done and under which authority. In 2011, when it came to RtoP, Brazil clearly accepted the "liberal" aspects of the international norm but not the ultimately hegemonic terms of its practical implementation. Providing one more ironic display of the longstanding relationship between liberal norms and hegemony, the then US Permanent Representative to the UN Susan Rice declared in an imperious statement that Brazil's and India's position on that issue was one that: "One might not have anticipated, given that each of them come out of strong and proud democratic traditions . . . [and] let me just say, we've learned a lot and, frankly, not all of it encouraging."[12]

Brazil's normative reaction to the Libyan crisis had its origins directly in the office of Foreign Minister Patriota. Under his direct supervision, some close associates drafted a concept note entitled "Responsibility While Protecting: Elements for the Development and Promotion of a Concept." The document, presented as a letter to the Secretary General and later extensively discussed in the UN and policy circles, was intended precisely as an articulation of the ideas described above. The document started with a reaffirmation of Brazil's support for the idea and practice of an RtoP but then moved to a detailed discussion of how some of the sharper edges of its uneven and hierarchical implementation could be softened. For the purposes of this chapter, two aspects of the proposal are worth noting. First, it proposed stable normative criteria for the "prudent and judicious" use of military force, namely the consideration of principles of last resort, proportionality, and its limited character as expressed in the objectives established by the Council. It further observed that the use of force should under no circumstances generate more harm than good, and that a careful assessment of potential consequences must be made prior to any authorization. Second, in a suggestion that would strengthen the institutional authority of the Security Council as a whole (rather than some of its individual members), the paper called for the enhancement of procedures for the monitoring, assessment, and accountability of those to whom authority is granted to resort to force by the Security Council.[13]

These proposals and Brazil's stance on Libya and the RtoP reflect wider foreign policy concerns that have been historically important in the composition of the Brazilian foreign ministry's self-image. They reflect broader concerns about the purposes of multilateralism and the importance of a rule-based international order that treats states equally. They are direct illustrations also of Brazil's views that liberal values and liberal norms are important ends, but they do not in any way justify the use of hegemonic means.

Conclusion

In his magnum opus *After Victory*, John Ikenberry proposed the hypothesis that less-powerful states worldwide embraced (US) hegemony in exchange for the benefits of an "open," user-friendly, liberal international order

(Ikenberry, 2001). This chapter has argued that at least in the case of Brazil, and in relation to the fundamental norm of non-intervention, this has not been the case. While in fact the aspects of contemporary international order that Ikenberry calls "liberal" (institutions, rule of law, etc.) are essentially welcomed by Brazil, the country has at the same time consistently rejected and resisted the hegemonic practices that so often have accompanied the practice of this "liberal order."

This resistance in Brazilian foreign policy has been manifest in two recurrent international postures. The first is the support for an institutionalized and rule-based international system. Brazilian foreign policy, which has been called "Grotian" (de Goffredo, 2005) commonly articulates its views in normative terms, and regularly emphasizes the rule of international law as a crucial aspect of its international outlook. Brazil's posture during the Kosovo crisis was indicative of this approach: an overwhelming concern with the political and institutional consequences of ignoring the legal authority of the Security Council with regard to the use of military force.

The second position is a fairly radical approach toward the absolute equality of states. For Brazilian foreign policy, reciprocity is the cornerstone of international social life and deserves close attention in both bilateral and multilateral settings. In the 1907 Hague Conference, Brazil defended the perfect equality of state representation in the proposed permanent court of justice, rejecting the proposal (and previously existing European tradition) of formally differentiating between great and small powers in international treaties. Over one hundred years later, similar ideas were defended during debates for the establishment of the Human Rights Council in Geneva. Brazil held a strong position that *all* countries should be subject to an international human rights evaluation through the Universal Periodic Review, rejecting *a priori* differentiation between countries that are supposedly "supportive" of human rights and those who are not. Reflecting on these ideas and projecting his own vision for international order, Brazilian foreign minister Antonio Patriota has stated: "What do we want? A multilateral system in which everyone is subject to the same rules" (2013).

It is evident that these ideas do not direct *all* of Brazil's behavior in international relations. Because foreign policy is a complex enterprise in which multiple actors push for their distinct visions and interests, no single concept provides perfect explanatory coherence. However, because these ideas are deeply ingrained and widely respected components of the foreign policy establishment's self-image, they are useful in elucidating some of the thinking behind Brazil's international attitudes.

In this context, it can be said that Brazil is not and has not been a revisionist state when it comes to the fundamental norms of international society, and specifically when it comes to the rule of non-intervention. While most liberal norms in international society are largely welcomed by Brazil's government and society, what they see as the hegemonic terms of their enforcement has produced substantial Brazilian dissent in international political debates on these issues. Celso Amorim, the most influential Brazilian foreign minister in decades, summarized this perspective by arguing: "We want neither multipolarity without the ballast of international law, nor multilateralism placed in the service of unipolarity. Strictly, what we seek is increased multipolarity with the juridical-parliamentary support of multilateralism. In other words, we want to preserve the UN framework, adapting it without disfiguring it to the new demands of contemporary reality" (1999).

Notes

1. According to Ikenberry (2009), crucial aspects of this order are "open markets, international institutions, cooperative security, democratic community, progressive change, collective problem solving, shared sovereignty, the rule of law."
2. United States Department of State, Foreign Relations of the United States: 1919 the Paris Peace Conference, 13 vols. (Washington: US Government Printing Office, 1942), vol. iii, p. 750.
3. In this chapter America is used in its traditional meaning, referring to the Americas in general, and not just the United States.
4. James Monroe, Message of President James Monroe at the commencement of the first session of the 18th Congress (The Monroe Doctrine), February 12, 1823; Presidential Messages of the 18th Congress, ca. February 12, 1823–ca. March 03, 1825; Record Group 46; Records of the US Senate, 1789–1990; National Archives.
5. This would change only with the proclamation of the Roosevelt Corollary in 1904, which marked the transformation of the United States into a world (and colonial) power and the establishment of new political dynamics in the inter-American system.
6. Ministério das Relações Exteriores, Resenha de política exterior do Brasil, Abril, Maio e Junho de 1975 (Brasília: Ministério das Relações Exteriores, 1975).
7. Celso Amorim was Brazil's Permanent Representative to the UN between 1995 and 1999. For his views on this issue see (Amorim, 1999).
8. UN Security Council, 3392nd Meeting. Wednesday, June 22, 1994 (S/PV.3392).
9. International Commission on Intervention and State Sovereignty.
10. Paragraph four authorized the use of "all necessary measures," beyond the already agreed-upon "no-fly zone." See United Nations, "Security Council Approves 'No-fly Zone' Over Libya, Authorizing 'All Necessary Measures' To Protect Civilians, By Vote of 10 In Favour with 5 Abstentions," March 17,

2001, http://www.un.org/News/Press/docs/2011/sc10200.doc.htm (accessed July 23, 2013).

11. Permanent Mission of Brazil to the United Nations, "Responsibility while Protecting," p. 3.

12. *New York Times*, September 13, 2011, cited in Spektor (2012).

13. Permanent Mission of Brazil to the United Nations, "Responsibility while Protecting," p. 4.

CHAPTER 6

Brazil's Ambivalent Challenge to Global Environmental Norms

Eve Z. Bratman

B razil's relationship to global environmental governance has long been fraught with contradictions. The nation is bounteous in biodiversity, forest, and freshwater resources, and it is a global leader in creating new conservation areas. Since 1992, when it hosted the Rio Earth Summit, Brazil has been a negotiation leader of the Global South on environmental issues. Yet at the same time, Brazil's position on environmental issues since the early 1990s has included the adoption of non-committal positions on climate change, increases in its energy production goals to keep up with demand, and the dilution of its forestry laws (Hochstetler and Keck, 2007; Teixeira, 2010).

How does Brazil interact with the evolving global liberal order on environmental issues? This chapter argues that Brazil generally adheres to the global liberal environmental order. Yet this is largely a reflection of the tenuousness and lack of rigor in the global liberal order's approach to environmental issues, rather than an affirmation of any outstanding proactivity in Brazilian environmental leadership. At home, Brazil's often contradictory stances can be ascribed to the low priority given to environmental issues and a lack of domestic consensus on environmental objectives. Other issues, most notably development and national sovereignty, have frequently been given priority over environmental policy, even as non-state actors have effectively influenced local and state environmental policies. The result is a tapestry of differing local, state, and national approaches to the environment. On the world stage, Brazil holds an ambivalent national position with regard to the "green economy," the notion, promoted by the United Nations (UN) since the economic crisis of 2008, of an economy that is low-carbon, efficient in the use of natural resources, and socially inclusive.

This chapter provides a brief history of these contradictions, and specifically examines the influence that non-state actors have exerted over Brazilian environmental politics. The argument proceeds in three parts. The first section describes liberal environmentalism, the predominant approach to global governance on environmental issues. Second, the chapter explains why Brazil's positioning on the green economy incorporates important points of resistance to global liberal environmentalism. The analysis is based on examination of different political actors and multilevel governance. Third, a focused empirical discussion follows, illustrating how changing spheres of influence have affected Brazilian environmental norms, yielding positions which are sometimes contradictory, and which may backslide from earlier positions because of their selective prioritization. The chapter concludes with observations on the interactions between different actors in Brazilian environmental governance and emphasizes the extent to which Brazil's role in global environmental governance is reflective of the norms of liberal environmentalism.

Liberal Environmental Norms: From Sustainable Development toward the Green Economy

Since the late 1980s liberal norms in global environmental politics have centered upon the concept of "sustainable development." The creation of a global liberal environmental consensus—first around sustainable development and, more recently, around the "green economy"—is one of the most important developments in the history of environmental governance, and is marked by the promotion of a liberal economic and political order within the shared goals and values that underpin environmental politics (Bernstein, 2000, pp. 464–512; 2002, pp. 1–16).

For scholars of global environmental governance, it is widely recognized that the norms established within the paradigm of sustainable development are predicated on liberal norms, understood as a championing of free trade principles, environmental cost accounting, and individualization of responsibility (Hobson, 2013, pp. 56–72). With the distinct affirmation of the sustainable development concept that took place at the Rio Earth summit in 1992, environmental governance began to more thoroughly embed the logic of state sovereignty and free market control. Notably, this was achieved through affirmation of the "polluter pays" principle (wherein environmental costs are assumed to be fully accounted for and responsibility is taken by private parties, rather than by strict regulation) and the "precautionary principle" (which establishes that in conditions where there is uncertain environmental harm, precaution should be taken) (Bernstein, 2002). At the summit, trade and the environment became institutionally viewed as having mutually reconcilable goals, captured within the discourse of sustainable development. The policies stemming from the Rio 1992 Earth Summit emphasized reducing state subsidies, resisting and reducing protectionism, internalizing environmental costs, and clarifying intellectual and other property rights (Bernstein, 2002). At the conference, Brazil largely transitioned from its historic "veto-state" attitude into a position as a more active participant, leading the bloc of nations from the Global South to ensure that environmental agreements would not compromise social priorities of development, poverty eradication, and technology transfers (Barros-Platiau, 2010).

While national strategies for sustainable development emerged and international cooperation followed from the Rio 1992 conference, many governments, including Brazil's, remain plagued by ongoing concerns over global economic, energy, food, and financial insecurity. These are further intensified by scientists' warnings about climate change and civilization surpassing multiple ecological limits. These are multiple and diffuse threats which beckon for international cooperation, suggesting a need for international engagement distinct from that of Cold-War era liberalism, dominated by the United States and Western European countries. However, the framework for international collaboration on those issues remains within the same institutions established in the earlier era of the global liberal order (Ikenberry, 2010).

The "green growth" and "green development" policy discourses—understood to refer to the UN's promotion of an economy that is low-carbon, efficient in the use of natural resources, and socially inclusive—are largely embedded within the sustainable development discourse, and represent a transforming, albeit still entrenched, variety of a global liberal regime. Like sustainable development, the "green" discourses are polemical among the environmental community, and are often criticized for overuse to the point of meaninglessness, as well as a lack of definitional precision in the first place. Sparked by the 2008 financial failures and economic crises, the green economy emerged as an alternative discourse to the sustainable development paradigm which earlier shaped much of global environmental politics (Brand, 2012, pp. 28–32; UNEP, 2011). It came into international prominence as the orienting framework for discussions at the Rio+20 Summit, which took place in Rio de Janeiro in June 2012. The discourse aimed to re-energize national policies, international cooperation, and sustainable development efforts (UN-DESA, 2012).

The green economy discourse posits a worldview wherein economic development is not seen in conflict with environmental priorities or social equity. Instead, these goals are construed as mutually supportive aims. Green development has been heralded as a means of achieving sustainable development, and as having significant analytical reach and policy applicability (Bowen and Fankhauser, 2011, pp. 1157–1159; UNEP, 2011). However, the framework positions the imperative of ecological sustainability predominantly through the lens of economic considerations (Ocampo, 2012; Rocky Mountain Institute, 1998). While the green economy centers upon the concept that economic growth and environmental sustainability have greater synergies than contradictions, critics have argued that in practice, the green economy has involved changing political actors and spheres of influence, encouraging more marketization, privatization, and the fostering of unequal social relations (Jacobi and Sinisgalli, 2012). The discourse of the green economy highlights environmental protection and innovation, but at the same time, may lead to a process in which nature is increasingly seen as a commodity, and where growth imperatives are left unquestioned (Becker, 2012, pp. 783–790). Brazil's role was central in drafting the final conference document, and in arguing for new funds for climate change and avoiding deforestation, as well as in encouraging the Sustainable Development Goals to be emphatic on social inclusion. Brazil's role in recent international environmental governance has been termed that of a "model exporter" (Barros-Platiau, 2010, p. 76), but the conference itself was considered to be a disappointment, especially given that the final document, "The Future We Want," lacked both ambition and detail in its response to continuing environmental degradation and worsening poverty and inequality (Watts and Ford, 2012). The green economy framework captures the notion of a transforming global liberal order, insofar as it is one where market-based principles predominate, and also, as Ikenberry (2010) suggests, the rising powers increasingly take on roles in international cooperation, and "poles" of state influence are more predominant than a central "anchor" of hegemony.

Global institutions such as the World Trade Organization (WTO) or the Organization for Economic Cooperation and Development (OECD), which operate under liberal environmental norms have had enormous difficulty in coping with environmental challenges (Bernstein, 2002, pp. 1–16). In the forestry sector, for example, the important role ascribed to the private sector has contributed to the difficulty of reaching common global accords on deforestation and forest management issues (Humphreys, 2006). Similarly, the ability of global environmental institutions such as the Kyoto Protocol of the Framework Convention on Climate Change (FCCC) to cope with the environmental externalities of private sector production has proven woefully inadequate, particularly in the face of climate change (Florini and Sovacool, 2011, pp. 57–74). Such failures highlight the importance of understanding how governments, civil society, and the private sector are responding to and experiencing the challenges of governance. They also raise questions about the effectiveness of the emerging powers to influence change and the norms that are established within the liberal environmental regimes which were previously dominated by developed countries.

Brazil's Contradictory Global Environmental Politics

Brazil has long been a central player in global environmental politics. Not only has the nation played host to some of the most notable conferences on environment, it is also a leader among nations of the Global South and Latin America within many such discussions. Furthermore, the nation's position on many global environmental issues has been one that seeks to take on responsibility within existing institutions. Its most notable roles as host were at the UN Summit on Sustainable Development (also known as the "Rio Summit") in 1992, and the Rio+20 Summit in 2012. Brazil's important place in global environmental governance is largely *sui generis* because of its wealth of natural resources: its biodiversity and wealth of Amazonian forest and freshwater resources give the nation global relevance on environmental issues. Brazil is generally considered an emerging or middle power in international relations. But in the environmental arena, Brazil is a central player, important historically, symbolically, and materially for its abundance of natural resources. With its increased prominence on the global stage during the twenty-first century, Brazil has increasingly sought to play a more prominent role in governance over environmental issues, most notably in climate change security and in food and agriculture (Barros-Platiau, 2010).[1]

Brazil has generally resisted the status quo in environmental agreements, which, in a general sense, has involved taking little action on most global environmental policy issues. Despite seeking a leadership position in negotiations and within global institutions, Brazil has not been radical in its stances on issues like climate change, where the country has acted in line with other developing countries by seeking common but differentiated responsibilities toward greenhouse gas emissions. Recent environmental dissonances within Brazilian domestic politics demonstrate how the sustainable development and the green economy frameworks are being resisted and re-interpreted in Brazil domestically and internationally, shedding light on the ambivalent ways Brazil interacts with the evolving liberal environmental order.

Brazilian energy and environmental policies have long prioritized development goals, often with an orientation toward modernization, which involves building significant infrastructure and promoting industrial growth. The political path of President Dilma Rousseff is emblematic of this national orientation. Prior to ascending to the presidency, Rousseff served as the head of the Ministry of Mines and Energy for Brazil. In this capacity, in 2004, she successfully won an international agreement that large dams should be considered as a clean energy source within the World Renewable Energy Conference. Wary of new energy technologies because they seemed to be pushed by the developed countries onto the developing countries, Rousseff took a stance at the 2009 Copenhagen conference on climate change about how the "right to develop" should not be impinged upon by tighter environmental strictures (Faleiros, 2011). Brazil has made strong commitments to promote national economic growth and increase the amount of energy available in the nation by 50 percent. As part of this strategy, the Rousseff government projects that over thirty new dams will be constructed from now until 2021, most of which will be located in the Amazon basin (Forero, 2013).

Despite this decidedly promodernization stance, between 2005 and 2010 there were several signs that the Brazilian government was making progress on climate change. The basis for these changes were substantial reductions in deforestation rates, the signing of a voluntary commitment to reduce emissions in 2009, and the sanctioning of a Brazilian climate bill (Law no. 12,187) in early 2010 (Viola et al., 2012). President Rousseff noted in her January 1, 2011 inaugural speech that the idea of the green economy would be central to her approach: "I consider that Brazil has a sacred mission to show the world that it is possible for a country to grow rapidly without destroying the environment."[2]

Early on in her administration, however, the nation also experienced some notable backsliding on environmental grounds. This concise synopsis captures the recent changes:

> the climate and environmental agenda has suffered considerable setbacks, like the expansion of the oil sector, the reform of Brazilian Forest Code, increase in gasoline consumption, the stagnation of ethanol, and the persistent expansion of individual/private transport. Policies at the federal level have abandoned the focus on issues of low carbon, in particular, and environmental, in general: not only has the implementation of the Climate Law barely advanced, but, in early 2012, the government also responded to the international crisis with a traditional carbon-intensive industrial stimulus package, focused on the car manufacturing sector and decided to eliminate taxation on oil consumption on the same day as Rio+20 ended, in June 2012. (Viola et al., 2012, p. 26)

Historian Andrew Hurrell notes that Brazil is currently faced with the predicament of putting more stock in existing formal institutions (such as the UN Security Council) than other emerging powers. But he also notes that since the Lula administration, domestic politics and informal institutions have become more politicized, reflecting a broader set of changes, which, he predicts, will erode the rather closed and top-down structures which comprised Brazilian foreign policy in the past (Hurrell, 2010, pp. 60–67). This phenomenon is particularly evident in the environmental arena.

The discussion which follows focuses on some of the most significant environmental norms in the nation through an analysis not only of presidential actions, but also of the sub-state and transnational activism over the environmental issues at stake. It illustrates the multiplicity of actors wielding power in governance processes, and contributes to an explanation of the persistence of the contradictory positions taken by the Brazilian government on these environmental issues. Underlying Brazil's ambivalence toward the green economy are two central foundations of Brazilian political thought highlighted by Maia and Taylor (Chapter 3, this volume): the primacy that the Brazilian government accords to economic development and the primacy of national sovereignty as an underpinning of Brazil's international engagements.

New People and Spaces of Environmental Governance

The field of international relations has long focused on central questions of agency and structure within the international system (Wendt, 1999; Wight, 2006). Some observers of international relations have noted the shifts in global power structures, such that East–West divergences and formal institutions are less relevant than they used to be in actually influencing change (Nye, 2011). Diplomatic norms and state practices are increasingly being questioned. At issue are not only the merits of hard versus soft power, but also who emerges as a relevant actor in international politics and what spaces exist for political action to take place (McConnell et al., 2012, pp. 804–814; Parmer and Cox, 2010; Sharp, 2009; Yeh, 2012, pp. 408–418). A recent focus of scholarship is on the contributions of political geography in approaching these same questions in terms of scale and spheres of action, with emphasis on how a wide range of actors and the extent of their actions influence both the locations and processes of global politics (Bulkeley, 2005; Meadowcroft, 2002; Sjoberg, 2008).

The concept of governance used here is based on understanding a variety of actors and their interactions. It focuses on their interdependence, shared objectives, and fluid frontiers between the public, private, and associated spheres of action, intervention, and control (Kooiman, 1993; Grandgirard, 2007). The borderlines between the public and private are increasingly diffuse in today's globalized world. "Domestically as well as internationally, private actors become politicized and public actors become marketized—'the public goes private and the private goes public'" (Bexell and Wirth, 2010, p. 218; Jonsson, 2013, p. 1). Informal groups of countries such as the BRICS (Brazil, Russia, India, China, and South Africa) are a part of this group of "atypical" actors in international relations, as are the private sector and civil society organizations.

Global environmental governance scholarship has long recognized the importance of domestic politics in influencing environmental outcomes at the global level. State dominance in affecting environmental norms has been significantly challenged, both by globalization politics and by global climate change realities (Barros-Platiau, 2010, p. 78). Civil society and epistemic communities have played central roles in engaging international processes for much of the past generation (Wapner, 1996). As Barros-Platiau noted:

> environmental politics is not ruled by hegemonic fixed structures or balance of power structures. Different actors have been playing unexpected important roles, from the private sector, like the supermarkets that banned GM food; from carmakers producing more efficient cars; from politicians, scientists, singers, movie stars, religious leaders, indigenous leaders, NGOs and so on. (2010, p. 86)

Urban networks and municipal leadership are increasingly important actors in governance in the wake of the failures of multinational accords on climate change (Bulkeley and Moser, 2007; Kern and Bulkeley, 2009; Lee, 2013; Toly, 2008). In the face of government failures to respond meaningfully to the challenges of global climate change and the associated problems of mobility and urban infrastructure, scholars have begun looking to cities as sites of more active responses to such challenges. As several scholars have suggested, the international norms that are adopted are not shaped purely in the international or transnational context; domestic factors play an influential role in determining what international norms are adopted and also the speed at which they come to be embraced (Schreurs and Economy, 1997; VanDeveer and Dabelko, 2001; Weiss and Jacobson, 1998). This is an important avenue for research, not least because of the commonly held view that global cities are especially destructive, as their inhabitants reach out into global markets for energy, consumable goods, and other inputs necessary for survival (Luke, 2003; Toly, 2011). A re-imagining of urban areas as more ecologically sustainable places is already taking place (Register, 2006), as cities are taking the lead in responding politically and with clear normative positions regarding global climate change, thereby urbanizing global environmental governance.

The concept of "paradiplomacy" is especially useful toward understanding the role that sub-national entities such as municipal governments and city leaders play as political actors (Milani and Ribeiro, 2011; Salomon, 2011). A broad analytic concept, paradiplomacy entails: "subnational governments' involvement in international relations through the establishment of formal and informal ties, be they permanent or ad hoc, with foreign public or private entities, with the objective of promoting social, economic, cultural or political dimensions of development" (Cornago, 2010, p. 13).[3] Some thirty medium and large size Brazilian cities and nearly all Brazilian states participate in paradiplomatic activities in substantive ways (Salomon, 2011). In spite of a handful of case studies examining urban contributions to global climate change regimes (Aall et al., 2007; Bulkeley and Betsill, 2003; Granberg and Elander, 2007; Holgate, 2007), little scholarship exists about the mutually constitutive relationships of influence that are formed between cities, civil society, and the private sector, as they function to influence governance in the global liberal order.

Brazilian cities' roles in engaging as paradiplomatic actors in global environmental governance have been notable. The state of Pará, which is ranked worst in Brazil for its deforestation rates, created a Green Cities Program (*Programa Municípios Verdes*) in 2011, aimed at curbing deforestation through establishing administrative limitations in all illegally deforested areas. The program that is in place in 97 of Pará's 144 municipalities functions to make a previously inexistent link between local policies of land regularization and the issuing of permits for logging concessions. While the program's effectiveness is not yet measurable, it does offer hope of a new strategy to prevent illegal deforestation, which is an issue of global concern and one where Brazil is especially scrutinized in global environmental politics (Rabello, 2013). In the southern state of Paraná, Curitiba's demonstrated effectiveness of Bus Rapid Transit (BRT) systems made it a leading city in ecological design, and the transit model was emulated in other global cities such as Seoul, Tokyo, and Bogotá.

São Paulo and many other Brazilian cities participate in the International Council for Local Environmental Initiatives' Cities for Climate Protection (CCP) program, the International Solar Cities Initiative (ISCI), and, most recently, the C40 Cities Climate Leadership Group, exemplifying their commitment to global environmental governance and to instituting environmental change at local levels (Toly, 2011). Amazonas passed a State Climate Change Policy into law in June 2007, well before the Conference of the Parties (COP-15) climate change conference in Copenhagen. The Acre state government extensively consulted civil society and businesses, prior to creating a sub-national regulatory framework for climate change policy, which included incentives for Reducing Emissions from Deforestation and Forest Degradation (REDD) and payments for ecosystem services (Shankland and Hasenclever, 2011). Rio de Janeiro's involvement in global events, such as hosting the 1992 Rio Earth Summit, the 2010 UN-Habitat World Urban Forum, and the 2012 UN Conference on Sustainable Development (Rio+20) are illustrative of the ways in which city leadership developed and strengthened global ties in the environmental policy arena.

While these efforts may be largely attributed to the roles of mayors and other city sub-national administrators as significant new actors in international relations, it is important to also extend the analysis beyond the sphere of elected officials and into civil society, so as to better understand the ways in which the geographical and political actors of international relations are affecting environmental norms. Scholarship has also long acknowledged the importance of civil society, epistemic communities, and transnational advocacy networks in driving global political change on environmental issues as well as a host of other concerns. It is also worth noting that identities and mutually constitutive processes of governmentality also influence the national and international context of environmental governance. That is, governmental control over the environment extends into decentered, self-regulating networks of knowledge/power relationships at individual levels (Agrawal, 2005; Hecht, 2011b). More directly, the business investment climate of China may influence Brazil's environmental policies and play an important role in shaping the liberal order more broadly. China is Brazil's main trading partner, having surpassed the United States in 2009, and Chinese foreign direct investment (FDI) was at a staggeringly high level of USD 13.69 billion invested in 2010 (Freitas, 2014). This brief observation conforms to Ikenberry's assertion that US hegemony is waning, while the role of China is one of the most significant features of the changing liberal order, even as other rising powers like Brazil also increase in prominence (Ikenberry, 2011b). Considering these different levels of actors and influences holds importance for our understanding of how global governance works, beyond the explanations offered both by international regimes theory and scholarship on transnational advocacy networks (Betsill and Bulkeley, 2006).

The ability of civil society to politically address national and international issues through activism and protest is also important in shifting norm structures. Susanna Hecht notes that in Amazonia, "environmentalities" of Amazonians' own movements (below the national government, what Hecht calls the "Amazon Nation") have had positive effects since 2004 in spurring reductions of deforestation and achieving new territorial protections for indigenous reserves and conservation areas. These have created and transformed regional political and social landscapes, such that tribal groups and organized civil society groups function to play the roles of vigilance over lands and proactive advocacy for land demarcation. Only a few decades ago this land demarcation was the sole obligation of the state (which often was unable to exert its authority over the distant lands of the Amazon, resulting in low-level conflicts). Today, in Brazil's post-authoritarian context, challenges to state power come through acts of public protest as well as through official legal challenges brought by the Federal Public Prosecutor's office (*Ministério Público Federal*) (Hecht, 2011b). Many of the nation's still-unresolved indigenous land disputes, such as the encroachment of non-indigenous miners and soy ranchers on Munduruku and Awá lands, are being worked out through a combination of autonomous direct action by the tribes and slow legal proceedings (Parracho and Stauffer, 2014). Thus, we see merits to the observation that governance, understood in the broad sense, is a process of asserting influence over the definition and pursuit of collective goals, based on a multiplicity of interacting actors and arenas of governance.

These manifestations from Amazonian residents are one of many important examples of the pivotal role that exists for sub-state actors in governance, beyond examinations of cities alone as geographic spaces or administrative units. Place-based social movement activism plays an important role in influencing both international relations and national politics. In the Brazilian context, the Congress and the president are ultimately the main actors of relevance in responding to activists' grievances. The effectiveness of such activism ultimately hinges upon the ways in which national-level institutions address their long-standing concerns such as corruption, inequality, fiscal balance, and many other political claims—including environmental policies.

Tensions between Industry and the Environment

Brazil's push for economic growth has largely been based in industrial agriculture for exportation, and also in extractive industries such as mining and fossil fuels. This reliance presents some tension for the Brazilian government's positioning on environmental issues both domestically and internationally, given that ecological concerns (and sometimes human rights questions) are raised when mining, logging, and hydroelectric dams are constructed in fragile ecosystems and sometimes on indigenous lands or inside conservation areas. While the vast majority of the electricity consumed in Brazil comes from renewable sources, which includes more than three-quarters from hydroelectric dams (Blount, 2013), non-renewables (e.g. fossil fuels, natural gas, coal) still outweigh renewable energy production by a few percentage points in the overall Brazilian energy market (EPE, 2013). Many infrastructure projects, including the Belo Monte dam, are being principally funded by the Brazilian National Bank for Economic and Social Development (BNDES) (*Reuters*, 2012). The scale of BNDES lending is not to be underestimated; in 2010, its lending volume was around USD 69 billion, a sum nearly three times greater than the loans of the World Bank (Lazzarini et al., 2011).[4] Within Brazil, infrastructure loans from the BNDES were 25 percent higher in 2012 than in the year prior, a notable indicator of the national commitment to rapid infrastructure development (*Wall Street Journal*, 2012). As such, institutionalizing greater sensitivity on environmental and social issues within the bank is an enormous challenge and one of substantial global importance, given the bank's international portfolio (Marinis, 2010).

Policies for energy concession contracting and natural resource use are germane to environmental governance insofar as they influence the nation's energy production and consumption and also as they relate to the power dynamics through which environmental governance takes shape. Brazil's position at the Convention on Biodiversity negotiations in 2010 supported a 10 percent marine protection target by 2020. However, an estimated 80 percent of Brazilian marine fisheries are overfished, and only 1.5 percent of its exclusive economic zone is protected (Scarano et al., 2012). Current estimates show that nearly 9 percent of the priority areas for fisheries conservation have been sacrificed to offshore oil exploration (*Greenpeace*, 2010). The pre-salt oil reserves discovered off the coast of Brazil will be controlled in large part by the state-owned oil giant Petrobras. The government has stipulated rules that guarantee that it will maintain a 30 percent stake in the concessions and function as the sole operator (*Dow Jones Newswire*, 2013). In this instance, the state's national energy production priorities trump its own environmental commitments, not only in terms of biodiversity but also through the priority given to fossil fuel extraction as the basis for growth.

Brazil's relationship with China and the growing trade relations between the two countries also suggest risks to the environmental safeguards present in existing global environmental governance regimes. The significant trade between Brazil and China has led to extensive collaborations in the oil and mining sectors, and is a centerpiece of Brazil's economic stability. In the past decade and a half, China has become Brazil's major geoeconomic and geopolitical partner—as well as core competitor—in Latin America, and managing the relationship with China is a central concern of Brazilian foreign policy (Vadell, 2013). The magnitude of Chinese investments in Brazilian energy infrastructure alone totaled over USD 18.3 billion between 2005 and 2012 (Husar and Best, 2013), influencing both fossil fuel and renewable energy developments. As the green economy's proposal to create a low-carbon, more inclusive, and resource-efficient future takes hold, Brazil's own government, as well as its private enterprises, will be pressed to institute normative and regulatory frameworks to guarantee that human rights and environmental protections are seriously directed toward those aims even as extractive industries and infrastructure expand their reach.

To illustrate this point, one need only look at the Brazilian mining company Vale SA. Vale operates in thirty-eight countries and is the second-largest mining company in the world. It won the ignoble Public Eye award in 2012 for its poor environmental and human rights record in mining operations in Brazil, Mozambique, and many other locations (Sousa and Hermann, 2013). Regulating Vale's actions on human rights and environmental grounds may well entail substantial confrontations and affect sensitive trade negotiations with China, whose hunger for commodities is well known and not likely to be easily assuaged. Avoiding such confrontations, on the other hand, gives greater credibility to the critiques that have been leveraged against the green economy, namely, that it is a framework which functions to promote the persistence of overconsumptive, unequal, and relatively undemocratic consolidations of control within the global economy, to the detriment of people and the environment.

Deforestation and Climate Change

Brazil's wealth of forests and extraordinary biodiversity make it a key player in global environmental governance. It jointly created the Megadiverse Like-Minded Country Group, which was the leading negotiation bloc at the Convention on Biological Diversity and in the Nagoya Protocol for Genetic Resources and Equitable Sharing of Benefits. Brazil innovated and garnered substantial international funds through the establishment of forest research and protection investment pools such as the Pilot Program to Conserve the Brazilian Rainforest (PPG7) and the Fundo Amazônia. Brazil also participates in regional environmental agreements such as the Amazon Cooperation Treaty (ACT), although these are relatively insignificant in their relation to the global environmental regimes (Barros-Platiau, 2010).

Despite such active participation in agreements aiming to quell the spread of deforestation, Brazil's position in climate change negotiations may be seen as something akin to a race for second place. While deforestation has declined remarkably in Amazonia since 2004 and even more significantly from 2008 to 2009, Brazil has missed an opportunity to become a global leader on climate change (Scarano et al., 2012). Brazil's positions were more ambitious on the issue of emissions reductions than those of India or China, but Brazil is not perceived by some other nations as being progressive on the issue of climate change. A 2009 US cable leaked through Wikileaks states, "The Government of Brazil (GoB) does not consider climate change an immediate threat to Brazil, and is not willing to sacrifice other priorities to address the problem" (King et al., 2012, p. 50).

Confirming this suspicion is the country's resistance to REDD+ financing,[5] which stems from concerns that it will introduce untoward foreign influence in the Amazon and allow other countries and industries to shirk responsibilities for greenhouse gas emissions (King et al., 2012). Still, the Brazilian government does support the general institutional framework for addressing climate change established in the Kyoto Protocol, especially through the top-down targets for developed countries and nationally defined targets based on historical emissions rates for developing countries (King et al., 2012).

Former Brazilian president Luiz Inácio Lula da Silva made a non-binding voluntary commitment at the 2009 Copenhagen climate conference (COP-15) that Brazil would reduce Amazonian deforestation by 80 percent by the year 2020. There is good reason to be skeptical about the feasibility of Lula's promise, however, given that Brazil will likely have several different presidential administrations between now and 2020. Around 50 percent of the Brazilian Amazon lands are protected in conservation areas and indigenous territories, leading to substantial reductions in deforestation rates. And though deforestation declined remarkably in Amazonia between 2004 and 2012, it has ticked up since then. The difficulty of credibly committing to further environmental restrictions suggests that there are good odds that future administrations will simply sidestep their Copenhagen commitments (Fearnside, 2012, p. 78).

Furthering skepticism about Brazil's likely success in combating deforestation, no land was placed into new protected areas, and the government even reduced the size of some already-established protected areas during Dilma Rousseff's first year as president (2011). This was the first time in more than fifteen years that such statistics did not go up (Scarano et al., 2012). A heated political process surrounded the revision of Brazil's Forestry Code in late April 2012, forgiving fines that had been issued for pre-2008 deforestation. The new Code loosely implied, moreover, that amnesty for violators would be encoded into the law through a stipulation that the rules could be reviewed within five years of the law taking effect (Rabello, 2013). Deforestation rates remain largely tied to market signals, although tightened scrutiny over beef exports and the ranching sector have helped to reduce illegal deforestation. With Brazil as the world's leading beef exporter, strict regulation will be key (Hecht, 2011b). Meanwhile, Brazilian indigenous groups, whose territories are recognized as being the strongest bastions of environmental conservation in the country, are continuously under threat from land invasions, unscrupulous carbon credit dealers (Harvey, 2007), and, most recently, proposed constitutional amendments which would roll back indigenous land protections and make demarcations of new lands significantly more difficult (*Amazon Watch*, 2013; Harvey, 2007).

A further example of these conflicting sources of environmental policy, and the federal government's strong but by no means monopolistic influence over Brazil's environmental policy, lies in the recent case of the Belo Monte dam project.

The Belo Monte Hydroelectric Project

The Belo Monte hydroelectric project has a long and complex history involving both government plans and oppositional activism (Bratman, 2014). It is also a high-stakes project of enormous salience to both proponents and opponents: when it is completed, likely in 2016, the Belo Monte dam is slated to be the world's third-most productive hydroelectric dam when operating at full capacity. It serves as an excellent illustration of shifting Brazilian environmental norms because of its symbolic importance, its physical importance in achieving the nation's energy production goals, and the extensive history of transnational, national, and local activism in response to the project.

The policy and planning responses to the Belo Monte hydroelectric project since the late 1990s have involved dynamics of pressure and political engagement from the sub-national and international spheres, alike. An important early fault line developed around norms of public involvement and environmental assessment within the debate over approval of the Belo Monte project. These norms are enshrined through the national environmental policy (*Sistema Nacional de Meio Ambiente*, or SISNAMA), which is stipulated in the Brazilian Constitution (Law No. 6.938, with a basis in Articles 23 and 225 of the constitution). The policy requires strong impact assessment measures as well as public participation. The government also signed on to the International Labor Organization's (ILO) Convention 169, an agreement that calls for the free, prior and informed consent of indigenous peoples who may be affected by nationally sponsored projects. Only after public involvement processes take place does Brazilian (and international) law allow for preliminary construction and operating licenses to be issued and public bidding processes for work contracts to take place (Baptista and Thorkildsen, 2011). The Belo Monte case history, however, has made these normative commitments appear disingenuous, as the discussion below elaborates.

The first approval of construction of the Belo Monte project was granted by the national Congress in 2004, with virtually no debate. This was prior to any updated consultations or environmental impact assessments, and was later found to be a violation of the National Environmental Policy, Law No. 6.938 (established in 1981). Then, in 2009, the environmental licensing process was found to have been inadequate by officials from within the national environmental agency. Two heads of Brazil's environmental agency (IBAMA), Roberto Messias Franco and Abelardo Bayma Azevedo, resigned in 2010 and in 2011, respectively, both allegedly over pressures to grant a full environmental license for the construction of the dam (Hurwitz, 2011). Of note, there was also a longer legacy of resignations among the government's environmental leadership. Between May 2008 and 2009, Marina Silva, the former Minister of Environment, resigned from her position, under pressure from agribusiness and energy sectors, which opposed legal barriers to new projects with potential environmental impacts. The presidents of IBAMA (Bazileu Margarido) and the Chico Mendes Institute for the Conservation of Biodiversity (ICMBio; João Paulo Capobianco) also resigned on claims of suffering political pressures running contrary to their own jobs (Novaes and França Souza, 2013).

Public hearings about the dam project made a mockery of the idea of public involvement,[6] since they were clearly being conducted more for tokenistic reasons than to seriously address any objections that might arise and slow the project down. Even before one set of public hearings had been held, the energy ministry announced the date when a preliminary license would be granted, and a 20,000-page Environmental Impact Assessment was released to the public only two days before another hearing (Marques, 2009; Salm, 2009). The close timing was not illegal, however, and it indicates how the Brazilian state has been able to strategically maneuver within existing environmental norms to attain greater flexibility in the regulatory regime. Additionally, IBAMA has increasingly adopted a licensing loophole of sorts, allowing for construction and operation licenses to be granted even though many stipulated social and environmental "pre-conditions" to the license remain unmet.[7] Failure to meet these pre-conditions results in the levying of additional fines but has not stopped this and other projects from moving forward (Borges, 2013). Such loopholes allow the state to achieve its agenda, while simultaneously appearing to uphold an image of democratic procedure and adherence to existing (and often very cumbersome) environmental rules.

The judiciary has been another battlefield in the process. Legal injunctions stopping the construction of the project from moving forward have frequently left the future of the project hanging in the balance. Ultimately, the judiciary has only delayed the project, rather than overturning it entirely. These judicial processes have re-affirmed the contradictions inherent in energy policy. One judge, while overruling an injunction against the dam, argued that Brazil's energy demands were so urgent that if the Belo Monte project was further delayed, other more expensive and polluting energy sources such as thermoelectric energy would be tapped (Graeff, 2012). Thus, in the name of "green" logic, the position that the dam should proceed triumphed over long-standing concerns about the lack of consultations of affected indigenous peoples or the environmental impacts of the dam itself (Borges, 2013). In addition, the dam's official estimated cost of some USD 13 billion has likely been exceeded, with estimates of the true cost ranging from USD 16 to USD 32 billion, making the project non-viable in financial terms (Rapoza, 2014). An evocative indicator of the state's commitment to the Belo Monte project, even in the face of high-profile attention and civil society pressure, came during the Rio+20 Earth Summit in June 2012, when anti-dam activists interrupted a session with high-level ministers and banking officials present. Environment Minister Izabella Teixeira engaged in a ten-minute shouting match with the protestors (Leitão, 2012; *O Eco*, 2012).

In addition to the protests at the Rio+20 Summit, local actions at the dam site taking place concurrently with the summit included a protest march with local high school students and residents, a few organizers of the Movement of People Affected by Dams (MAB, or Movimento dos Atingidos por Barragens), the NGO Movimento Xingu Vivo organizers, and a Brazilian telenovela actor. At the dam site itself, a protest also took place, which included local tribes and Munduruku indigenous peoples (who came out of concern that Belo Monte was the gateway dam for the Tapajós river dams, slated next for construction, which would affect their own areas), some young foreigners from the Rainbow Family, and an assortment of national and international NGOs, including the Instituto Socioambiental, Amazon Watch, and International Rivers. Later occupations of the dam site included a number of indigenous tribes from the Xingu River basin. While government officials from local municipalities were not present at the protests, their relationship to the project has shifted over time: at first they supported the project, then cautioned against it, as the energy consortium's promises for certain important local benefits remained unmet. As the Belo Monte project has become perceived as inevitable, local activist coalitions have splintered, creating a fragmented set of civil society opposition actors who are increasingly impotent in their efforts (Bratman, 2014).

The fracturing of social movements is a key factor in the state's success in proceeding with the Belo Monte project, but the project is far from minimal in its social and ecological consequences. Over a dozen local tribes of the Xingu River basin will be affected by the project, including the Xinkrin, Kayapó, Asurini, Arara, Araweté, Paracanã, and Juruna. Most of these tribes, as well as the traditional fishing and rubber-tapping populations of river-based peasants living along the Xingu River, will experience significantly lower water levels as a result of the dam, affecting their transportation and lifestyles. Additionally, over 20,000 urban residents in the city of Altamira, Pará, will be displaced by the flooding from the project. Many of these communities have experienced human rights violations in conjunction with the project.

Claiming violations of the free, prior, and informed consent stipulations that are a part of the ILO's Convention 169 (as well as consultation stipulations in Article 231 of the Brazilian Constitution and the UN Declaration on the Rights of Indigenous Peoples), many of the indigenous tribes of the Xingu River basin issued a complaint to the Inter-American Commission on Human Rights (IACHR), which is part of the Organization of the American States (OAS). In April 2011, the IACHR ruling demanded that Brazil suspend the dam's construction, based on violations of the ILO Convention 169. President Rousseff rejected the decision and retaliated by suspending payment of Brazil's dues (USD 800,000) to the organization and recalling Brazil's OAS ambassador (Soltis, 2011). In this instance, the Brazilian government's position was clear; the national priorities for sovereignty and development trumped its international commitments. In a later ruling, the IACHR modified its position, and noted that "the debate between the parties on prior consultation and informed consent with regard to the Belo Monte project has turned into a discussion on the merits of the matter, which goes beyond the scope of precautionary measures" (IACHR, 2011). Brazil's place in the liberal environmental order, in this instance, might be viewed as one of leadership only when the international order aligns with other national priorities, a position seemingly in conflict with Brazil's simultaneous aspirations to be an international champion of human rights and multilateralism (Sotero, 2012).

The current state of the Belo Monte project and activism against it suggests that pains are being taken by the government to maintain basic compliance with domestic laws and democratic commitments. However, there is a simultaneous unwillingness to yield to changes that would involve more concerted public participation, legal proceedings, impact assessments, and consultation for the Belo Monte project, yielding dissonance between policies and practices. Domestic policy changes and creative legal maneuvering have occurred over the course of the project, enough to shift the character of several important normative structures including indigenous consultations, licensing procedures, and prior environmental impact assessments. Despite attempts by both domestic and transnational civil society to exert pressure on the state, the environmental norms and human rights safeguards at stake in the Belo Monte case have been overcome by the state's imperative to increase energy supply, even if this comes at significant environmental, cultural, and even economic cost.

Brazil's Environmental Ambivalence

In spite of the emergence of new spheres of influence such as cities and the importance of transnational and sub-national activism, Brazil's positions on global environmental norms emphasize the politics of a strong national developmental state. The national state's dominance arises out of its strong regulatory role, commitment to sovereignty, and desire for economic stability. Ultimately, the state gives top priority to economic concerns, but still takes pains to make discursive commitments that recognize environmental governance globally. While still wishing to maintain international favor and legitimacy through its commitments and environmental discourses, Brazil's environmental stances ultimately take a back seat to other concerns, making Brazilian positions in global environmental governance appear disingenuous and frequently contradictory.

This chapter has discussed a wide range of actors and influences upon Brazil's role in the green economy. On the global stage, the green economy represents a deepening of liberal norms and a shifting liberal international order in which Brazil has a notable role. A few observations help to summarize Brazil's interactions with global environmental governance. First, urban areas in Brazil, and the urbanization phenomenon more broadly, are significant factors within global environmental governance. Not only do Brazilian cities function as paradiplomatic actors, but they are also a sphere for public action, catalyzing attention and action on mobility, inequality, and environmental issues at the national and international levels in formative ways. Second, domestic and transnational civil society activism against substantial infrastructure projects such as the Belo Monte dam, has not been effective in terms of its ability to spur normative shifts or reinforce existing environmental and human rights norms. Instead, the Brazilian government has taken on normative stances which demonstrate the limits of its environmental commitments. This brings into high relief the question of whether infrastructure growth, environmental protection, and social inclusion can indeed be triangulated in a balanced way. Moreover, state control over many extractive industries and the privileging of extractive industries and their substantial infrastructure overall within the Brazilian political economy indicate that Brazil's priorities will likely involve a national prioritization of non-renewable resources within the green economy for many years to come. Deforestation rates may be improving and renewable energy remains one of Brazil's most laudable environmental achievements, but even these are not without their costs. Amazonian dams such as the Belo Monte project qualify as renewable energy projects, but entail significant environmental and human rights concerns. Finally, the lack of social and environmental safeguards and transparency in Brazilian mining, petroleum drilling, and infrastructure investments domestically and internationally remains in conflict with many of the nation's stated international commitments toward environmental protection.

While this discussion has shown that the urban sphere, social movement activism, and private enterprises are taking on important roles in global environmental governance, these observations should not be interpreted to mean that the national state is obsolete. Indeed, far from it, all of the characteristics of Brazil's positioning in global environmental governance are dependent upon the national government's responsiveness and oversight. Infrastructure, energy, and urban policies may be quite strongly influenced by the challenges of activists or the investments of private corporations. However, between the strong national development bank, the Brazilian courts, and the ability of the federal government to pass legislation in rapid response to public outcry, the federal government remains the central actor in Brazilian environmental governance. Brazil's stance toward the liberal environmental order on the global stage is shaped in significant ways by the national government's energy protectionism, prioritization of modernization and economic development, and its emphasis on national sovereignty. Dissonance between policies and practice, both domestically and internationally, are common in Brazil. In spite of its spotty domestic and international track record on mining, climate change, renewable energy, and deforestation, Brazil has continued to confidently champion its environmental achievements, remaining both symbolically and pragmatically a central player within the changing liberal order of the green economy.

Notes

1. Other works on Brazilian environmental policy and its implications for global environmental governance focus on the specific issues of climate change, biodiversity, and low-carbon development policies (Lampreia et al., 2011).
2. Rousseff (2011).
3. See also Duchacek (1990).
4. "Performance: The Evolution of BNDES' Disbursements." 2013. *BNDES* http://www.bndes.gov.br/SiteBNDES/bndes/bndes_en/Institucional/The_BNDES_in_Numbers/
5. A strategy for addressing REDD, which also includes forest management practices, enhancing existing carbon stocks, and including the role of conservation as a form of payment for avoiding deforestation. For more information, see: http://www.un-redd.org/aboutredd/tabid/102614/default.aspx

6. Interview with author, Biviany Rojas (lawyer, Instituto SocioAmbiental, July 3, 2012).

7. Decreto no. 7.340, October 21, 2010. The Belo Monte case involved over forty social and evironmental conditions within the Preliminary License. When the conditions were not all met on schedule for the installation licensing process, IBAMA set a new precedent and granted an exception in January 2011, allowing that the installation license be approved even though these preliminary conditions had not been met. Lawsuits and appeals from the federal prosecutor's office requesting the suspension of this license have been overruled by the high courts in Brasília. The basis for these rulings is that interfering with the project will harm the public order and the economy. For more, see Graeff (2012).

CHAPTER 7

Brazil and the Global Nuclear Order

Togzhan Kassenova[1]

B razil fascinates nuclear analysts. It is the only non-nuclear-weapons country in the world to work on a nuclear-powered submarine. It is one of only few countries worldwide with a capacity to engage in all stages of the nuclear fuel cycle—a process of producing nuclear fuel. In the area of commercial nuclear trade, it finds itself among the members of a rather exclusive club of countries with advanced nuclear industries—the Nuclear Suppliers Group (NSG). In Latin America, Brazil is one of only three countries to generate electricity from nuclear power, the other two being Argentina and Mexico.

Internationally, several factors make Brazil an important player in the global nuclear order. Brazil together with its Latin American and Caribbean neighbors established a regional nuclear-weapon-free zone under the provisions of the Tlatelolco Treaty. Together with Argentina, Brazil developed a bilateral safeguards mechanism implemented by the Brazilian–Argentine Agency for Accounting and Control of Nuclear Materials (ABACC). Yet at the same time, Brazil opposes signing the International Atomic Energy Agency (IAEA) Additional Protocol designed to enhance nuclear safeguards,[2] which creates tensions in Brazil's relationship with the global non-proliferation regime. In the realm of multilateral diplomacy, the country actively promotes global nuclear disarmament.

Brazil is seeking to shape the global nuclear order, and its presence on the global nuclear scene has become increasingly visible in recent years. In 2010, together with Ankara, Brasília reached out to Tehran and attempted to broker a nuclear deal between Iran and the West that resulted in a trilateral Tehran Declaration.

For Brazil, the global nuclear order is a microcosm of the global order more broadly. Brazil's interaction with the nuclear order follows the same pattern as its interaction with other global governance structures. Brasília believes the country has reached a point where the size of its economy, the pace of its development, its role in the region, and its international credentials have to be formally reflected and acknowledged in global order. It seeks that acknowledgment by pursuing acceptance in the exclusive club of the United Nations (UN) Security Council permanent members. Brasília also argues that institutions such as the UN, the World Bank, the International Monetary Fund (IMF) and others fail to adequately represent the rising South and developing countries. Similarly, Brazil seeks to see more democratic and just governance structures in the fields of environment and multilateral trade—even though critics argue that Brazil is primarily interested in its own inclusion in exclusive decision-making bodies rather than in more profound changes.

Brazil's push for global governance structures to evolve manifests itself in the area of nuclear order. Brazil emphasizes the unfairness of the global nuclear order and points out that the existing nuclear order benefits the nuclear-weapon states and puts undue pressure on countries that do not possess nuclear weapons.[3] A lack of progress toward nuclear disarmament and questionable policy choices of nuclear states provide Brazil with an opportunity to claim that non-nuclear-weapon states should not be expected to do more for the health and strength of the global nuclear order. Nuclear justice and the fight against "double standards" are at the heart of Brasília's beliefs and rhetoric. Brazil would prefer for the global nuclear order to be remade, but if such an overhaul does not happen, it wants to be at the high table. It seeks a greater role for itself in the global nuclear order, whether or not that order is just.

This chapter explores Brazil's evolving nuclear identity and its role in the global nuclear order. It does so by first looking at Brazil's past, which helps explain its policy decisions today. The chapter proceeds with describing the main elements of Brazil's nuclear policy relevant for the global nuclear order. They include the nuclear submarine program, nuclear fuel cycle, and expansion of nuclear energy, as well as Brazil's role in the international treaties and regimes. The chapter highlights how Brazil is navigating between normative considerations and its national interests in constructing its nuclear policy. Finally, the exploration of Brazil's role in the Tehran Declaration highlights the country's quest for a greater say in the global nuclear governance and the tensions between established and emerging powers in the nuclear field.

Past Matters

In order to understand Brazil's nuclear policy today one should look into the past. The roots of Brazil's disillusionment with the global nuclear order run deep and go back in history. The country's struggle to import foreign nuclear technology and the external pressure (mostly, from the United States) that limited or attempted to limit development of its nuclear program inform Brazil's views, even decades later.

The country's attempts in 1953–54 to acquire key components of the nuclear fuel cycle—uranium enrichment technology—from France and West Germany did not succeed. The transfer of technology from West Germany was hampered under pressure from the United States, which was concerned about potential proliferation (Flemes, 2006, p. 10; Patti, 2012, pp. 41, 45). And plans for cooperation with France were disrupted due to political turmoil in Brazil following the suicide of then president Getúlio Vargas in 1954.

For a brief period from the mid-1950s to the early 1970s, Brazil reverted to cooperation with the United States under the Atoms for Peace program. In 1955 Brazil and the United States reached an agreement on building a nuclear research reactor in Brazil, the first in Latin America.[4] By 1971 Brazil's Nuclear Energy Commission (Comissão Nacional de Energia Nuclear, CNEN) signed an agreement with the US Atomic Energy Commission and the US company Westinghouse on building Brazil's first nuclear power plant, Angra 1. Under the terms of agreement, Westinghouse would build the plant, and the Atomic Energy Commission, the sole provider of enrichment services in the United States, would supply nuclear fuel for the life of the imported reactor.

After 1973 Brazil also sought to acquire the full fuel cycle, including capacity to enrich uranium, from Westinghouse. Brazil did not sign the Treaty on the Non-Proliferation of Nuclear Weapons (NPT) at that point, a matter of concern for the United States. In compliance with the US non-proliferation policy, Westinghouse denied Brazil's requests but offered to supply more nuclear reactors on the condition that Brazil continued to rely on the United States for nuclear fuel (Skidmore, 1988, p. 193).

Two developments in 1974—India's nuclear test and reorganization of the US enrichment industry—resulted in far-reaching repercussions for the global nuclear market and had a negative impact on Brazil. India's nuclear test triggered a review of US non-proliferation policy and resulted in further strengthening of restrictions on sensitive nuclear technology transfers.

Meanwhile, the US government pushed for the reorganization of the US enrichment industry in order to make it more commercially viable. As a result, the US Atomic Energy Commission changed the rules of nuclear fuel supply abroad. If before, the United States guaranteed fuel supply for the life of the reactor (as with Angra 1 in Brazil), now such guarantees did not come automatically and countries had to commit to purchasing fuel for a specified timeframe. This resulted in an artificially inflated demand for US nuclear fuel and forced the Atomic Energy Commission to suspend the signing of new contracts and to classify existing contracts of supply as "conditional." As a result, Brazil's first nuclear power plant built by Westinghouse—Angra 1—suddenly did not have guaranteed access to fuel with which to run. Moreover, the changes in the United States meant that negotiations between Brazil and Westinghouse on building up to twelve additional reactors fell through (Skidmore, 1988, p. 194). The crisis with fuel supply was both "bad and good," Brazilian observers would say. The first Brazilian secretary of the ABACC Carlos Feu Alvim explained: "We became aware of the importance of autonomy."[5]

In its continued quest for a nuclear fuel cycle, Brazil engaged in negotiations with France and West Germany, and cooperation with West Germany was heralded as a real breakthrough for Brazil. Under a 1975 agreement West Germany committed to building up to eight nuclear reactors in Brazil and to transfer full nuclear-fuel-cycle technology to Brazil. Washington, concerned with potential proliferation risks of sensitive technology, once again put pressure on Bonn to cancel cooperation with Brazil. Bonn did not succumb to coercion completely but did put limits on what types of technology Brasília could receive. As a result, Brazil could only receive uranium enrichment technology based on the "jet-nozzle method," which at the time was in its early stages of development. Meanwhile, US president Jimmy Carter came to power in 1977, further strengthening US non-proliferation policy and putting even stronger pressure on Brazil and West Germany to step away from cooperation in the nuclear field.

US efforts aside, cooperation between Brazil and West Germany in the nuclear field did not bring Brazil closer to acquiring a full nuclear fuel cycle. Brazil benefited from Germany's assistance with reactor construction but ran into problems with adopting the under-developed "jet-nozzle" enrichment technology. According to Alvim, "Germany's jet-nozzle technology did not work well and, in the best scenario, would be uneconomical. The Brazilian scientists were against it."[6]

In 1978 the United States adopted the Nuclear Non-Proliferation Act, which meant that countries like Brazil could not rely on foreign partners when trying to develop their own nuclear industries. The act imposed further restrictions on countries wishing to import nuclear technology from the United States because it required recipient states to adopt nuclear safeguards.

Those episodes from the past are relevant even decades later. Tensions between Brazil and the United States in the nuclear non-proliferation field reveal mutual distrust. From the vantage point of the United States, tougher non-proliferation controls and the resulting pressure on other countries were necessary to prevent an uncontrolled spread of sensitive nuclear technology. At the international level, India's nuclear test in 1974 served as a reminder that countries could exploit access to nuclear technology from other states to quietly build a nuclear bomb. Several factors made the United States, a country heavily invested in preventing nuclear proliferation, concerned about Brazil. Brazil did not sign the NPT, while at the same time it demonstrated keen interest in acquiring a full nuclear fuel cycle and in conducting peaceful nuclear explosions.

From Brazil's point of view, the United States unfairly interfered with its development of nuclear industry. As Brazilian scholar Paulo Wrobel wrote, Brazil viewed those efforts "as attempts at denying industrializing countries access to the socio-economic benefits of nuclear energy and technology" (1996, p. 341).

Partly out of frustration with unsuccessful efforts to acquire nuclear technology from abroad, in the late 1970s the Brazilian military launched its own "parallel" nuclear program. All three branches of the Brazilian military participated, but it is the Navy's pursuit of uranium enrichment and nuclear submarine development that resulted in the most determined and sustained efforts of the entire program. The Navy's efforts laid the foundation for Brazil's present nuclear program.

In addition to similarities in tensions dividing Brazil and the United States over nuclear issues then and now, the past demands attention because it continues to inform Brazil's nuclear policy today.

Brazil's Nuclear Policy: Key Elements for the Global Nuclear Order

When it comes to the global nuclear order, Brazil is not just any other ordinary participant. With its advanced nuclear program and an assertive voice in global nuclear matters it is a country worth watching.

Nuclear-Powered Submarine Program

External observers, especially in the non-proliferation community, are perplexed by Brazil's nuclear submarine program. The underlying question for most of them revolves around the purpose and utility of a nuclear submarine. Why is Brazil seeking a nuclear-powered submarine and not just conventional submarines?

Almost every country pursues projects or policies that do not make sense to outsiders, but not all of them receive the same level of scrutiny as Brazil's nuclear submarine program. Such heightened attention is due to the fact that the nuclear aspect of the program makes it a sensitive project. The external discourse focuses on two potential threats: first, that Brazil itself might acquire latent nuclear capability; and second, that Brazil's example might spur other countries, with lesser non-proliferation credentials, to follow suit (e.g., Iran).

A hypothetical proliferation scenario concerns production of nuclear material to fuel a submarine. Nuclear power plants mostly run on uranium fuel enriched to less than 5 percent. Nuclear submarines, however, can run on low-enriched uranium (LEU), uranium enriched up to 19.9 percent, or highly enriched uranium (HEU), uranium enriched to more than 20 percent.[7]

The question of levels of enrichment of uranium is not trivial in the nuclear debates. Production of 20-percent-enriched uranium in non-nuclear-weapon states is generating some controversy in non-proliferation circles (negotiations with Iran on its enrichment program being the most vivid example). That is because once uranium is enriched to 20 percent, most of the isotope separative work needed to reach 90 percent enrichment (weapons grade) is done. The NPT, furthermore, does not prohibit production of weapons-grade uranium by non-nuclear-weapon states for the purposes of naval nuclear reactors. Some US experts view this as a serious loophole that might be exploited by countries in the future (Thielman and Hoffman, 2012).

All indications are that Brazil will power its submarines with fuel produced from uranium enriched to 18–19 percent, a figure mentioned in an interview a few years ago by the then Chairman of Brazil's National Nuclear Energy Commission (*Comissão Nacional de Energia Nuclear*, CNEN), Odair Gonçalves (Huntington, 2005, p. 37). As a matter of principle, however, Brazilians stress that it is Brazil's sovereign right to decide what type of fuel to use.

Production and use of additional nuclear fuel enriched to higher levels than needed for nuclear power plants makes the question of safeguards ever so important to the international community. This is necessary to provide the international community with confidence that no nuclear material will be diverted for non-peaceful purposes. The relevant IAEA document (INFCIRC/153) states that nuclear material can be withdrawn from general safeguards for "non-proscribed military activity" which would include use in naval propulsion. Brazil plans to apply safeguards on submarine fuel in accordance with the Quadripartite Agreement between Brazil, Argentina, ABACC, and the IAEA that requires "special procedures" for nuclear material removed from regular safeguards for purposes such as naval propulsion.[8]

Reportedly Brazil is already engaged in relevant safeguards conversations with the IAEA. Yet this will be a challenging endeavor because Brazil will be the first non-nuclear-weapon state to operate a nuclear-powered submarine, and no precedent exists for a relevant safeguards system. From Brazil's point of view, the challenge is how to implement safeguards without disclosing sensitive information (e.g., the location of the submarine). As a matter of fact, Brazil's operation of a nuclear-powered submarine implies that there would be no continuity of safeguards because there would be periods when the submarine was at sea.

Another common thread in the external discourse revolves around Brazil opening the way for other non-nuclear-weapon states to follow suit. Some fear that countries might use the pretext of a nuclear-powered submarine to produce weapons-grade uranium. In June 2012, Iranian Navy official Abbas Zamini announced that Iran took "the first steps in the direction of building nuclear-powered submarines" (Afkhami, 2012, p. A12).

The difference between the external narrative fueled by concerns about potential proliferation and Brazil's internal thinking on the rationale for the program provides a vivid example of the perception gap. In general, external observers do not "buy into" the official narrative behind the program that emphasizes the defense rationale. Not understanding the purpose of the program makes them nervous about its ultimate purpose. Yet on closer examination, a range of drivers, including many of a purely domestic nature, help to explain the program.

The driving forces behind Brazil's nuclear submarine program are multiple, not always connected, and at times contradictory. They can be divided into three major categories: strategic, bureaucratic, and technological. But above all, Brazil's quest for a nuclear submarine reflects a desire to attain a greater place in the international system. The program is indicative of how Brazil perceives the outside world and how it perceives itself within the system.

Strategic and Defense Drivers

Within Brazil, the narrative on why the country needs a nuclear submarine revolves around strategic and military-defense reasons. The dominant themes in conversations with Brazilian government officials and experts and in the doctrinal documents include protection of the coastline, protection of natural resources in off-shore waters, and protection against potential enemies.

Protection of the coast emerges as an undisputable and overarching rationale for the program. Brazil's National Defense Strategy (2008) stated: "The priority is to ensure the means to deny the use of [the] sea to any concentration of enemy forces approaching Brazil from the sea" (Ministry of Defense, 2008, p. 20).

Brazil's desire to protect its coastline is understandable. Brazil has an 8,000-kilometer-long coast and almost 70 percent of the population lives within 300 kilometers of the coastline. The country is the largest and most powerful on the South American landmass, so none of its neighbors is likely to pose a major threat by land. Larger powers, which could theoretically threaten Brazil, would need to come by sea, as the colonial powers did centuries before.

The second common theme in Brazilian explanations of the nuclear submarine program is the necessity to protect off-shore oil resources, the discovery of which the government announced in 2007. The formal narrative within Brazil stresses concern that rich natural resources in the seabed off its coast might attract unwanted attention from foreign powers.

Yet, developing a nuclear submarine to protect off-shore oil resources can be questioned because the big discoveries were made in 2006, decades after the submarine program was launched. Foreign specialists question the practical utility of nuclear submarines for protecting off-shore oil platforms (Gasparre, 2009; Taylor, 2009). And in fact, some Brazilian defense experts, not affiliated with the Navy, seem to believe the Navy is overselling the utility of nuclear submarines. As one Brazilian expert summarized, "protection of oil and other resources at sea is at the heart of the defense rational of the submarine program," but he cautioned that such explanation could be qualified more as "an effort of propaganda," and not the primary purpose for the nuclear submarine.[9]

In considering uncertain threats in the future, Brazil is not alone. It is not totally unheard of for a country to seek naval military capabilities without reference to a particular country that might threaten it. In the post–Cold War period Brazilian naval thinking started to shift away from concepts of "hypotheses of war" with any particular country in mind in favor of the concept of "strategic vulnerabilities." The core of the new concept is the emphasis on all points in which a country is vulnerable to any external enemy. Within the broader context of Brazil's desire to be prepared for uncertain threats in the future there is unease about potential military presence of the North Atlantic Treaty Organization (NATO) and the United States in the South Atlantic. Brazil has observed with uneasiness several developments.

For example, the inconclusive debates within NATO on whether it should expand its security cooperation to areas outside of the North Atlantic prompted Brazil's top officials to express concern. In 2010 Brazil's defense minister at the time, Nelson Jobim, warned about NATO's ability to "interfere anywhere in the world on the pretext of counter-terrorism, humanitarian actions, or prevention of threats to democracy or environment" (*O Estado*, 2010).

No official statement or doctrinal document links Brazil's nuclear submarine program with concerns about any specific threat from the United States, but the conversations with Brazilian experts often feature Brazil's northern neighbor. The re-establishment of the US Fourth Fleet in 2008, to renew operations in Central and South America and the Caribbean, triggered concern among South American governments about potential US involvement in their internal affairs and US projection of power in the region. After initial expression of concern, the Brazilian government seemed to walk away from alarmist rhetoric, but the Brazilian expert community and the media continue to bring up the resurrection of the Fourth Fleet in conversations about threat perceptions. In a similar vein, Brazilian analysts point out that the United States failed to ratify the UN Convention of the Law of the Sea, which "protects states' control over special economic zones stretching up to 200 nautical miles from the baselines from which the breadth of the territorial sea is measured."[10]

It is hard to tell how strongly the sentiment of a potential threat from the United States and NATO feeds into thinking behind the nuclear submarine program. Do the Brazilian Navy and the rest of the official establishment rely on the future submarine force to increase their country's security against these specific potential threats? The anti-submarine warfare capabilities of the United States and NATO would negate potential Brazilian nuclear submarine power, and that raises questions about this particular rationale.

Bureaucratic Drivers

A closer examination of the most often cited strategic and defense motivations for the nuclear submarine program reveals that they alone cannot neatly explain the rationale for the program. The threat assessments in Brazil's defense thinking underwent significant changes from the late 1970s, when the program began. The Falklands/Malvinas War frequently raised by Brazilian experts as a motivation for their country's nuclear submarine program happened after the Navy launched the program. Brazil's off-shore oil resources that the Navy claimed it would protect with the help of the submarine force were discovered well after the program's establishment. What remained constant throughout almost four decades has been the Navy's interest and commitment to the program.

The organizational interests of the Navy provide a strong impetus for the program, a fact not fully appreciated outside of Brazil. Since late 1970s the submarine project has provided the Navy with a stable source of funding (the levels of funding fluctuated throughout the years but the program itself was sustained). As Brazilian defense analyst Rodrigo Moraes pointed out, the nuclear submarine is "the sole project for many Navy engineers."[11] In this context, the Navy's narrative that Brazil is vulnerable to sea-based threat appears more natural.

External observers perceive the nuclear submarine project as a top-down project promoted by the Brazilian government. In this author's opinion, the Navy drives the project and the government plays a secondary role, by supporting it. The Navy has successfully married the defense and developmental objectives of Brazil in the field of nuclear energy. The National Defense Strategy lists development of uranium deposits and nuclear power plant construction along with fuel-cycle development for nuclear submarine as strategic tasks, transcending "the limits of defense and development" (Ministry of Defense, 2008, p. 33). Even in semantic terms, the Navy chose the right strategy. It calls territorial waters "Blue Amazon," referencing a sense of vulnerability and a determination to protect Brazil's territory that the inland Amazon forests evoke.

The Navy's interest in driving a technologically challenging project fits into the broader role that the Brazilian military has historically played in science and technology development in areas such as aeronautics, engineering, and telecommunications. Some of Brazil's most successful technological projects originated from military projects. The military adopted French air traffic control technology CINDACTA (*Centro Integrado de Defesa Aérea e Controle de Tráfego Aéreo* or Integrated Air Traffic Control and Air Defense Center) and with time, the Brazilian commercial market fully absorbed the technology. Embraer's regional jets built with Italian Aeritalia and Aermacchi were spinoffs of a military project on ground attack aircraft produced by AMX, a joint Italian–Brazilian venture.

Modernity, Technology, and Prestige
In addition to strategic drivers and the Navy's bureaucratic interests, Brazil's search for modernity, technology, and prestige sustain the program. The nuclear submarine program, and the nuclear program more broadly, fit into Brazil's quest for modernity.

Pursuit of technological prominence and independence from external actors adds to the explanation of why Brazil has been pursuing a nuclear submarine program. As Emanuel Adler observes in his writings, "The general ideological consensus about industrialization as the way to progress, . . . the proliferation of antidependency ideas during the 1950s and 1960s in places of intellectual and political influence, . . . the basic nationalist views of scientists, and . . . the ad hoc alliance between the military and technocrats in pursuit of a common nationalist goal" were important ingredients for the country's success in the field of science and technology (1987, p. 199). The nuclear submarine program promised not only submarine technology but technology to enrich uranium.

Historically Brazil has sought to develop advanced technology indigenously. Brazilian academic literature on defense matters notes that since the 1970s "naval thinking was concentrated on the tendency of the new order to consolidate what was configured as a kind of technological apartheid" (Martins Filho and Zirker, 2007). Brazil's 2012 National Defense White Book singled out nuclear submarine development as a key driver of national technological process (Ministry of Defense, 2012). The 2008 National Defense Strategy lists the development of a nuclear-powered submarine among the country's projects that "require technological independence in terms of nuclear energy" (Ministry of Defense, 2008, p. 12). As a former senior Brazilian diplomat noted, "Brazil wants to know how to do things, rather than being forever dependent on foreign technology."[12]

A nuclear submarine is also a status symbol. Brazilians imply that a nuclear submarine is a token of a technologically advanced, geopolitically important country. During the 2013 inauguration of the submarine shipyard at Itaguaí, President Rousseff remarked that Brazil was entering "the select club of countries with nuclear submarines: the United States, Russia, France, Britain and China" (Defense News, 2013).

Nuclear Fuel Cycle and Nuclear Energy

Brazil's advanced nuclear program, including nuclear fuel capabilities, both strengthens the country's position in the global nuclear commercial market and makes it an important stakeholder in the global nuclear order. But the fuel cycle also has inherent proliferation challenges because of the dual-use nature of advanced nuclear technologies.

Brazil's civilian nuclear energy program and the nuclear submarine program are closely inter-related. Two organizations—a state-owned company INB (*Indústrias Nucleares do Brasil*) and the Navy—run the two programs. The multistage nuclear fuel cycle includes uranium mining and milling, conversion, enrichment, and production of fuel pellets and fuel assemblies. Brazil finds itself among a very small number of countries that have technology to implement all stages of the fuel cycle. Brazil is endowed with uranium reserves and has mined for uranium since 1982. Brazil's uranium reserves are estimated at between 277,000 and 1.1 million tons, which represents 5 percent of the world's total (World Nuclear Association, 2013). The country has three major uranium mines—Caldas, Caetité, and Itataia —with Caetité currently in operation.

Brazil possesses technology for uranium conversion and enrichment, which involves converting uranium to its gaseous form and then increasing the concentration of U-235 in natural uranium (0.7 percent) to higher levels. Nuclear fuel for nuclear power plants typically requires an enrichment level of 3–5 percent while Brazil's future nuclear submarine will likely require production of nuclear fuel enriched to just below 20 percent. While it possesses technology, the country has yet to industrialize both conversion and enrichment processes. It relies on foreign partners to meet its domestic demand for these services.

Brazil's Navy remains the key player as far as the uranium enrichment is concerned. It was the Navy that mastered enrichment technology in the 1980s. The Navy leases uranium enrichment technology to INB and INB depends on the Navy for supply of enrichment centrifuges. So far, INB enriches uranium to cover only 5 percent of its needs. The Navy has built a demonstration plant for uranium conversion at its Aramar Experimental Center in Iperó. And INB plans to build a uranium conversion plant at its Nuclear Fuel Factory at Resende.

Brazil has the capacity to implement the final stages of fuel fabrication—producing fuel pellets, loading the pellets into fuel rods, and bundling the fuel rods together into fuel assemblies. In South America, only two countries generate electricity from nuclear sources—Argentina and Brazil. Brazil operates two nuclear power plants, Angra 1 and Angra 2, with a third plant, Angra 3, under construction. Yet the extent to which Brazil will expand nuclear power production in the coming decades is not clear. Previously ambitious plans to build several new nuclear power reactors appear to be shelved, at least, for now, partly as a result of the Fukushima accident.

Despite the challenges with industrializing uranium conversion and enrichment and a slowed-down pace of nuclear power expansion, overall, Brazil's nuclear development makes it a nuclear actor worth watching. A relatively ambitious domestic nuclear program goes hand in hand with an assertive voice on global nuclear matters.

Brazil's Evolving Nuclear Identity

Brazil challenges the global nuclear order to evolve, and with its growing economic, political, and diplomatic might, its ability to do so has been increasing. In the discourse on nuclear disarmament and non-proliferation Brazil positions itself as being on higher moral ground. From Brazil's point of view, it has an impressive record both in terms of disarmament and non-proliferation. Not only does Brazil maintain a strong vocal position in support of disarmament, it has also made practical contributions to the cause: it joined the NPT as it introduced a ban on nuclear weapons in its Constitution, it became a member of a regional nuclear-weapon-free zone, and it has formally closed the chapter on the secret "parallel" nuclear program that its military maintained during the military dictatorship.

On the non-proliferation front, Brazil, together with Argentina, maintains a strong safeguards system through ABACC, which should instill confidence in the international community. Brazil criticizes nuclear-weapon states for failing to live up to their obligations to have meaningful progress toward disarmament. And Brazil argues that nuclear-weapon states let their national interests trump fairness, justice, and common good objectives, such as a more balanced global nuclear order or a nuclear-weapon-free world.

Yet, on closer inspection of Brazil's policies and choices in the nuclear field, its record appears more nuanced. Brazil challenges a global nuclear order that is inherently unfair, but in this process, it, too, chooses its actions based first and foremost on its national interests.

Brazil, the Tlatelolco Treaty, and the NPT

In terms of multilateral treaties, Brazil's interaction with the Tlatelolco Treaty and the NPT expose how it navigates between its normative beliefs and its national interests. Brazil's path to fully adhering to the Tlatelolco Treaty, which established a nuclear-weapon-free zone in Latin America and the Caribbean, was not straightforward. Brazil pioneered the zone in 1962 when its representative to the UN proposed the idea. During the negotiation process, Brazil, together with Argentina, ensured that the treaty would specifically allow for peaceful nuclear explosions, in which both countries had keen interest.

Brazil signed and ratified the Tlatelolco Treaty in the 1960s, but the treaty did not enter into force for decades. The treaty's text stipulated that a number of conditions had to be met, such as ratification by all state parties, before it could enter into force and become binding for all the signatories. At the same time, there was a provision allowing each individual country to waive these conditions; in case of the waiver, the treaty would enter into force for that particular country.[13] Brazil did not waive those conditions. Both Brazil and Argentina had doubts about the scope of safeguards to be applied under the treaty, whether all Latin American countries would adhere to it, and whether nuclear powers would sign the relevant protocols to the treaty. As a result, only in 1994 did Brazil fully embrace the Tlatelolco Treaty.

The NPT provides the foundation for the global nuclear regime. Open for signature in 1968, the treaty promotes non-proliferation of nuclear weapons, materials, and technology; development of nuclear energy for peaceful purposes; and global nuclear disarmament. Countries could join the NPT either as nuclear-weapon states or non-nuclear-weapon states. Only five countries qualified as nuclear-weapon states according to the treaty's criteria (nuclear weapon tests conducted before 1968)—China, France, the Soviet Union, the United States, and the UK. The Soviet Union, the United States, and the UK signed the NPT in 1968, while China and France delayed joining the treaty until 1992.

Brazil for a long time did not join the NPT. In fact, among the non-nuclear-weapon states it was second-to-last to join the treaty, in 1998, followed by Cuba in 2002. Brazil's reservations about joining the NPT are symptomatic of how it relates to the global nuclear order, which it sees as unfair and unbalanced. Brasília, like other capitals, criticized Washington and Moscow for drafting the treaty without consulting others. It was critical of the imbalance between the obligations of the nuclear and non-nuclear-weapon states (Rosenbaum and Cooper, 1970, p. 79). In fact, Brazil believed that the treaty's fundamental flaw was a lack of commitment to global nuclear disarmament. Importantly, as Carlo Patti writes based on Brazilian government documents, Brasília did not wish to accept restrictions on nuclear explosions, the use of which it considered valuable in "mining, opening of ports, canals, and earthmoving." Patti notes that Brazil and Argentina were eager to insert the same provision in the NPT on these explosions as the ones they were able to insert into the Tlatelolco Treaty. Brazil, like other countries, also could not ignore the fact that at the time two out of five nuclear-weapon-states (France and China) had failed to join the NPT (Patti, 2012, p. 70).

Brazil's eventual adherence to the NPT in 1998 did not have unanimous domestic support. Influential voices argued that Brasília should have maintained principled opposition to a treaty it saw as fundamentally unfair. From a practical point of view, they reasoned, Brazil had already made equivalent commitments. It had adhered to a nuclear-weapon-free zone in Latin America (under the Tlatelolco Treaty); it had a safeguards regime with Argentina and the IAEA; and it had a prohibition against pursuing nuclear weapons enshrined in its Constitution.

Those who supported Brazil joining the NPT contended that adherence to the near-universal treaty would provide Brazil with greater access to peaceful nuclear technology. They maintained that Brasília would also gain political benefits from not being an NPT holdout in the company of a handful of nuclear-armed countries—Israel, India, and Pakistan.

But in fact, it is more common to hear Brazilian experts argue that Brazil gained little from joining the NPT than the opposite. Thomaz Guedes da Costa, who in the 1990s worked on defense and strategic issues within the Brazilian government, argues that Brazil might have made a strategic mistake by signing the treaty. According to Guedes da Costa, Brazil received neither substantive technological nor political gains from joining (Arnson and Sotero, 2010, p. 6). Antonio Jorge Ramalho, a prominent Brazilian analyst and an advisor to the government on defense issues, noted: "Brazil was in a unique position not to sign the NPT. It alone could argue a principled position not to sign it. Brazil had always denounced the Treaty's discriminatory substance and renounced going nuclear."[14]

Brazil, as many other non-nuclear-weapon states in the world, firmly believes that the current global nuclear order is unfair. A majority of non-nuclear-weapon states abhor the fact that while the expectations of their non-proliferation obligations continue to rise, the nuclear-weapon states continue to rely on nuclear weapons, and the prospects of global nuclear disarmament remained dim. The order, largely based on the NPT, divides the world into official nuclear "haves," five permanent members of the UN Security Council possessing nuclear weapons, and nuclear "have-nots," countries that did not have nuclear weapons when the NPT came into being.

The main premise of the treaty rests on the following principles: non-nuclear-weapon states have an obligation not to develop or acquire nuclear weapons, and in exchange, receive access to nuclear technology for peaceful purposes; and nuclear-weapon states have an obligation to work toward nuclear disarmament. The legal implications, the exact nature of parties' obligations, and the conditions of the NPT "bargain" remain a matter of heated discussion in international fora, largely driven by the countries' status under the treaty.

The discourse of the nuclear-weapon states emphasizes the non-proliferation obligations of the non-nuclear-weapon states and frames the discussion around progress toward disarmament. Meanwhile, the non-nuclear-weapon states emphasize that nuclear-weapon states should achieve disarmament, rather than simply seek progress toward it. They also argue that the non-nuclear-weapon states accepted an obligation not to acquire nuclear weapons of their own, in exchange for access to nuclear technology for peaceful purposes and the eventual disarmament of nuclear-weapon states.

The rhetoric of official "nuclear haves"—the United States, Russia, China, France, and the UK—on nuclear disarmament varies. In the United States, President Barack Obama appears to be personally invested in the idea of disarmament. In his 2009 speech in Prague he shared his vision of a nuclear-free world. But US domestic politics, negative reaction from the fellow nuclear states and from countries benefiting from the US nuclear umbrella, all but killed the initial optimism surrounding Obama's speech.

Russia relies on its nuclear weapons as the only remaining symbol of its great-power status. In the most recent snub to the idea of nuclear disarmament and possibly to Obama's rhetoric, on the fifth anniversary of Obama's Prague speech in 2014, the Russian government disbanded its foreign ministry's department on security and disarmament. Instead, a department on non-proliferation and arms control was created, noting that disarmament was a thing of the past.[15] China argues that Russia and the United States, possessors of 95 percent of the world's nuclear weapons, should reduce their nuclear arsenals before China can join the disarmament process.[16] French diplomats often do not even attempt to appear interested in nuclear disarmament (Perkovich and Acton, 2009, p. 26). The UK's policy states that its nuclear deterrent "remains an important element" of its national security. The British government echoes other nuclear-weapon states: "We will continue to take steps towards a safer and more stable world where countries with nuclear weapons feel able to relinquish them" (Hammond, 2013).

Brazil, like many other non-nuclear-weapon states, challenges the logic of nuclear-weapon states who argue they need to feel safe before they can give up on their weapons. Brazil's representative to the NPT RevCon 2015, Antonio Guerreiro, contended:

> Waiting for a Kantian universal and perpetual peace to commit to foreswear atomic weapons simply runs counter to the ultimate objective of the NPT which is the total and irreversible elimination of nuclear weapons. We should all realize that the present discriminatory, and even invidious, state of affairs is unsustainable in the long run.[17]

Brazil's disillusionment with the nuclear-weapon states is palpable. Even Obama's Prague speech, in which he promoted the goal of the nuclear-free world, did not elicit any enthusiasm in Brazil. In the case of Brazil, the tensions brewing among the NPT states over the obligations of nuclear-weapon states and non-nuclear-weapon states are especially pronounced over the issue of Brazil's refusal to sign the IAEA Additional Protocol.

Brazil and the Safeguards Regime

The effectiveness of the nuclear non-proliferation regime depends on an efficient method to generate confidence that unauthorized weapons-related activities can be detected in time. Nuclear safeguards serve this purpose. States, including Brazil, sign comprehensive safeguards agreements with the IAEA to provide the first layer of confidence. Under such agreements, the IAEA can verify that what states report to the IAEA about their nuclear material and nuclear activities is correct and truthful.

In the early 1990s, the IAEA recognized that the existing safeguards system required strengthening and expanding its verification capabilities beyond the facilities and material declared by states. That realization came as a result of the IAEA's failure to detect undeclared nuclear activities in Iraq and North Korea in a timely manner. The IAEA promoted a system of strengthened safeguards by developing an Additional Protocol. Under an Additional

Protocol, the IAEA receives greater access to countries' nuclear facilities and can conduct more intrusive inspections. All facilities involved in fuel-cycle activities as well as any sites where nuclear material may be present become subject to inspection.

Brazil is among a small number of countries with significant nuclear activities that have not signed an Additional Protocol. The list includes Algeria, Argentina, Egypt, Syria, and Venezuela. Brazil finds itself under quite a bit of pressure from the outside, especially from countries like the United States, to sign an Additional Protocol (Hibbs, 2013). A combination of normative and practical reasons fuel Brazil's opposition to signing the IAEA Additional Protocol. As a matter of principle, Brazil is reluctant to accept any additional non-proliferation measures as long as nuclear-weapon states do not achieve meaningful progress toward disarmament. By opposing the IAEA Additional Protocol, Brazil demonstrates its objection to the global nuclear order that promotes too much non-proliferation and too little disarmament. Like many non-nuclear-weapon states, Brazil detests the fact that nuclear "have-nots" are expected to adopt more and more stringent non-proliferation measures while nuclear "haves" keep nuclear weapons at the heart of their defense and national security strategies.

In its official rhetoric, the above principled position is emphasized the most. Yet a number of other factors contribute to Brazil's lack of desire to embrace an Additional Protocol. Some Brazilian experts believe that provisions of the Additional Protocol, such as unannounced inspections and complete access to all facilities in the country, are not compatible with Brazil's nuclear submarine program. For example, short notice inspections would pose a challenge since the location of a nuclear submarine at sea, including the distance from the coastline, is sensitive information. Some in Brazil express concern that by signing an Additional Protocol and opening up all of its facilities to intrusive inspections would make Brazil vulnerable to industrial espionage. Finally, Brazil maintains that safeguards implemented on the basis of Brazil's agreement with Argentina and the Quadripartite Agreement between Brazil, Argentina, ABACC, and the IAEA provide sufficient reassurance of the peaceful nature of Brazil's nuclear activities. In fact, some Brazilian experts believe that the IAEA Additional Protocol is not fully compatible with the ABACC system and that if Brazil and Argentina sign the Additional Protocol, "its application would practically result in abandoning the bilateral system" (Feu Alvim et al., n.d., p. 10).

Brazil's interaction with the global nuclear order in the context of nuclear safeguards manifests itself in an interesting way within the NSG, as well. The NSG recognized safeguards implemented by Argentina and Brazil with the help of the ABACC as sufficient to allow Brazil and Argentina to engage in the exchange of sensitive nuclear technology associated with uranium enrichment and reprocessing. Until 2011, the NSG guidelines stated that members should exercise restraint in transferring these technologies. In 2011, the group adopted more specific criteria guiding transfers, one of which was that enrichment and reprocessing technology could only be transferred to countries that have ratified the IAEA Additional Protocol.

The important deviance from this rule was to allow enrichment and reprocessing transfers to countries "implementing appropriate safeguards agreements in cooperation with the IAEA, including a regional accounting and control arrangement for nuclear materials, as approved by the IAEA Board of Governors." The latter is a direct reference to the ABACC safeguards (Hibbs, 2011). Indeed, the NSG agreed to this provision at the insistence of Brazil and Argentina, in order to obtain required consensus for the adoption of new formal rules for the transfer of sensitive technologies.

Brazil's existing safeguards rooted in the bilateral context are critical to the non-proliferation regime, and they constitute an important source of confidence building at the regional and international level. But the existing safeguards are not equivalent in scope to the Additional Protocol. ABACC's authority is limited to verifying declared nuclear activities and material. The NSG/ABACC episode serves as an example of Brazil (together, in this case, with Argentina) managing to successfully promote its interests in the context of a global nuclear governance structure. It also demonstrates how emerging powers attain greater influence on the global nuclear scene without which they would not be able to nudge rules to reflect their interests.

As the next section describes, Brazil's concerns about the global nuclear order are no longer restricted to its own nuclear program. In the standoff between Iran and the Western powers in 2010, Brazil leveraged its rising ambitions and soft power to play an unexpected role in attempting to resolve the impasse, much to the consternation of traditional Western powerbrokers.

Established Powers versus Emerging Powers: The Tehran Declaration

In May 2010, Brasília and Ankara made major news by unveiling, together with Iran, a Joint Declaration, dubbed the Tehran Declaration. The Declaration announced an agreement on a nuclear fuel-swap scheme: Iran agreed to part with some of its LEU, in exchange for foreign nuclear fuel to power its research reactor in Tehran. The scheme was not a novel idea; it had been tried in several iterations before by Western powers seeking to minimize the amounts of LEU that Iran could potentially use for weapons purposes. In October 2009 the P5+1 (the five permanent members of the UN Security

Council plus Germany) and Iran agreed "in principle" that Iran would ship out approximately 1,200 kilograms of LEU at or below 5 percent enrichment in return for 120 kilograms of fuel for the Tehran Research Reactor. The 1,200 kilograms equaled roughly 80 percent of Iran's total LEU stockpile. According to the preliminary understanding, Iran would ship all 1,200 kilograms of LEU in one batch before the end of 2009; Russia would enrich Iran's LEU to 20 percent level of enrichment; and France would produce the fuel rods using enriched uranium and would supply them to Iran approximately one year after the conclusion of agreement.[18]

The final agreement never materialized. More radically minded figures in Iran's political elites, who were also keen to undermine their political rival President Ahmadinejad, opposed the proposed arrangement and persuaded the Supreme Leader Ayatollah Ali Khamenei to reject the proposal. Both Ahmadinejad's team and the international community were keen to pursue the fuel-swap route, but Iranians needed conditions better than those offered in 2009 in order to obtain domestic support. But at the same time the P5+1, burned by the 2009 experience, were not ready to go down the same river twice.

Meanwhile, international tensions surrounding Iran's nuclear program continued to escalate, with discussions about a new round of sanctions against Iran and scenarios of military action against Iran intensifying. It is in this context that Brazil and Turkey launched their own attempts to revive the fuel-swap proposal. After complex and controversial negotiations, Brazil and Turkey agreed with Iran on the following: Iran would ship 1,200 kilograms of its 5 percent LEU to Turkey in exchange for 120 kilograms of fuel for the Tehran Research Reactor from the Vienna Group (made up of the United States, Russia, France, and the IAEA). The Tehran Declaration spelled out the steps in basic terms. Iran would deposit 1,200 kilograms of LEU in Turkey, and pending a positive response from the Vienna Group, Iran and the Vienna Group would further spell out the delivery of 120 kilograms of fuel supplied by the Vienna Group to Iran.[19]

But the United States, the other members of the Vienna Group, and somewhat surprisingly, a majority of Brazilian strategic thinkers dismissed the Tehran Declaration. The swiftness and harshness with which the United States brushed the Tehran Declaration aside surprised Brasília. The day after Brazil and Turkey secured Iran's agreement and signed the Tehran Declaration, on May 18, Washington announced that it secured the support of Russia, China, and the rest of P-5 on a draft resolution to impose a new round of sanctions against Iran. And the P-5 sent the draft resolution for consideration to the rest of the Security Council the same day (MacAskill, 2013). To the Brazilian government, this was the opposite of giving diplomacy a chance.

Brazil's foreign minister at the time, Celso Amorim, admitted that Brazil knew the United States was pursuing both tracks—a diplomatic solution and sanctions—and, in his words, "maybe when Lula went to Iran, the sanctions track became more feasible." Indeed, US observers confirm that Russian and Chinese support for a new round of sanctions was not a given until the last moment. Nonetheless, as Amorim added, "It is not that at any point anything changed. This is what is intriguing. Even for me."[20]

Lack of straightforward communication between Brazil, Turkey, and the United States contributed to the final result. Brazil and Turkey were taken aback with the harsh response from the United States to their diplomatic endeavor, and the United States played into the hands of its critics by dismissing emerging powers. The leaders of the three countries communicated directly only once during the Nuclear Security Summit in Washington in March 2010. President Obama sent letters to his Brazilian and Turkish counterparts after the conversation in Washington as a follow up. The letter, likely a product of an inter-agency effort, was not straightforward. On the one hand, it warned Brazil and Turkey of being led on by Iran but, on the other, it did not dismiss a diplomatic solution to the Iranian nuclear crisis. As a result, Brazilin leaders could selectively interpret it as a "green light" from President Obama to engage with Iran.[21]

The context in which the Tehran Declaration had been conceived may have impaired its success from the very beginning. The challenges of dealing with substantive issues resulted in a ten-paragraph document that was thin on the actual implementation of the arranged swap. Unlike the 2009 attempted deal, it did not (and could not) spell out specifics regarding which countries would supply Iran with reactor fuel or during which period.

The Tehran Declaration did not address the fact that Iran started enriching uranium to 20 percent after the failure of the 2009 negotiations. This development was a significant proliferation concern because once uranium is enriched to 20 percent, most of the isotope separative work needed to reach weapons-grade 90 percent enrichment is done. The Tehran Declaration also did not reflect the fact that while in 2009 the negotiated 1,200 kilograms of 5 percent LEU represented 80 percent of Iran's stock, it now accounted for just over 50 percent of Iran's LEU holdings (Institute for Science and International Security 2010, p. 1). In other words, while the essence of the Tehran Declaration was close to the attempted deal in 2009, the immediate value of the agreement was significantly diminished by changed circumstances.

According to Amorim, Brazil and Turkey in no way ignored the important steps necessary for resolving a standoff with Iran, such as sorting out the issue of 20 percent enrichment. But as Amorim underscores, the goal of the Tehran

Declaration was to start building trust so that in the future, the international community's goals could be reached. Amorim added that he talked to Ahmadinejad in late 2009 before Iran started enriching to 20 percent levels. He asked Ahmadinejad to postpone starting enrichment at this level, and Ahmadinejad agreed to delay it by two months. Amorim noted with regret: "The West did not pay much attention."

Writing together in the *New York Times*, Brazil's Amorim and Turkey's foreign minister, Ahmet Davutoğlu, emphasized that solving all problems "was never the purpose of the original agreement." Rather, the efforts to engage Tehran in early 2010 were designed to "provide essential confidence-building, the key missing component" (Davutoğlu and Amorim, 2010).

Beyond the issues of the increased amount of LEU and Iran's new capability to enrich uranium to 20 percent, certain parts of the Tehran Declaration were bound to be problematic for the United States and key Western states. For example, Brazil and Turkey proclaimed their appreciation of "Iran's commitment to the NPT and its constructive role in pursuing the realization of nuclear rights of its Member States." The declaration included a provision allowing the return of all of Iran's LEU from Turkey if the declaration's provisions were "not respected." Noting that the declaration called for the international community to refrain from "measures, actions and rhetorical statements that would jeopardize Iran's rights and obligations under the NPT," such a provision meant that Iran could have easily decided to walk away from the deal under the pretext of jeopardizing rhetoric coming from the international community.[22]

Why Did Brazil Engage?

The experience of the Tehran Declaration showcased Brazil's potential to play a more assertive role in the global order, but it also exposed the limitations of that role. Brazil's involvement in the hot issue of Iran's nuclear program could be seen as both expected and unexpected. That is because some of the drivers behind this initiative were a natural extension of Brazil's foreign policy and world outlook, while others were more of a one-off occurrence, namely, the unusual combination of the Lula-Amorim power duo.

Brazil's foray into a high-profile international negotiation was consistent with Brazil's growing desire to be involved in global governance. Reaching out and attempting to mediate between Iran and the Western powers could also be seen as a manifestation of Brazil's increasing confidence in its "soft power" credentials. Building on its experience and relative success with engaging in multilateral issues such as trade, environment, and health, Brazilian leaders felt ready to try the country's diplomatic skills in the nuclear arena. Brazilians, proud of being "a nation of no enemies," counted on their ability to talk equally comfortably with all parties, including Iranians, Americans, and Europeans.

Brazil sees the global nuclear order as dominated by the established powers, much like the broader global order. The idea that emerging powers, such as Brazil and Turkey, could make a meaningful contribution to solving an international problem appealed to Brazil. If nothing else, the time felt ripe for the nuclear field to bring in new players. Brazil, unlike the United States, believed that a new round of sanctions would damage the chances for a negotiated solution on Iran. And it feared that absent a diplomatic breakthrough, the situation could deteriorate to the point of a military conflict in the Middle East. Brazil likely hoped that making Iran agree to a fuel swap would alter the increasingly negative context in which Iran and the international community were negotiating. Brasília potentially anticipated that the new landscape created as a result of a fuel-swap agreement would push the P5+1 to adopt a different view on how to deal with Iran.

Throughout its diplomatic history Brazil has maintained a skeptical view of sanctions, a perspective that hardened after the controversial experience with Iraq. Celso Amorim, who served on the UN Security Council's Iraq panel, reached the following conclusions on the limited effectiveness of sanctions: "The sanctions were having no result from the point of view of the weapons of mass destruction, but certainly were creating havoc in the civilian population in Iraq . . . it's not that sanctions are useless and they may not be used, but . . . you have to calibrate them in a proper way" (Amorim 2011a).

Unlike the United States or European countries that ratcheted up pressure on Iran, including through adoption of sanctions, Lula's Brazil adopted a policy of engaging Iran as an important Middle Eastern partner. Brazil, home to millions of citizens of Middle Eastern descent, turned toward Iran as a part of deepening South–South relations. Brazilian leadership also saw Iran as an important market and a potential recipient of Brazilian investments (Amorim 2011b, p. 59).

But why would Brazil be so anxious about the standoff with Iran, a country that remained remote from Brazil geographically, politically, and culturally? While the Brazilian government never openly compares itself to Iran, Brazilian experts point out that their government is sensitive to how the international community views Iran's uranium enrichment program. Some Brazilians fear that Brazil, a non-nuclear-weapon state with an advanced nuclear fuel cycle, including the capacity to enrich uranium, might be the next to come under scrutiny and have its right to uranium enrichment "denied."

As a matter of principle, Brazil could not be further away from Iran. Brazil was never accused of violating its non-proliferation obligations, as Iran was.

Yet the uranium enrichment programs of Brazil and Iran share an important element: they are not driven by considerations of economic feasibility. Both countries believe in the importance of self-sufficiency in the nuclear field, and both have invested in developing indigenous nuclear fuel cycles.

The discourse surrounding nuclear energy helps to explain Brazil's interest in the evolution of the standoff between Iran and Western countries. The Iranian government managed to expand the conversation about its own nuclear program into a broader debate on the right to peaceful nuclear energy. For developing countries, Brazil included, this debate hits a nerve. Many developing countries see nuclear energy as an important component of their development; they worry that the non-proliferation agenda promoted by developed countries might limit their own access to nuclear technology. Their worries are exacerbated by the general disillusionment of developing countries with the global nuclear order, in which a handful of countries possess nuclear weapons while the rest are expected to comply with their non-proliferation obligations.

Even though Brazil had strong drivers to engage in the negotiations with Iran—its growing confidence on the international scene and interest in a diplomatic solution of the Iranian problem among them—these alone are not sufficient to explain Brazil's nuclear entrepreneurship. Personalities served as an important catalyst for Brazil's entry into the hottest international dispute: popular, self-confident, and ambitious, Lula and his equally confident foreign minister Amorim created quite a dynamic duo, combining qualities that embodied Brazil's long search for greatness (*grandeza*).

All in all, Brazil's effort was significant in many ways. Its attempt to serve as an intermediary in a complex international impasse reflected the Brazilian leadership's intent to expand its role in the international security arena, reaching beyond the realms of multilateral trade, the environment, and global health. The Tehran Declaration also crystallized two broader trends: the growing ambition and potential of emerging powers to play an ever-increasing role in the global nuclear order and the increasing evidence that neither emerging powers nor the established powers are completely prepared for this evolving trend.

Conclusion

For decades Brazil has invested into developing its nuclear industry. Today it has reached a level of nuclear development that makes the world see it as an important stakeholder in global nuclear affairs. A quest for independence, self-sufficiency, technological progress, and greater recognition animates Brazil's nuclear policy. Those drivers explain Brazil's persistence in developing a full nuclear fuel cycle, building a nuclear submarine, and expanding the share of nuclear power in its energy mix, as well as its attempts to play a more active role in global nuclear politics.

Brazil's views on the global nuclear order are informed by the sentiment of distrust toward technologically advanced countries that in the past have sought to deny countries like Brazil access to nuclear technology. Brazil sees the global nuclear order as a reflection of the world order: unfair and antiquated. In the nuclear realm Brazil pursues a strategy similar to its policy in the fields of multilateral trade, finance, and world governance more broadly. Brazil pushes for greater representation of developing countries in structures like the World Trade Organization, World Bank, IMF, and the UN Security Council. While Brazil calls for greater democratization of these institutions, it is ready to accept that they might not evolve to a sufficient degree and in that case, Brazil is keen to be among the powerbrokers.

Brazil's nuclear policy-making reveals that occasionally the country's inclination to be seen as being on higher moral ground conflicts with its immediate national interests. Brazil places high value on multilateralism, international institutions, and norms, but practical considerations coupled with a general sense of disillusionment with the global nuclear order have pushed it to adopt policies that meet its immediate interests. Brazil's reticence to join the NPT, adhere to the Tlatelolco Treaty, and sign the IAEA Additional Protocol are among the examples of this tension in Brazil's nuclear identity.

Speaking about the sense of disillusionment with the global nuclear order, countries like Brazil are growing increasingly assertive in questioning the current status quo; and tensions between established and emerging powers on questions of nuclear disarmament, non-proliferation, and nuclear energy have become more pronounced. These tensions are not new, but they are becoming harder to ignore. In the past, established nuclear powers could more easily dismiss complaints from non-nuclear states about the lopsided order, but the non-nuclear states have gradually become more active and vocal, pushing the order to evolve and making outright dismissal of their demands more difficult.

Brazil's growing confidence and desire to play a more hands-on role in global nuclear affairs manifested itself in negotiating the Brazil-Turkey-Iran Tehran Declaration. The initiative left a contradictory legacy and added to tensions between Brazil and the United States, but at the very least, Brazil's bold attempt at brokering a complicated international standoff made observers curious about Brazil's ambitions and potential. Brazil is still in the process of establishing itself on the global scene including in the nuclear realm. Brasília, for the foreseeable future, will face the paradox of criticizing the unfairness of nuclear order while attempting to carve out a role for itself in it.

Notes

1. This chapter is based on Togzhan Kassenova, *Brazil's Nuclear Kaleidoscope: An Evolving Identity* (Washington, DC: Carnegie Endowment for International Peace, 2014).
2. Nuclear safeguards are technical measures to verify the correctness and the completeness of the declarations made by states about their nuclear material and activities (based on IAEA methodology).
3. Statement by Ambassador Pedro Motta Pinto Coelho, Permanent Representative of Brazil to the Conference on Disarmament, Preparatory Committee for the 2015 Review Conference of the Parties to the Treaty on the Non-Proliferation of Nuclear Weapons, NPT PrepCom, 2014, at http://www.reachingcriticalwill.org/images/documents/Disarmament-fora/npt/prepcom14/statements/28April_Brazil.pdf
4. Interview with Carlo Patti, email communication, June 2013 (Patti, 2012, p. 41).
5. Author interview with Carlos Feu Alvim, Rio de Janeiro, July 2012.
6. Author interview with Carlos Feu Alvim, Rio de Janeiro, July 2012.
7. The United States and the UK use uranium enriched to 90 percent in their submarines, while Russia uses uranium enriched to more than 20 percent. France moved from using HEU to LEU in its submarines, and China reportedly uses LEU to power its fleet. India, a nuclear-armed state outside of the NPT, started sea trials of its first indigenous nuclear submarine in late 2014 (Pandit, 2014).
8. Agreement between the Republic of Argentina, the Federative Republic of Brazil, the Brazilian–Argentine Agency for Accounting and Control of Nuclear Materials, and the International Atomic Energy Agency for the Application of Safeguards, ABACC, http://www.abacc.org.br/wp-content/uploads/2009/10/quadripartite_ingles.pdf
9. Author's interview with a Brazilian defense expert, Brasília, July 2012.
10. UN Convention on the Law of the Sea, Article 57.
11. Author interview with Rodrigo Moraes, Brasília, July 2012.
12. Author interview with a former senior Brazilian diplomat, email communication, January 2013.
13. Treaty for the Prohibition of Nuclear Weapons in Latin America and the Caribbean (Treaty of Tlatelolco), Article 28, http://cns.miis.edu/inventory/pdfs/apttlat.pdf
14. Author interview with Antonio Jorge Ramalho, Brasília, 2012.
15. Announcement for mass media on structural changes in the Ministry of Foreign Affairs (in Russian), Ministry of Foreign Affairs, April 4, 2014, at http://www.mid.ru/brp_4.nsf/newsline/9AAB4F0A53803C2A44257CB0004EB2D9
16. Ministry of National Defense of the People's Republic of China, "Arms Control and Disarmament," http://eng.mod.gov.cn/Database/ArmsControl/
17. Statement by Ambassador Antonio Guerreiro, Permanent Representative of Brazil to the Conference on Disarmament, Head of the Brazilian Delegation to the I Preparatory Committee for the 2015 Review Conference of the Parties to the Treaty on the Non-Proliferation of Nuclear Weapons, NPT PrepCom, 2012.

18. "History of the Official Proposals on the Iranian Nuclear Issue," updated January 2013, Arms Control Association, www.armscontrol.org/factsheets/Iran_Nuclear_Proposals

19. Joint Declaration by Iran, Turkey, and Brazil, May 17, 2010, available at http://www.fas.org/nuke/guide/iran/joint-decl.pdf

20. Author's interview with Celso Amorim, Brasília, July 2012.

21. For a more comprehensive analysis of Obama's letter to Lula, please refer to Kassenova (2014), pp. 72–73.

22. Joint Declaration by Iran, Turkey, and Brazil, May 17, 2010.

CHAPTER 8

Brazil's Place in the Global Economy

Arturo C. Porzecanski

B razil is a country with long-standing ambitions for a major role in the world economy, but its footprint remains relatively modest. This chapter documents the extent to which Brazil's economy remains fairly inward-looking and isolated from global markets, despite the modernizing reforms of the past generation. It then discusses some of the causes, which include both contingent economic factors and conscious foreign policy choices. It concludes with a discussion of potential policy changes that could enable Brazil to bridge the gap between global ambitions and achievements.

Brazil's Significance in the World Economy

Brazil has enjoyed political and economic stability and an increasingly favorable external environment during the past two decades, but its economic accomplishments at home and on the world economic stage have been relatively modest, and thus the country's influence and prestige have remained quite limited.

Its impressive geographical and economic size is indisputable: Brazil is the world's fifth-largest country in terms of territorial extension, coming after Russia, China, the United States, and Canada; the fifth most populous country, surpassed only by China, India, the United States, and Indonesia; and in terms of the value-added of its economic output, adjusted for international differentials in purchasing power, it is the seventh-largest economy, after the United States, China, India, Japan, Germany, and Russia.

However, despite these oft-cited headline indicators, Brazil casts a much smaller shadow when put in its proper context. The country's extensive land area (8.5 million square kilometers), as continental-sized as it is, represents but 6.5 percent of the world's total area, and includes just 5 percent of the planet's arable land.[1] Its territory is relatively lightly settled, such that Brazil's 200 million residents account for less than 3 percent of the world's total population, significantly less than China's 19 percent and India's 17.6 percent shares of the total. Brazil's production of goods and services, even once adjusted for purchasing-power differentials, is likewise valued at less than 3 percent of the world's total, as opposed to the United States, which accounts for nearly 20 percent and China's over 15 percent of global output.

Other relevant indicators of Brazil's economic dimension in the world cut a relatively unimpressive figure (Table 8.1). The country's merchandise exports multiplied from an average of $1.5 billion per annum during 1950–53 to over $60 billion by 2000–03, but because other countries' exports expanded even faster during that half-century, Brazil's share of world exports actually dropped from over 2 percent to under 1 percent of the total. In the past decade, Brazilian exports have vaulted to the vicinity of $250 billion per year during 2011–13, and although this surge led to relative gains, and the country's market share rose, Brazil currently accounts for only around 1.2 percent of total world exports.[2]

Moreover, Brazil remains a particularly inward-looking economy even in comparison with other large, continental-sized nations, which naturally tend

Table 8.1 Main Indicators of Brazil's Place in the World

Rank	Land area*		Population**		GDP***	
1	Russia	16.4	China	1,357.4	United States	16.8
2	China	9.3	India	1,252.1	China	13.4
3	United States	9.1	United States	316.1	India	5.1
4	Canada	9.1	Indonesia	249.9	Japan	4.7
5	**Brazil**	**8.5**	**Brazil**	**200.4**	Germany	3.2
6	Australia	7.7	Pakistan	182.1	Russia	2.6
7	India	3.0	Nigeria	173.6	**Brazil**	**2.4**
8	Argentina	2.7	Bangladesh	156.6	United Kingdom	2.4
9	Kazakhstan	2.7	Russia	143.5	France	2.3
10	Algeria	2.4	Japan	127.3	Mexico	1.8
	World	**129.7**	**World**	**7,124.5**	**World**	**87.0**
	Of which: Brazil	**6.5%**	**Of which: Brazil**	**2.8%**	**Of which: Brazil**	**2.8%**

* Millions of square kilometers in 2012
Source: World Bank, *World Development Indicators*, 2014.
** Millions of inhabitants in 2013
Source: World Bank, *World Development Indicators*, 2014.
*** GDP in 2013 based on purchasing-power-parity (PPP) valuation of country GDP, in trillions of US dollars
Source: International Monetary Fund, *World Economic Outlook Database*, April 2014.

to be more self-sufficient and thus less dependent on cross-border trade and financial flows than medium-sized—never mind small—economies. In countries such as Canada, Mexico, South Africa, and Russia, exports of goods and services are equivalent to around 30 percent of their GDP; and in India, Indonesia, and Turkey, the export sector represents about one-quarter of their GDP. In Brazil, in contrast, exports of goods and services have represented less than 13 percent of GDP throughout 2009–13.[3]

Mineral, agricultural, and other primary products account for over half of Brazil's total exports, with many products that are classified as "manufactured" actually involving the processing of raw materials; for example, exports of orange juice are counted under manufactured goods. It is estimated that the proportion of total Brazilian exports embodying "high technology" has decreased from over 10 percent of total exports in 2000 to 5 percent by 2010 (Canuto et al., 2013). The share of manufactured goods incorporating these high technologies, in turn, has likewise shrunk from roughly one-fifth of total manufactures in 2001 to a mere one-tenth by 2012.[4] Even manufactured export goods incorporating low levels of technology slid from over 13 percent to under 10 percent of total exports between 2000 and 2010. And this decrease in the content of technology in Brazilian exports was not solely the result of the intervening boom in commodity sales abroad; rather, it also reflected slow growth in exports of manufactured goods embodying technology (Canuto et al., 2013).

Brazilian exports are also characterized by the fact that they involve a relatively small proportion of imported inputs, a sign that Brazil is only marginally integrated into global production chains. For instance, estimates of the contribution of off-shored intermediate inputs to the production of goods that are then exported show that Brazil is one of the most self-sufficient of nations, with no more than one-tenth of the value-added of its exports incorporating foreign-made inputs. This very low share compares to more than one-fifth of export value-added in the case of Canada and India, and about one-third of the same in China and Mexico.[5]

Brazil's self-sufficiency means that its economy is not as connected to global production as those of its peers, and thus the country is slow to benefit from quality improvements, technological upgrades, and price reductions taking place elsewhere in the world. Indeed, Brazil has served as a platform for national and multinational producers to satisfy the needs of the large (and relatively protected) domestic market, or else as a platform to export primary and manufactured goods made almost entirely in Brazil. The resulting self-sufficiency has contributed to Brazil's relative isolation from the world's multiplying production chains and thus to the country's comparatively low international economic profile.

Brazil also cuts a very modest figure in terms of international financial, and not merely trade, connections. To begin with, the local currency, the real (BRL), is hardly traded in the international currency markets, a further sign of the economy's marginal integration into the global market. According to the latest and most authoritative survey of currency turnover in the world, the BRL figured in 0.6 percent of all spot transactions taking place during the sample month of April 2013. This compares to a 1.7 percent share for the heavily regulated Chinese yuan (CNY), 1.8 percent for the Russian ruble (RUB), and 2.8 percent for the Mexican peso (MXN). Even the Indian rupee (INR), the Turkish lira (TRY), and the South African rand (ZAR) trade more frequently in the spot currency market than does the Brazilian real.[6]

In the foreign exchange swap market, which is marginally larger than the spot market—the equivalent of $2.2 trillion/day in swaps, versus $2.0 trillion/day in spot transactions—the BRL was involved in an insignificant 0.04 percent of all transactions taking place around the world during the sample month of April 2013. This compared to a swap-market presence of 1.8 percent of total transactions for the (partially inconvertible) Chinese yuan and 2.6 percent of total for the (fully convertible) Mexican peso, just to mention two more heavily traded emerging-market currencies.[7]

In terms of the international reserves and other foreign assets owned by the Brazilian public and private sectors—foreign currencies, stocks, bonds, real estate, and the like—these amounted to an estimated $731 billion as of the end of 2012—more than double those in 2006, and by far the largest number in Brazil's history. However, this wealth represents a mere 0.56 percent of what all other countries own in terms of their combined cross-border assets. Brazil's $731 billion was also one-seventh of mainland China's international assets, and roughly one half of Russia's cross-border assets as of the same date.[8]

Brazil's FDI around the world (viz, investments entailing at least a 10% ownership stake) were estimated at about $373 billion as of end-2012, and foreign portfolio investments at the equivalent of $271 billion. To put them in proper perspective, these components of Brazil's international assets were 3.19 percent and 0.93 percent, respectively, of the world total of such cross-border investments.[9] In other words, Brazil's multinational companies and investments may have expanded a great deal abroad in the past decade, but they represent a small dot in the huge universe of cross-border direct and portfolio investing (Table 8.2).

In terms of the international liabilities owed by the Brazilian public and private sectors to foreign direct and portfolio investors, and also to foreign banks and suppliers, these amounted to an estimated $1.6 trillion as of the end of 2012. This figure is likewise more than double the amount of external

Table 8.2 Additional Indicators of Brazil's Place in the World (as of 2012, except as noted)

	Amount ($ billions)	% of World total
Merchandise trade, 2013	**487**	**1.27**
Merchandise exports, FOB	242	1.21
Merchandise imports, CIF	245	1.34
International assets	**731**	**0.56**
Official international reserves	373	3.19
Outward foreign direct investment	271	0.93
Outward foreign portfolio investment	22	0.06
International liabilities	**1,583**	**0.73**
Inward foreign direct investment	745	2.57
Inward foreign portfolio investment	639	1.30

Source: International Monetary Fund, *International Financial Statistics*, June 2014.

liabilities the country had in 2006, and by far the largest number in Brazil's history. There is no question that in recent years Brazil has attracted many foreign investors to its shores. Nevertheless, the $1.6 trillion captured by Brazil represents a mere 0.73 percent of the cross-border loans and direct and portfolio investments that all of the world's countries had managed to attract as of end-2012.[10]

In sum, despite Brazil's recent rise in global rankings of GDP (on a purchasing-power adjusted basis), which moved the country from eighth in the world in 1990 to seventh place by 2013, a comeback from the sixth place it had held back in 1980, the figures above document the continued inward-looking nature of the economy.[11] Brazil is one of the most self-sufficient economies in the world. To state this in less-positive terms: it is one of the least internationalized of the large economies, with its manufacturing base increasingly marginalized from global production chains. While Brazil's scale provides it with the luxury of a large and expanding domestic market, the rapid rise of a modernizing China and the increasing competitiveness of East Asian, Western and Eastern European, and Latin American countries suggest that Brazilian industry is and will likely remain at a disadvantage despite well-meaning policies enacted in Brasília.

Brazil's Economic Statecraft

How has this come to pass? Brazilian policymakers, after all, came to recognize during the 1980s the limits of state-led, import-substituting industrialization. They have since sought a "middle way" between the continuation of past nationalist, interventionist economic policies and the neo-liberal alternative that became fashionable in much of Latin America—never mind in the formerly Communist countries, most of which embraced free-market capitalism with gusto. This section suggests a number of causes for Brazil's economic policy choices, some more strategic than others, which have culminated in Brazil's relative isolation from global markets, and for the adoption of public policies that are not up to the task.

Economic Performance

First and foremost, Brazil's footprint on the world economic stage is light because, whether as a cause or consequence, by world standards its economic performance has been mixed. In the long period from 1980 through 2013, per capita incomes in Brazil, measured on an inflation-adjusted basis, increased by a total of 35 percent (Figure 8.1). The economy actually experienced a contraction in per capita GDP in 12 out of the 33 years, or in more than one-third of the time elapsed. Thus, Brazil has made economic progress in what could be characterized as a "two steps forward, one step back" pattern—certainly so up until the mid-2000s.[12]

Meanwhile, during the same period, the simple (unweighted) mean performance delivered by 109 emerging and developing countries excluding Brazil was a doubling of their GDP per capita—specifically, a 105 percent cumulative surge—and the median performance was a 60 percent increase. China was the star performer by a long shot: the country managed to multiply its 1980 per capita income by 16 times during the intervening 33 years, never

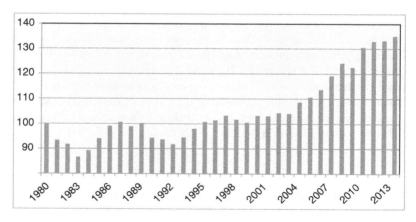

Figure 8.1 Brazil's GDP Per Capita, Constant Prices (1980 = 100)
Source: International Monetary Fund, *World Economic Outlook Database*, April 2014.

experiencing a single recession year. Vietnam multiplied its GDP per capita by five times—not a single recession year there, either—and India and Thailand, notwithstanding a major setback in 1998, achieved a nearly four-fold increase in their living standards. Malaysia and Indonesia almost tripled their per capita incomes between 1980 and 2013, despite becoming victims of the Asian financial crisis; Chile registered a more than time-and-a-half (170%) increase—impressive only by Latin American standards; and Poland doubled its economic standard of living even though it went through a wrenching transition from communism to capitalism.[13]

Neo-developmentalism

Second, as Villela and Maia and Taylor (Chapters 9 and 3 this volume) also note, despite the changes of the past generation, Brazilian policymakers have followed an economic development strategy that remains heavily influenced by the structuralist-inspired policies of the 1950s. Although policymakers in the 1980s and 1990s recognized the futility of autarchy and began to work toward opening the economy and lessening the burdensome role of the state, Brazil has embraced this policy set less than enthusiastically. Policymakers have retained the most important state-driven mechanisms of development, including the substantial role of the national development bank, BNDES, as the large-scale source of subsidized credit for companies deemed strategic, as well as the granting of tax breaks and protection from imports as tools of industrial promotion.

The administration of President Luiz Inácio Lula da Silva (2003–10) reintroduced the concept of a strategic industrial policy with the launch of the *Política Industrial, Tecnológica e de Comércio Exterior* (Industrial, Technological, and Foreign Trade Policy, or PITCE) in November 2003, this time with an export-promoting, rather than import-substituting, development objective. It was supplemented in May 2008 by a *Política de Desenvolvimento Produtivo* (Productive Development Policy, or PDP), administered by the BNDES, to help position Brazilian companies (e.g., in the mining, steel, aviation, and biofuels sectors) to become global leaders. Ever since then, BNDES has been picking and promoting suspected winners through generous long-term loans at concessional interest rates (Rojas, 2013).

Most recently, this tendency is epitomized by the effort to build a domestic shipbuilding industry in the northeastern state of Pernambuco, as part of the drive to exploit the pre-salt oil finds in Brazilian coastal waters. The Brazilian government, which has been the principal investor (through a subsidiary of Petrobras), has implemented local-content restrictions, and has borne the costs of a production process that has been longer and considerably more expensive than purchasing ships from international competitors—all in the name of developing local shipbuilding capacity that might later be used in developing the (state-owned) coastal oilfields (DuBois and Primo, 2013).[14]

In her inaugural year in office, President Dilma Rousseff, Lula da Silva's successor, quickened the pace of industrial policy and turned it sharply inward, starting in August 2011. The government first announced the *Plano Brasil Maior* (Plan Larger Brazil), a package consisting mainly of tax breaks, in most cases conditional upon the use of Brazilian-made goods or on export performance objectives.[15] The following month, the authorities imposed a 30 percent increase in the tax on manufactured products (IPI) for vehicles with less than 65 percent of their value-added originating in Brazil, Argentina, or Mexico (Brazil has preferential regimes for autos with Argentina and Mexico, the former in the context of Mercosul).

Subsequently, in October 2012, increases on 100 tariff lines were announced mainly affecting imported machinery, plastics, iron and steel, chemicals, paper, and wood articles. Tariffs were raised between 2 and 18 percentage points, which resulted in new tariff levels of between 14 percent and 25 percent for affected imports. According to a recent report by the European Commission, Brazil, together with Argentina, South Africa, and Indonesia, is responsible for more than half of all new protectionist measures introduced in the period from October 2008 to May 2013—and this even though they were little affected by the global financial crisis which impacted Europe, above all.[16]

All of these efforts have been given theoretical backing by a revised version of state-fostered economic development known as "neo-developmentalism," a term coined by Brazilian economist and former policymaker Luiz Carlos Bresser-Pereira to define a twenty-first-century alternative to the "Washington Consensus" orthodoxy (Ban, 2013; Bresser-Pereira, 2009). Harkening back to the heady growth of the late 1960s and early 1970s, Bresser-Pereira describes a national developmentalist policy set that combines nascent industry protection and state promotion of investment in potential industrial champions. The objective is to promote export-led industrialization supported by government intervention (including keeping the exchange rate competitive) in what appears to be a reprise of the East Asian model of development in the 1970s and 1980s.

The siren song of neo-developmentalism and the practical policy choices of the Lula and Rousseff administrations have set Brazil on a path reminiscent of the inward-looking policies that dominated policymaking from the 1930s through the debt crisis of 1982, albeit perhaps with slightly more emphasis on export promotion than on sheer import substitution. As Musacchio and Lazzarini (2014) note, these policies have developed their own homegrown constituency of proponents, including state-owned firms and their employees, as well as the large private-sector firms that have bene-fited from these policies and from various forms of government support, including national champions from diverse fields, from major construction multinationals to various banking giants. Furthermore, as we have already seen, the boom in commodity exports since 2003 provided the most sus-tained growth in per capita GDP since Brazil's return to democracy, at least until it petered out in 2011. Correctly or not, this growth spurt was credited to the neo-developmentalist agenda, providing it with credibility that is prov-ing increasingly difficult to sustain now that domestic and international cir-cumstances are no longer as favorable, and given limits to expansionary fiscal and monetary policies in Brazil.

The Mixing of Foreign Policy and Economic Policy

A third and perhaps unexpected motivation for Brazil's inward-looking development policies results from choices made in the realm of economic diplomacy. Brazil is somewhat paradoxical in this regard. On the one hand, in terms of its economic statecraft—namely, the harnessing of global eco-nomic forces to advance Brazil's foreign policy, and the use of foreign policy tools to further the country's economic potential—the political and business elites in Brazil have responded to the centrifugal forces of economic globaliza-tion through a commitment to multilateralism. At the same time, however, for reasons that often have less to do with economic motivations than geopo-litical strategy, the government has responded to the centripetal forces of regionalization by constraining itself via commitments to Mercosul, and to a lesser extent to Portuguese-speaking Africa.

As other contributors to this volume note, Brazil has long pursued the resolution of world problems through multilateral approaches to economic development, international trade, and international security issues. In eco-nomic policy, Brazil has sought both greater influence and greater autonomy with some success, increasing its quota share in international financial insti-tutions and building up the Group of 20 into an influential participant in global economic policymaking. Brazil and other developing countries became influential voices in the Uruguay Round of trade negotiations that was launched in 1986 under the aegis of the General Agreements on Tariffs and Trade (GATT, the predecessor of the WTO, the World Trade Organization). Brazil also played an important role in the start of the Doha Round of 2001, the latest—and so far incomplete—attempt to curb protectionism affecting trade in agriculture, services, and intellectual property. Among developing countries, Brazil and India have been heavily involved in guiding the agenda and negotiations (Fishlow, 2011, pp. 168–73).

Indeed, as Miles Kahler (2013, p. 721) notes, Brazil has high capabilities in global economic governance. Through coalition building, the use of informal norms, and the extensive employment of formal dispute-resolution mechanisms, Brazil has become one of the most active and influential participants in the WTO. Despite failure to build consensus on a comprehensive trade deal, the earnest efforts of Brazil's envoy to the WTO, Ambassador Roberto Azevêdo, gained him the credibility and gave him the visibility to be elected Director-General of the WTO for a four-year term in September 2013. This election marked the first time that a national of Brazil became head of any of the global economic-governance institutions. He was only the second of eight prior Directors-General of the GATT/WTO to come from a developing country, which is no mean feat.[17] While resuscitating the moribund Doha Round is likely to be a herculean task, Azevêdo's election is nonetheless a sign of Brazil's ability to build influential coalitions within global economic institutions.

Simultaneously, however, Brazil has committed to regional economic organizations that constrain its ability to participate effectively in global institutions. The reasons for doing so often have more to do with geopolitics than with economic self-interest. Perhaps most emblematically, in the last several decades, Brazil has supplemented its allegiance to multilateralism with a commitment to regional economic projects in South America and in Portuguese-speaking Africa. In the mid-1980s, a relationship blossomed between Brazil and Argentina as both countries celebrated the restoration of democracy and the end of a military-era nuclear development race, and as both found themselves coping with a heavy legacy of government indebtedness, galloping inflation, and lack of access to foreign capital. Presidents José Sarney and Raúl Alfonsín grew close as each experimented with unconventional stabilization plans (the Cruzado Plan and the Austral Plan, respectively) and toyed with the idea of a unified response to foreign bank and official creditors. Adoption of more orthodox domestic economic policies led to coincidental trade-liberalization initiatives in both countries during 1988–91, whereby tariff walls were cut in half. This made it possible for Presidents Fernando Collor and Carlos Menem to enter into an alliance whereby tariff levels would be lowered further only for intra-regional trade (Fishlow, 2011, pp. 141–43). In March 1991, the Treaty of Asunción was signed, incorporating Paraguay and Uruguay into the trading arrangement that became known as Mercosul in Portuguese and as Mercosur in Spanish.

From the outset, Mercosul was as much a regional economic bloc as it was an effort to tame historical tensions with Argentina. Soon after the treaty came into effect, however, Brazilian economic diplomacy began to envision that Mercosul could serve a larger, strategic purpose: Brazil would be able to boost its bargaining power in multilateral trade and other negotiations if it built a block of supporters in South America and beyond, perhaps in Portuguese-speaking Africa (Bernal-Meza, 2002). Mercosul provided the way to reconcile a pivot to regionalism with continued allegiance to multilateralism. "There is no doubt that a continental integration [process] will reinforce considerably our country's potential development and international position" (Nogueira Batista, 2008, p. 237). Besides, multilateralism "does not have the universality [of application] that it had hoped to achieve some day" (Souto Maior, 2004, p. 187).

Moreover, the search for regional prominence "was also an end in itself, which reflected historical beliefs among Brazilian foreign policy elites regarding the distinct destiny of their country. It was in particular a reflection of their awareness that beyond its potential to occupy a central or hegemonic position among its neighbors, Brazil was large enough to play a relevant role in the international order" (Gomez-Mera, 2005, pp. 131–32). Under President Lula da Silva's tenure, Brazil added a complex cooperation structure with other South American countries to its overall foreign policy agenda, and together with Argentina, pushed forcefully to include Venezuela in Mercosul, achieving full-member status in 2012. Simultaneously, it joined the newly founded Union of South American Nations (UNASUR) to pursue regional integration projects (Saraiva, 2010b).

The geostrategic realities of Brazil's expanding role in the Global South, and particularly within Latin America, have placed it in the awkward position of being forced to absorb some important economic losses. Some of these losses have been taken willingly: an expansion of Brazilian exports to and investment in Africa in the past decade has been promoted to a large extent by Brazilian government loans to African importers and borrowers, channeled mainly via an export financing program known as PROEX, Brazil's equivalent of the US Export–Import Bank, and also by BNDES. An unknown proportion of these loans are of dubious quality, and it is estimated that more than $1 billion in loans to African obligors have already had to be written off (Pereira da Costa and da Motta Veiga, 2011; World Bank/IPEA, 2011, p. 99). But Brazil sought influence in Africa and was willing to spend a portion of its national wealth on this geostrategic priority.

Other losses have been less willingly entered into. Over the past two decades, as Brazil has sought the role of regional and Southern leader, it has not infrequently found that its erstwhile partners were not welcoming of its new leadership role (Kahler, 2013, p. 725). The nationalization of Petrobras refineries in Bolivia in 2006 angered the Lula administration, for example, but it decided that in the name of regional comity, and so as to avoid the appearance of being an imperious regional hegemon, this slap would be tolerated.

The most complicated relationships are turning out to be those that Brazil has cultivated with Argentina and Venezuela. During the past decade, both those countries have been run by increasingly authoritarian governments that have mismanaged their economies, discouraging investment and disregarding property and contractual rights through high-profile nationalizations, discriminatory taxes, and suffocating controls on consumer prices, utility rates, foreign trade, and capital movements. In both Buenos Aires and Caracas, governments have undermined fundamental institutions like the judiciary, the press, the central bank, labor unions, business associations, and civil society generally through acts of intimidation and abuse of power.

For reasons that are described in greater detail in previous chapters, Brazilian policymakers have not sought to interfere in the internal workings of these countries, even when failing to do so has had an increasingly deleterious economic impact on Brazil. Beyond the impact of restrictions on imports and controls on access to foreign exchange on bilateral trade and tourism, there has been the damage done to Brazilian investments, as seen in the high-profile cases of Vale, Petrobras, and América Latina Logística (ALL) (*Valor Econômico*, 2013). Brazilian companies with still sizeable trading relationships and investment in Argentina and Venezuela are currently finding it hard to get their bills paid (*Valor Econômico*, 2014).

The relationship with Bolivarian Venezuela has been the most complex of all bilateral relations in the region, leading Brazilian diplomats into a series of potentially expensive regional commitments—such as the creation of the Banco do Sul, an "energy ring" of gas pipelines, and a joint Brazil–Venezuela oil refinery in Pernambuco—which coopted the late Hugo Chávez and reduced his most confrontational postures, but could be gradually whittled away by inaction. As Burges (2013, pp. 588–89) notes, this was a calculated strategy: "Brazil adopted a more co-optive negotiating attitude in order to slowly suffocate unwanted Venezuelan initiatives and proposals. [President] Chávez was left free to talk and dream with little in the way of commentary from Brazil. The Brazilian approach was to let the weight of technical details rein in Chávez and quietly maintain Brazil's pre-eminence." The UNASUR and Community of Latin American and Caribbean States (CELAC) groupings, similarly, were seen as a way of simultaneously removing the United States and Canada from regional discussions, increasing Brazilian influence in the hemisphere, and coopting some of the Bolivarian discourse into a larger regional grouping that ideally would be headed by Brazil.

While these geostrategic objectives may seem worthwhile to Brazilian policymakers, there can be little doubt that they are expensive, particularly in terms of foregone opportunities elsewhere around the world. With the benefit of hindsight, one can certainly question whether the South American and

African countries on which Brazil has hung its hopes have made a tangible contribution to whatever influence Brazil has gained in the world in recent years. For example, while the value of Brazil's exports and imports with its Mercosul partners has tended to increase over time, it has grown far less rapidly than Brazil's trade with the rest of the world (Figure 8.2). Specifically, Brazil's trade with Mercosul increased by $40 billion between 1990 (the year prior to the signing of the Asunción Treaty) and 2013. During that same period, however, Brazil's trade excluding Mercosul increased by a mammoth $390 billion, and thus the share of Brazil's trade with Mercosul in total trade has shrunk to a low of 9 percent in 2013 from a peak of nearly 17 percent in 1988.[18] Therefore, regardless of any efficiency—or inefficiency—effects which the trade alliance may have generated, it can be said that in the past decade Mercosul has been more of a drag, rather than a stimulant, in terms of propelling Brazil forward to a greater role in global trade.[19]

This contrasts sharply with the economic strategies followed by other nations in the hemisphere. The North American Free Trade Area (NAFTA) has been a useful complement to the maintenance of the United States' commanding role in world trade. US trade with Canada and Mexico has increased at a faster pace relative to that of US trade with the rest of the world: specifically, trade with Canada and Mexico has grown four-fold between 1993 (the year prior to NAFTA going into effect) and 2013, whereas US trade with countries other than Canada and Mexico has expanded by about

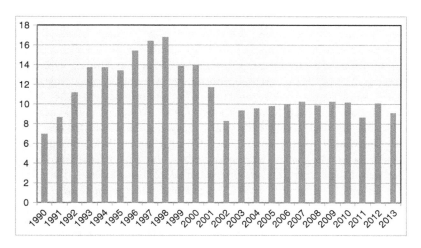

Figure 8.2 Brazil's Merchandise Trade with Mercosul (percent of total trade)
Source: Secretaria de Comércio Exterior (SECEX) Database, July 2014.

three-and-a-half times. NAFTA's share in US trade has thus been maintained at almost 30 percent of total during the decade 2004–13 versus a pre-NAFTA share of 28 percent in 1993.[20] Therefore, beyond the efficiency effects which this trade alliance has generated, it can be said that NAFTA has been useful in terms of helping to maintain US leadership in global trade.

The geostrategic gains from Mercosul—including a claim to hemispheric leadership and the containment of Bolivarian Venezuela—are also offset by the considerable constraints that membership in the imperfect customs union places on Brazil's freedom of action in international trade. Indeed, during the couple of decades that Brazil has chosen to wait for the consolidation of a block of regional supporters in order to sit down and negotiate key trade and other issues with the likes of China, Europe, Japan, and the United States, many other countries have already gone ahead on the basis of their own achievements—without relying on regional alliances—and they have attained impressive economic-statecraft objectives.[21] By way of example, Chile and Colombia have negotiated preferential trade agreements with about 60 countries each, and Mexico and Peru with some 50 countries each.[22] They all have free-trade treaties with the United States, the European Union, and all but Mexico also with the most important countries in Asia. They also have many investment promotion and protection agreements with dozens of partners around the world.

In sharp contrast, Brazil, directly or indirectly through Mercosul, has negotiated and ratified trade agreements only with a handful of other South American countries and with Israel.[23] Brazil has also negotiated few, and has ratified no, bilateral investment treaties of the kind that have become very popular around the globe. Trade negotiations between Mercosul and Europe have been dragging on for 15 years, and despite recent movement on this front, still have little to show. European trade preferences expired at the start of 2014 for all Mercosul countries except Paraguay, since Argentina, Brazil, and Uruguay were deemed to be too well off to deserve them. A deal with Europe has been held back especially by Argentina and Venezuela, which are not ready to make the same concessions that their Mercosul partners are willing to entertain.[24] Since "Brazil can't be [held] hostage [by] Argentina or Venezuela," as retired Ambassador Rubens Barbosa rightly declared in his new role as representative of the powerful São Paulo Federation of Industries (FIESP),[25] the time seems ripe for Brazil to forge ahead on its own, if need be.[26]

Indeed, in Mercosul and more broadly, Brazil seems likely to be forced into a rethinking of the priority it has traditionally ascribed to geopolitics over economic statecraft. Even defenders of the status quo seem to have recognized that the country's economic potential is being hampered by its limited achievements on the international economic stage. The National Industrial Confederation (CNI), whose members have in the past advocated protectionist, inward-looking industrialization policies, has shifted gears in recent years to argue that Mercosul needs to be made more flexible, that other trade negotiations must become a government priority, and that a bilateral agreement with the United States should receive consideration.[27] There seems to be increasing recognition by Brazilian companies that, without further integration into the global economy, they will not generate the kind of high-quality jobs that depend neither on the ups and downs of commodity prices nor on the elimination of distortions and restrictions to trade in agricultural products.

Furthermore, there is a widespread perception among business leaders that Brazil may be left by the roadside in the current rush to form major regional trade blocs around the world. There is a deep irony here, not least because many of these groupings are coming together precisely in order to bypass some of the stickiest roadblocks to the deepening of WTO Doha Round negotiations: just when Brazil has gained a leadership role in the WTO and thus an opportunity to shape these negotiations, the world seems to be walking away from the WTO playground.

In Latin America, the founding of the Pacific Alliance in mid-2012, by Chile, Colombia, Mexico, and Peru, is leading to the rapid elimination of trade barriers among its members and the increasingly free circulation of goods, services, capital, and even people. Costa Rica and Panama are in the process of accession and some 30 other market-friendly economies (from Canada to Uruguay but not Brazil, and others mainly in Asia and Europe) have observer status—and some of the observers are likely to decide in favor of membership.[28]

Similarly, the Trans-Pacific Partnership (TPP) involves the United States plus 11 other countries, including Chile, Peru, and Mexico, and there is a parallel negotiation between the United States and Japan on bilateral market access to the TPP. It looks to be the most important economic initiative to unite the Americas with South-East Asia. The countries in the TPP share a commitment to concluding an ambitious agreement that will address many of the issues that have proven too difficult to resolve during the Doha Round, like rules for free trade in services and technology. As of late 2014, they had gone through about 20 negotiating rounds, making significant progress on an accelerated track toward conclusion of a comprehensive agreement in the months to come.[29] Brazil has so far expressed no interest in joining this bloc, even though the grouping looks on target to become the largest in the world, including countries representing at least 40 percent of global GDP (depending on Japan's incorporation).

Finally, there is the Transatlantic Trade and Investment Partnership (TTIP), in which the United States and the EU have been engaged since mid-2013. TTIP is aiming to be an ambitious, comprehensive, and high-standard trade and investment agreement between parties who already trade a great deal with one another on the basis of very low tariffs, and thus it is focused on costly non-tariff barriers, including on agricultural goods, and on differences in health and environmental regulations and standards that impede the free flow of goods and services across the Atlantic Ocean. As of late 2014, the United States and the EU had completed six negotiating rounds.[30]

At some point, these developments will probably force a change in Brazilian economic strategy, although any such change will be constrained by domestic economic realities, previous foreign policy commitments, and the challenge of negotiating accession into previously formed clubs that may be suspicious of Brazil's latecomer status. Two paths seem most plausible, and both will require Brazil to modify its current economic and geostrategic policy priorities.

The first path involves an acknowledgment that the world is heading toward a global economy made up of several super-blocs: the TTP, the TTIP, the EU, China's own economic bloc with its neighbors, and within Latin America, the Pacific Alliance. There is much to be gained from Brazil's joining a bloc such as the Pacific Alliance, which might open up the country to its western neighbors, and through them, further build bridges to Asia. Doing so, however, would require a serious commitment to phasing out Brazilian protectionist policies, as well as the dilution of its geopolitical ambitions for, and economic commitments to, Mercosul.

If Brazil wishes to stay out of the super-blocs, then the second path involves placing all its bets on a strengthened multilateral approach to global trade governance, in which case Brazil's private sector and political elites will have to double down on their support of Roberto Azevêdo and the WTO's agenda. To be consistent with this wager on multilateralism, however, Brazil would likewise have to tame its "neo-developmentalist" policies and be prepared to make serious liberalizing concessions.[31] In the wake of the last WTO ministerial which took place in Bali in December 2013, a fresh negotiating approach is needed, without which the Doha Round will remain moribund. The recent, limited progress in what is now a modest, WTO trade-facilitation agenda threatens to leave Brazil marginalized in a world that is marching on and does not seem to be constrained by a deadlocked WTO.

Notes

1. Arable land for 2011 as percent of world's total (5.2 percent) from World Bank, *World Development Indicators*, 2014.
2. Calculated from 2013 data in the International Monetary Fund, *International Financial Statistics*, June 2014, available at http://elibrary-data.imf.org
3. Inter-Agency Group of Economic and Financial Statistics, *Principal Global Indicators*, 2014, available at www.principalglobalindicators.org
4. World Bank, *World Development Indicators*, 2014, available at http://databank. worldbank.org/data/views/variableselection/selectvariables.aspx?source=world-development-indicators#
5. OECD, *Interconnected Economies: Benefiting from Global Value Chains* (Paris: OECD, 2013), p. 26. Data cited are for 2009, available at http://dx.doi.org/ 10.1787/888932834397
6. Bank for International Settlements, *Triennial Central Bank Survey: Global Foreign Exchange Market Turnover in 2013*, February 2014, pp. 2–5, available at www.bis. org/publ/rpfxf13fxt.pdf
7. Ibid., pp. 6–9.
8. International Monetary Fund, *International Financial Statistics*, June 2014, available at http://elibrary-data.imf.org
9. Ibid.
10. Ibid.
11. International Monetary Fund, *World Economic Outlook Database*, April 2014.
12. Ibid.
13. Countries currently classified by the IMF as emerging and developing countries plus Hong Kong, Israel, South Korea, and Taiwan, calculated from International Monetary Fund, *World Economic Outlook Database*, April 2014.
14. Estaleiro Atlantico Sul (EAS) has become Brazil's largest manufacturer of large-scale crude carrier and offshore platforms and structures and is currently in the midst of numerous high-profile shipbuilding projects for Petrobras, including tankers and drill ships for oil and gas development. See Camarotto (2013).
15. See www.brasilmaior.mdic.gov.br
16. European Commission, Directorate-General for Trade, *Tenth Report on Potentially Trade-Restrictive Measures Identified in the Context of the Financial and Economic Crisis, 1 May 2012–31 May 2013*, available at http://trade.ec.europa. eu/doclib/docs/2013/september/tradoc_151703.pdf
17. The previous one was Thailand's Supachai Panitchpakdi (2002–05).
18. Calculated from Secretaria de Comércio Exterior (SECEX) data, Ministério do Desenvolvimento, Indústria e Comércio Exterior, 2014, available at www. desenvolvimento.gov.br/sitio/interna/interna.php?area=5&menu=2081. Prior to 1991, Argentina, Paraguay, and Uruguay accounted for 7 percent of Brazil's total foreign trade.

19. An early empirical study found that Mercosul was not internationally competitive in sectors where intra-regional trade grew most rapidly. "Domestic producers reoriented exports to local markets, presumably in order to charge the higher prices associated with the most restrictive trade barriers. This reduced the potential exports of third countries to Mercosur and under many circumstances may have reduced their welfare relative to an equivalent nondiscriminatory trade liberalization" (Yeats, 1998, pp. 25–6).

20. Calculated from Bureau of the Census data, US Department of Commerce, 2014, available at www.census.gov/foreign-trade/balance. In relative terms, US trade with its NAFTA partners peaked in 1999–2001, when trade with Canada and Mexico accounted for almost one-third of total US trade.

21. An important objective is poverty reduction on the basis of employment growth rather than government handouts. Empirical studies simulating the potential effect of liberalized trade in Brazil illustrate that while protectionism favors capital-intensive manufacturing relative to production in agriculture and manufacturing that is intensive in unskilled labor, trade liberalization raises the return to unskilled labor relative to capital and helps the poor disproportionately. "The percentage increase in the incomes of the poorest households is three to four times greater than the average percentage increase in income for the economy as a whole" (Harrison et al., 2004, p. 314).

22. Chile: Dirección General de Relaciones Económicas Internacionales, Ministerio de Relaciones Exteriores, available at www.direcon.gob.cl/acuerdos-comerciales; Colombia: Ministerio de Comercio, Industria y Turismo, available at www.tlc. gov.co/publicaciones.php?id=5398; Mexico: Sistema Integral de Información de Comercio Exterior, Secretaría de Economía, available at www.siicex.gob.mx/ portalSiicex/SICETECA/Tratados/Tratados.htm; Peru: Ministerio de Comercio Exterior y Turismo, available at www.acuerdoscomerciales.gob.pe

23. The country's "South-South [trade] agenda has left Brazil without preferential access to the world's major markets, while failing to sign enough and significant South-South agreements to at least reduce the disadvantages of not making inroads in the North. Even Brazil's most significant achievement in the South, Mercosur, faces significant problems of misguided expectations and dysfunctional incentives, the latter due in great part to Brazil's unfinished job in opening its economy" (Moreira, 2009, p. 155). Data on trade agreements from Ministério do Desenvolvimento, Indústria e Comércio Exterior, www.desenvolvimento.gov. br/sitio/interna/interna.php?area=5&menu=405&refr=405

24. See "Merkel wants hurdles removed to EU-Mercosur free trade pact," *Reuters*, June 15, 2014, available at http://www.reuters.com/article/2014/06/16/us-germany-brazil-mercosur-idUSKBN0ER05D20140616

25. "Brazil can't be Hostage of Argentina or Venezuela in Mercosur/EU trade negotiations," *MercoPress*, January 29, 2014, available at http://en.mercopress. com/2014/01/29/brazil-can-t-be-hostage-of-argentina-or-venezuela-in-mercosur-eu-trade-negotiations

26. An econometric study confirms that Brazil's agricultural sector would be a major beneficiary of an agreement with the EU which would liberalize the entry of foodstuffs into the European market (Vieira et al., 2009). The question is whether the Brazilian industry would accept the government entering into a deal that would open it up to greater competition from European industry.

27. "The proliferation of preferential trade agreements in which Brazil does not participate erodes the access that Brazilian exports have in the markets of countries which are involved in the exchange of trade preferences included in said agreements." Confederação Nacional da Indústria, *Mapa Estratégico da Indústria 2013–2022* (Brasília: CNI, 2013), p. 57, available at www.fieb.org.br/Adm/Conteudo/uploads/Mapa-Estrategico-da-Industria-2013-2022_id_27__x16b1139d6caf4d0ba837f952e449b33e_1162013083441_.pdf

28. See The Pacific Alliance, available at http://alianzapacifico.net/en/observer-states-of-the-alliance-key-companions-in-the-process-of-regional-integration

29. See Office of the United States Trade Representative, available at http://www.ustr.gov/about-us/press-office/fact-sheets/2011/november/outlines-trans-pacific-partnership-agreement

30. See European Commission, available at http://trade.ec.europa.eu/doclib/press/index.cfm?id=1132

31. "Brazil must contribute not only to the maintenance of multilateralism, but also to its renewal and re-launch in a manner that is compatible with the demands of the global agenda" (Castello Branco et al., 2011, p. 48).

CHAPTER 9

Ever Wary of Liberalism: Brazilian Foreign Trade Policy from Bretton Woods to the G-20

André Villela[1]

Over the past two centuries, the world has witnessed two major waves of globalization, defined as involving increased flows of goods, capital, people, and ideas across nations and continents. The first, which spanned the second half of the "long" nineteenth century, was shaken by World War I and collapsed in 1930. The second wave began in the early 1980s and is still with us today. In-between, the world experienced a brutal period of deglobalization.

Brazil's role in each of these three phases varied. During the classic wave of globalization and then the toughest years of the subsequent deglobalization (1930–45), the country was relatively in line with the rest of the world: it was, in theory (if not entirely, in practice), a freetrader in goods, capital, and labor until 1930 and a closed economy thereafter and until the end of the war. It was only post–World War II that Brazil would choose a particular form of engagement with the international liberal trade order then being constituted, one which would often prove to be at odds with the tenets of American-led multilateralism (free trade, non-discrimination, adoption of a competitive exchange rate, etc.).

This chapter seeks to explain the origins of Brazil's reluctance to fully embrace the liberal international order from its inception, after World War II, to the present. It will focus exclusively on one aspect of this order, namely, foreign trade relations. The main argument of the chapter is predicated on one generally accepted fact, explored in the previous chapter—namely, that over the past century Brazil has been a relatively closed economy, a feature that remains to this day[2]—and that this fact has brought more harm than benefit to the country's economic performance in the long run.[3] Following the author's comparative advantage, the approach will be, essentially, historical. For the same reason, the conclusions are admittedly speculative.

Brazilian Foreign Trade Policy—A Historical Overview

Antecedents

Throughout the first great wave of globalization (c. 1870s–1930), Brazil largely behaved like an archetypical peripheral economy, exchanging commodities for manufactured goods from the North. At the same time it was the destination for millions of European immigrants as well as for capital flows from Europe and, to a lesser degree, North America. To this extent, it would be fair to say that the country's engagement with the liberal world order in place at that time was very much in line with the pattern set by the then-prevailing international division of labor.

Nevertheless, this otherwise liberal stance went hand in hand with some of the highest tariff levels in the world (Coatsworth and Williamson, 2004). Implicit tariffs—measured as the ratio between collected duties and the value of imports—ranged from 25 percent to 38 percent in Brazil between 1880 and 1928 (Abreu, 2004a, p. 7). At the product level, measures of the so-called *ad valorem* equivalent tariffs (which take into account the combined effect of specific tariffs, the exchange rate, and the collection of part of import duties in the form of "gold") could reach 400 percent for some classes of cotton textiles imported into the country in the early twentieth century (Villela, 1993).

This last point begs one to question the objectives of Brazilian tariff policy in the closing years of the Empire and during the First Republic (1889–1930). While mostly used to maximize customs revenues, it is also true that tariff policy would increasingly reflect the outcome of political disputes pitting protectionist industrialists against free traders in government.[4] In light of the high tariff levels prevailing on the eve of the Great Depression, it appears that protectionist interests were gaining ground during an era otherwise dominated by liberalism, both in Brazil and abroad.

This, of course, would change dramatically as the Great Depression set in. The process of "deglobalization" that engulfed the world economy in the early 1930s hit Brazil in the shape of a moderate decline in the volume of coffee exports combined with a sharp decrease in their value, as oversupply in Brazil led to the collapse of the price-support schemes that had been in place for over two decades. The Provisional Government that took power in the 1930 Revolution, headed by Getulio Vargas, proceeded to launch a policy of purchase and deliberate destruction of part of the coffee crop, in an attempt to avert a total collapse of Brazil's leading economic sector and foreign exchange earner. In combination with the massive exchange rate devaluation which followed early departure from the gold standard, this countercyclical fiscal policy ensured that the Brazilian economy recovered fairly quickly from the throes of the Depression. In the process, the nature of the Brazilian economic "model" itself was transformed, leaving behind four centuries of outward orientation and ushering in a shift in the "dynamic center" (of the economy).[5] In a nutshell, this shift comprised a reorientation of the Brazilian economy toward the domestic market, which, henceforth, would be increasingly supplied by local industry, instead of imports.

As expected, Brazilian foreign trade policy would have to adapt to this new environment. And such was the case when a new Tariff Law was enacted in 1934. Partly as a result of intense lobbying by industrialists in the Constitutional Assembly convened in that year, modifications were introduced in the government's original bill. The tariff, when finally implemented, included two tariff lines—40 percent and a lower level, covering items imported from countries with which Brazil had trade agreements. Both the government and industrialists deemed the new tariff protectionist (Leopoldi, 2000, p. 124).

A trade agreement signed with the United States in 1935, which included an unconditional "most favored nation" clause, would seem to conflict with the spirit of the 1934 tariff while indicating official adherence to the multilateralism promoted by the US Department of Commerce. On closer inspection, however, this agreement appears to have been more a byproduct of the United States' leverage over Brazil (as the main destination of Brazil's coffee exports), amid a lull in the foreign exchange constraint after years of severe balance of payments adjustments. A concurrent bilateral compensation trade agreement with Nazi Germany, lasting from 1934–38, captured more fully the then-prevalent illiberal atmosphere in Brazil.

In the long term, though, it was *exchange rate* policy, rather than tariff policy, that would help shape the course of the Brazilian economy—and its relationship with the world at large—from the outbreak of the Great Depression to the late 1950s. Indeed, a bevy of import controls and different schemes for allocating scarce exchange "cover" would act as powerful levers in the import-substituting industrialization drive from the 1930s to the 1950s. Implemented initially as an immediate response to balance of payments constraints, exchange rate policy was increasingly perceived—and used—as a forceful instrument for the promotion of selected industrial sectors in Brazil.

Postwar Industrialization and the Liberal World Order

Brazil's involvement in the Allied war effort was both military and economic. On the military side, the country harbored naval and air bases in the northeastern region, and from 1944 sent combat troops to fight alongside the US 5th Army in Italy. The economic "front" was no less important, with Brazil serving as an important supplier of foodstuffs, cotton, textiles, and strategic ores to the Allied war effort. After a very bad start, the Brazilian economy picked up steam and boomed from 1942 to 1945. Throughout the conflict the country managed to post average GDP growth of the order of 3 percent annually, with the manufacturing sector growing at twice this rate.

In many ways, the war served to reinforce the pattern of inward-looking (and technologically backward) industrialization experienced by Brazil in the aftermath of the Great Depression. Moreover, the conflict witnessed a strengthening of the special relationship forged with the United States. This, in turn, meant that in the postwar period the country would not be able to exploit to its benefit political and commercial rivalries between the great powers, as it had done in the 1930s (Bonelli, 1996, p. 95).[6]

One of the side effects of the war on Brazil—in light of the country's ability to increase its manufactured exports amid the disruption brought about by the conflict on industrial countries' foreign trade—was the relieving of the chronic balance of payments constraint that had beset it for more than a decade. Foreign reserves (including monetary gold) reached USD 760 million in 1946, against USD 67 million at the start of the war. However, the bulk of these were made up of strategic gold reserves, complemented by mostly inconvertible or blocked currencies, such as sterling, subject to limits as to their use in peacetime (Bonelli, 1996, p. 99).

Import demand after the war, as one would expect, was considerable. Years of limits on imports for both businesses and the public at large meant that by 1946 there was considerable demand for all sorts of consumer goods, industrial inputs, and machinery. The incoming Dutra administration reacted to this by relaxing import controls. This decision was motivated not only by the desire to meet the existing backlog of imports, but also by other considerations. Internally, Dutra sought to distance himself from deposed president Getulio Vargas, whose previous inward-looking policies had helped alienate part of the urban middle class electorate. A greater level of imports, it was deemed, would also help in fighting inflation—the latter a major rallying cry for the opposition in the closing moments of the Vargas regime.[7]

The decision to pursue a liberal foreign trade and investment policy in the immediate aftermath of the war—and, it must be stressed, a year before General Agreement on Tariffs and Trade (GATT) negotiations would start in Geneva, and amid continuing capital controls in all major economies—was based on strategic considerations as well. The hope was that commercial liberalization would serve to modernize and expand industrial capacity, via increased imports of capital goods. This, in turn, would serve to boost domestic supply, thus helping dampen inflationary pressures, while also fostering industrialization.[8]

As to liberalization of the capital account, the idea was that in the long run, freer entry and exit of foreign capital would, on balance, attract overseas investment into Brazil and therefore help develop its infrastructure and industry. The postwar dollar shortage, of course, put these hopes in due perspective: a massive surge in imports, combined with capital flight, all but exhausted Brazil's convertible foreign exchange reserves. As a result, in 1947 the government was forced to restore import controls, thus reverting to the inward-looking policies that had been in place since the onset of the Great Depression.

The failure of this fleeting experiment with liberalism in the early days of the Dutra administration would help shape the course of Brazilian foreign trade (and investment) policy over the next two decades. Indeed, it could be said that from the mid-1940s to the mid-1960s, Brazilian foreign economic policy was characterized by growing illiberalism, comprising tariff and, especially, exchange rate policies that sought to control the value, and influence the direction, of imports.[9] The reason this course of action was taken is straightforward: for the bulk of the period Brazil was under a binding balance of payments constraint, as it forged ahead with import-substitution industrialization (ISI) amid a limited supply of foreign exchange cover (either as a result of its extreme reliance on the exports of a single commodity—coffee— or due to the limited inflows of foreign capital, especially before the mid-1950s).

ISI in Brazil was pushed ahead with on a scale with few parallels in the world in the twentieth century. At first, the process was essentially market-driven and led by the private sector. In other words, the private sector responded to changes in the rate of exchange by either increasing imports of capital goods (and, hence, investment) or, when the domestic currency lost value, to seek shelter from competing manufacturing imports. This was clearly seen in Brazil during successive waves of import substitution, as in the early 1890s, during World War I, and, yet more forcefully, in the 1930s.

As time went by, however, the State acquired the technical capacity and the will to steer the ISI process. To this end, it resorted to import controls, which became the preferred tool, in lieu of tariff policy, for selecting imports according to their "essentiality."[10] In practice, this meant maintaining an exchange rate that was overvalued in real terms (as this also helped to curb inflationary pressures) while, at the same time, confining imports to capital and intermediate goods which local industry was not yet able to produce. Consumer goods, in this order of things, were considered "superfluous"— again, given the permanent balance of payments constraint which operated between the mid-1940s and mid-1960s, especially in the first half of the period, when somewhat volatile coffee exports comprised the bulk of foreign exchange earnings in Brazil.

The anti-export bias implicit in such an arrangement—which relied, crucially, on keeping an artificially overvalued real exchange rate in place—meant that before the late 1960s Brazil essentially retained the centuries-old status of a commodity exporting economy. To put it differently, in spite of the significant strides it had made at least since the 1930s—in transforming itself from a rural, agrarian society into an increasingly urban and industrial economy—Brazil's engagement with the booming international economy during the so-called Golden Age of the postwar decades was rather timid.[11]

How did this situation come about? In other words, how was it that during the formative decades of the postwar world order Brazil (an original participant, it must be noted, in both the Bretton Woods meetings and the negotiations surrounding the GATT) distanced itself from the tenets of the American-led liberal project, by restricting the free flow of goods from abroad?

While a more comprehensive answer to this question will have to wait until the next section of this chapter, one must bear in mind, from the outset, that at the time Brazil was not alone in pursuing inward-looking trade and industrial policies. Indeed, this policy mix found favor with several countries in both the Third and Second (communist) Worlds after the war. Furthermore, it is also a well-known fact that controls on the current account of the balance of payments were not lifted in the major European economies until the late 1950s, and in 1967 in the case of Japan. In this light, Brazil's insistence on the imposition of import controls at the time does not stand out as some sort of idiosyncrasy.

As regards trade policy in particular, Brazil's (and other developing countries') use of import controls after 1947 was made permissible under international treaty by recurrently invoking Article XVIII:B of the GATT, that allowed the imposition of such controls in cases of balance of payments vulnerability (Abreu, 2004a, pp. 14–15).[12] These import controls, in conjunction with varying arrangements for the allocation of scarce exchange rate cover, were the norm in Brazil from the mid-1940s to the mid-1960s. As such, they acted as powerful instruments for the inducement of import substitution industrialization, by facilitating the importation of much-needed machinery and industrial inputs, while at the same time staving off competition in the domestic light manufactured goods sector.

This combination of quantitative (import) restrictions and selective allocation of exchange rate cover would be complemented, in 1957, by a new, protective, tariff adopted by the Juscelino Kubitschek (1956–61) administration. The main trappings of the autarkic development "model" were thus in place: an overvalued exchange rate, import controls, selective allocation of exchange rate cover, and a high tariff wall. Varying combinations of these instruments—at times complemented by recourse to the Law of Similars (which forbade the importation of manufactured goods that were already being produced locally) or the outright prohibition of imports of over 1,000 articles under the infamous Foreign Trade Department of the Banco do Brasil (CACEX) Annex C—were the mainstay of Brazilian foreign trade and industrial policies well into the 1980s, despite timid attempts at reform during the Castelo Branco government (1964–67).

In fact, the first military government after the 1964 coup, led by General Castelo Branco, was imbued with a reforming zeal that led to a substantial overhaul of the institutional framework and policy guidelines inherited from the Vargas Era. As a result, many areas of public policy were subject to changes broadly consistent with a more market-oriented agenda. In the case of foreign trade, this comprised the adoption of a single, competitive, rate of exchange, complemented by the introduction of a host of incentives geared toward the promotion of non-coffee exports. This policy shift was carried further by the subsequent military governments, allowing for massive growth in the value of Brazilian exports. From the 1970s onward, Brazilian exports would become increasingly dominated by manufactured goods, leaving behind a centuries-old reliance on the export of agricultural commodities alone.

On a broader level, this increase-*cum*-diversification of Brazilian exports from the late 1960s onward served to mitigate the anti-export bias that had been introduced in the 1930s and reinforced thereafter. At the same time, however, it saddled the economy with a double distortion in the foreign trade realm, as a still artificially overvalued currency (a result, mostly, of anti-inflationary considerations) helped divert resources from the export sector, prompting the government to attempt to compensate by granting generous subsidies to exporters of manufactured goods. In the end, policies such as these cost up to 5 percent of GDP and could only be maintained as long as the government remained solvent. This big "if" would begin to change in the early 1980s, as the Mexican debt default laid bare the fragile state of Brazilian public finances. The party was over, although it would take almost 15 years for the mess to be cleaned up in full.

The Crises of the 1980s and the (Partial) Change of Course

Brazil's postwar, inward-looking growth model began to collapse under the weight of the debt crisis of the early 1980s. Deep recession and budget cuts combined to sap a system that since the 1960s had become increasingly dependent on an array of tax breaks and subsidies provided by the central government in order to promote industrial exports. Furthermore, the scope for further advancement of ISI itself had all but been exhausted, as the country had become virtually self-sufficient in the production of most manufactured goods.

The international context conspired to undermine even further Brazil's autarkic development strategy. Changes in US trade policy toward advanced developing countries (where it sought to limit free riding by demanding, in return, reciprocity from its partners), in conjunction with difficulties experienced by developing countries in the run-up to the Uruguay Round of trade negotiations (as developed countries forced the so-called new themes—services, intellectual property rights, high technology products, etc.—onto the agenda) caught Brazil in a particularly fragile position.

Indeed, in the early 1980s, Brazil still retained its defensive approach to multilateral trade negotiations and, as such, maintained a policy of obstruction toward the GATT. However, at a time when macroeconomic deterioration and the first signs of exhaustion of the ISI model set in, foot-dragging on the "new themes" became increasingly incompatible with Brazil's interests as a *demandeur* in agriculture, an area where the country had been gaining comparative advantages (Abreu, 2004b, p. 3). In the end, though, it was macroeconomic meltdown—which took the form, *inter alia*, of rampant inflation, recession, and the debt crisis—that dealt the final blow to the decades-old import-substitution strategy and forced Brazilian officials to consider following liberalization moves already under way in, among others, Argentina and Mexico (Abreu, 2004b, p. 25).

Starting in the late 1980s, trade liberalization in Brazil progressed, roughly, in three consecutive waves. First, tariff redundancies were removed in 1988–89, resulting in a reduction in the average (unweighted) nominal tariff from 57.5 percent to 32.1 percent. The second—and most important—wave (1991–93) brought the average tariff level down to 13.5 percent and, crucially, removed a substantial portion of the non-tariff barriers that had hampered imports into Brazil. Finally, further reduction in the tariff level was introduced in 1994, as part of the Real (stabilization) Plan and amid implementation of the Mercosur Common External Tariff (Abreu, 2004b, pp. 7–8).[13] In practice, the latter established a timetable for bringing down the high tariff levels on capital and informatics/telecom goods imported into Brazil, leading to a convergence with the lower levels then prevalent in partner countries (Abreu, 2004b, p. 8).

In late 1994 a sharp deterioration in the balance of payments following currency appreciation and the onset of the Tequila Crisis led to a reversal of this policy, with average tariff levels increasing moderately for the rest of the decade. A change of government in 2001—with the Workers' Party (PT) replacing the Social Democratic Party (PSDB) in the presidency—brought fears that further tariff increases might follow, but this was not to be. However, the incoming administration indicated clearly that any additional liberalization or rationalization of Brazil's tariff structure would have to be negotiated multilaterally within the Doha Round, which, for practical purposes, was making little progress by then. The bilateral avenue to liberalization, involving regional trade agreements such as the Free Trade Area of the Americas or the European Union–Mercosur agreement, proved equally elusive as negotiations were virtually stalled (Moreira, 2009, p. 3).

By the early twenty-first century Brazil's tariff levels were much lower than they had been for most of the postwar period (or since the early twentieth century for that matter). Yet, comparatively speaking, Brazil still ranked among some of the countries with the highest median nominal tariffs in the world (Moreira, 2009, p. 4). This (relative) protectionist stance is further evidenced by high tariff rates charged on imports of capital goods and automobiles, for example.

To sum up, the country has come a long way since the heyday of ISI, when it pursued an overtly illiberal foreign trade policy. Still, high nominal and effective import tariffs, combined with a great variance in tariff levels between different industrial sectors (indicating the power of sector-specific interest groups) and the parlous state of the Mercosur seem to suggest that now at the dawn of the twenty-first century the country still appears as a wary participant in the world trading system. The next section of the chapter seeks to explain the history (past and present) of the country's mostly anti-liberal trade bias.

Interpreting Brazil's Anti-Liberal Bias

Brazil's cautious approach to the postwar liberal trade regime found exception on very few occasions, namely, in 1946–47, 1964–67, and from the late 1980s to the mid-1990s. Excepting these interludes, Brazilian foreign trade policy may be fairly characterized as illiberal. What accounts for this wariness on the part of Brazilian officials (and, as argued below, Brazilian society in general) toward fuller engagement in expanding trade and investment flows, which would bring benefits to a developing economy? Three interrelated forces help explain the cautious stance displayed by Brazil in its foreign economic relations for most of the postwar period.

First, the very inward-looking development "model" followed by Brazil after 1930 precluded, almost by definition, the adoption of a more liberal attitude toward international trade and financial flows. A second, political-economic, explanation for Brazil's defensive position amid increasing liberalization on the world stage involves recognizing the clout of protectionist lobbies. In practice, this meant that the interest groups who fought most vigorously for the implementation of an ISI strategy were, of course, those most likely to benefit from protection and, therefore, oppose freer trade. Finally, the third force that must be included in any explanation of Brazil's mostly illiberal trade policies relates to the other two and has to do with the role of ideas, namely the scant political support for liberalism that exists in Brazilian society to this day.

Starting with the point about the inevitable relationship between policy and the domestic and international environment in which it is implemented, it is clear that Brazil's foreign trade policy must be seen in the context of the development model that started to evolve post-1930. In this light, one cannot but agree with the claim that any interpretation of the *rationale* behind the actual shape taken by Brazil's foreign economic relations must derive from an understanding of the "social and political bases that supported the Brazilian state and of the social relations of production at the time" (Malan, 1986, p. 105). This is simply the fairly obvious claim that the postwar context—both domestic and international—must be considered when trying to make sense of the policy decisions eventually taken in the realm of foreign trade.

The international context, of course, was one characterized by "embedded liberalism" or, in John Ikenberry's terms, Liberal Internationalism v. 2.0 (Ruggie, 1982; Ikenberry, 2009). In practice, such an arrangement differed considerably from the *laissez-faire* liberalism of the "long" nineteenth century, by offering substantial leeway for national governments to adopt more or less *dirigiste* ("Keynesian") policies. Brazil, of course, took advantage of this and followed this course of action. Brazil was, arguably, an extreme case of state-led, inward-looking industrialization in the postwar decades. And its illiberal foreign trade (and industrial) policies were vigorously pursued into the late 1980s, well past their shelf life. Yet in no way should the country's policies be seen as an aberration in the international context. Brazil was an outlier, perhaps, but not a country following policies that departed radically from those deemed acceptable (especially for the then so-called Third World economies) at the time.

As state-led ISI progressed in Brazil; in the 1950s to 1960s, it became increasingly apparent that the selective use of instruments that combined the granting of access to "essential" imports, while limiting those deemed "superfluous" (i.e., which competed with domestically produced goods), was part of a broader strategy which sought to fully industrialize a once backward, rural economy. The anti-export bias that an artificially overvalued currency entailed would start to be counterbalanced, from the mid-1960s onward, with generous fiscal stimuli directed at exporters of manufactured goods. This double distortion—and the anti-liberal bias which it imparted upon foreign economic policy in Brazil until the late 1980s—only makes sense in view of the broader inward-looking, autarkic, industrialization model adopted during most of the second half of the twentieth century.

As for the second force, the political economic logic behind Brazil's defensive engagement with the international trade order, one needs only to take a step back in history to understand the virtual absence of political support for a more liberal trade regime. As noted in the literature, organized defense of protectionism has historical roots in Brazil (Abreu, 2007). Part of the reason for this stems from the fact that, unlike their counterparts in, say, Argentina or the United States South, Brazilian export farmers never served as a meaningful force opposed to industrial protectionism. This was particularly the case of the all-powerful coffee *fazendeiros* who, as price makers in the international market, could pass on to foreign consumers price (cost) increases derived from high import tariffs at home (Abreu, 2007). Indeed, it should not come as a surprise that protectionist interests have been so entrenched in Brazilian trade policy from early on, given the fact that *fazendeiros* and industrialists were often one and the same group, in light of the diversification of coffee profits undertaken by planters in the starting decades of the twentieth century.

As the shift in the "dynamic center" of the Brazilian economy in the 1930s brought manufacturing industry unequivocally to the fore, representatives of this sector became increasingly involved in shaping tariff and, more broadly, foreign trade policy (Diniz, 1978; Leopoldi, 2000). Needless to say, this allowed interest groups to "capture" official policy and use it in their favor, in order to ensure—and, ideally, increase—private gains associated with rent-seeking behavior.

Rent-seeking accounts for notable anomalies in Brazilian trade policy to this day, such as the so-called Automotive Regime, "peaks" in Brazil's tariff schedule, and the existence of sundry special import regimes. The automotive sector, for instance, is the beneficiary of the highest nominal tariffs charged on imports into Brazil (which are complemented by additional levies that confer further protection from foreign competition). It must be noted that both the business and the all-powerful metalworkers' unions benefit from such an arrangement, which, of course, burdens consumers with the bulk of welfare losses. As for the various "peaks" in Brazil's current tariff schedule, they appear to faithfully represent industrial sectors with superior lobbying skills. These sectors also tend to benefit from special import regimes, thereby paying lower import duties on inputs and capital goods.[14]

Political (even more than political economic) logic appears to have underscored those brief periods after 1945 in which liberal trade policies were pursued in Brazil. For instance, the liberalization of both the current and capital accounts of the balance of payments in the early days of the Dutra administration can only be understood in light of liberal opposition—in both the political and economic spheres—against the Vargas dictatorship that was toppled in 1945.

In the case of the modest liberalization undertaken in the early months of the Castelo Branco government in the mid-1960s, credit must be given to liberal-minded technocrats at the helm of the economic policymaking establishment. The decision to press forward with a liberalizing economic agenda must also be seen as a reaction to what was perceived by the incoming government as excessively interventionist and anti-liberal policies inherited from previous administrations. Collor's (1990–92) bold tariff reduction and privatization policies, on the other hand, appear to reflect the "outsider" nature of the new president, who came from a backward state and lacked political support from the established parties.

Finally, further trade liberalization under President Cardoso, with hindsight, appears more like a case of expediency, in the sense that opening up the economy to imports was perceived as instrumental in supporting price stabilization. Further evidence of the, relatively, secondary role played by trade liberalization during the Cardoso government was that once the Real Plan was put at risk by a succession of international crises, pro-liberalization technocrats in the Ministry of Finance and the Central Bank prioritized stabilization, leaving industrial and commercial policy to protectionist elements in the administration. To a great extent, this helps explain the about-face in the so-called Automotive Regime, or a more distant approach toward initiatives such as the Free Trade Area of the Americas. In both cases a more defensive stance in trade matters—or, as was the case regarding the Automotive Regime, outright reversal to protectionism—serves as a reminder of the cross-party influence of the *Paulista* industrial lobby. Not only that, it illustrates the atavistic nature of protectionist—or, more broadly, anti-liberal—*ideology* in Brazil. This is, I believe, the final element explaining the country's wary approach toward liberal internationalism in the foreign trade arena.

The failure by liberal ideology to take hold in Brazil has received the attention of Brazilian scholars of varying persuasions. Among others, it was diagnosed by Oliveira Vianna as stemming from the fact that the country built a society which was, essentially, non-liberal (Vianna, 1954).[15] Raymundo Faoro, from a Weberian perspective, argued that the patrimonialism that characterized the formation of Brazilian society meant that over the centuries "politically-oriented" capitalism (or pre-capitalism) ended up incorporating "modern capitalism," which is grounded in individual liberty (Faoro, 2000, p. 263). Marxist literary critic Roberto Schwarz, in turn, famously claimed that liberalism was an ideology that was "out of place" in a slave-based nineteenth-century Brazil (Schwarz, 1992a).

Regardless of the ultimate reason(s) for the failure of liberal ideology to take root in Brazil, a cursory look at Brazilian history reveals the ambiguous nature of liberal *practice*—a feature that probably militated against the acceptance of this ideology by a greater proportion of society. Indeed, defense of private property rights in nineteenth-century Brazil was meant to include slave property as well, thus exposing the frailty of liberal arguments in this crucial matter. Likewise, price-support schemes for the coffee sector during the First Republic were blatantly inconsistent with the free trade doctrine apparently espoused by contemporary liberal elites.

When, finally, the Great Depression set in—and, at its heels, the shift in Brazil's "dynamic center" from agriculture to manufacturing industry—it might be said that at last a proper bourgeoisie was beginning to take shape. This was a class, according to Wanderley Guilherme dos Santos, that could be potentially organized with a view "to shaping the State apparatus and structuring society according to the logic of the market" (1998, p. 52).

The problem is that this potential "vanguard of liberalism" was, actually, part and parcel of the illiberal post-1930 tide which, barring short spells in 1946–47, 1953–54, and 1964–67, would extend well into the late 1980s. Rather than liberalism, the overarching ideology that bound this bourgeoisie and the Brazilian state together was in fact *developmentalism*.

In the best study done on this topic, Ricardo Bielschowsky defined developmentalism as "the ideology geared towards overcoming underdevelopment by means of capitalist industrialization, planned and supported by the State" (1988, p. 503). It was, therefore, a very practical type of ideology, increasingly espoused by industrialists, academics, and bureaucrats, who were ultimately responsible for implementing an agenda that shunned liberalism and its defense, *inter alia*, of free trade and the gains from specialization. Beginning in the 1930s, amid a vigorous industrial spurt and the political centralization of the Vargas Era, this ideology would turn into the dominant intellectual underpinning for the autarkic model that would characterize Brazilian economic history for the next half a century.[16]

From then on, liberal thought would be relegated to the sidelines, only occasionally entering public debate through the lonely voice of Eugenio Gudin and a few of his followers.[17] Indeed, from the 1930s to the 1980s mainstream thought in relevant policy circles in Brazil would be dominated by the developmentalist credo and its wariness of the outside world.[18] It would take the "lost decade" of the 1980s—with its combination of runaway inflation, fiscal disarray, and exhaustion of the ISI model—and the election to the presidency of a mercurial political outsider (Collor de Mello) for this ideological edifice to suffer its first major fissures.

Still, two decades on—and despite further liberalization promoted by Cardoso—developmentalist ideology still trumps liberalism by a long shot in the minds of government officials, politicians, and academics in Brazil. Not only that, the mercantilism that undergirds this ideology permeates the perception of the average citizen as to the pros and cons of a more liberal engagement by the country in the international economy. In short, it would be fair to say that, overall, Brazilians tend to perceive more threats than opportunities stemming from economic liberalism, and this translates into a defensive stance toward a further opening of the economy to the outside world.

Looking Ahead

Standing here in 2013 and looking at the same forces that, it has been argued, help explain Brazil's cautious/wary approach to liberal internationalism in the sphere of trade policy, one is inclined to conclude that this state of affairs is likely to remain in place for the near future, at least. Indeed, although ISI as a development strategy was virtually buried in the 1990s, recent moves by the Lula and, especially, Rousseff administrations remind us that old habits die hard. Official backing of "national champions," subsidized public credit channeled to "strategic sectors," minimum local content rules in procurement policies, to name but a few, serve to show that protectionist feelings still run high in Brasília.

The world, of course, has changed since the bad old days of the 1970s and 1980s,[19] so that room for illiberal policies in the foreign trade/industrial policy realms has been curtailed either by Brazil's commitments to World Trade Organization (WTO)-agreed rules or, more generally, by globalization and the emergence of China as a formidable competitor on the world stage. Furthermore, recent deindustrialization[20] in Brazil has served to dampen the voice of industrial lobbies in public debate as compared, for instance, to their high profile during the heyday of the autarkic model. To this one could add two recent developments that might serve to check the ease with which industrial interests influence Brazilian foreign trade policy. The first one is not so new and has to do with the emergence of Brazil as a global superpower in the agribusiness sector. This fact alone places Brazil in a new role as a *demandeur* in international trade negotiations and, as such, it has exerted increasing influence over official strategy in trade negotiations. If it is to achieve its pretensions for agriculture, Brazil may be pushed to shift its policy stance in a more liberal direction through concessions that might have to be made in the way of market access for manufacturing imports or in the area of services.

The second novelty involves the rise of the so-called new middle class in Brazil, comprising millions of formerly poor families who over the past 10–15 years have joined the consumer market, on the back of substantial real income growth among the lower rungs of the income distribution ladder. The very definition of this class mostly (if not exclusively) in terms of its access to durable consumer goods suggests that a relapse into more protectionist and illiberal trade policies—and the higher domestic prices that this would entail—might face greater political opposition than any government might wish for.

This final point, however, hinges crucially on the extent to which a liberal *ideology* is successfully incorporated into political discourse in Brazil. In fact, a clear lack of political backing for a further opening of the economy suggests there is little sign that the current political establishment in Brazil will embrace a foreign economic policy which departs substantially from the one currently in place. If this is, indeed, the case, then liberals in Brazil have an uphill struggle if they wish to see further tariff reduction, elimination of special import regimes, or more official restraint in granting subsidized credit to "national champions." And to some extent this has to do with the absence of significant support for a freer market among any of the major political parties in Brazil. Indeed, both the PSDB and the PT, which have dominated Brazilian politics for the past two decades are, essentially, of the Center-Left and, as such, have historically championed protectionist policies.[21] The absence of a competitive conservative party—which in democratic regimes tends to advocate pro-market policies, including freer trade—acts to stifle informed debate on the benefits of different policy choices in the sphere of foreign trade.

The role of the dominant anti-liberal, or anti-market, ideology in preserving the status quo cannot be overestimated. Indeed, the notion that imports are, intrinsically, "evil" and, therefore, something to be avoided (if possible) is very much ingrained in the minds of average Brazilians. If one were to ask a layperson—or, worse, a government official or most economists—in Brazil to choose between exports or imports (or between a trade surplus and a deficit) the answer would most likely be "exports" (or a trade surplus). This is despite the fact that there is nothing in economic theory which indicates that, all other things being equal, either one is preferable to the other. Exports are, quite simply, one way of importing and, therefore, consuming goods or services that are not produced locally—or, at least, not in sufficient amounts to satisfy domestic consumption. At the end of the day, it is the amount of the latter—*consumption* (either immediate, or deferred, through investment)—which helps to indicate whether a given country is more or less prosperous, and not the value of its exports or its trade surplus.

The deep-rooted mercantilism that underpins most Brazilians' opinion on matters of foreign trade shows little sign of losing its allure among policymakers or the average man/woman in the street.[22] This fact does not bode well for those who expect significant domestic support for a liberal engagement by Brazil in the international trade order anytime soon.

Notes

1. I wish to thank Andrew Balanda and Marcelo de Paiva Abreu for their comments on an earlier version of this chapter. Workshop participants provided additional criticism and suggestions, for which I am very grateful.
2. As of 2012, Brazil ranked twenty-fifth in the world in terms of the value of its exports, despite being the world's seventh largest economy. As for the share of imports in GDP, it figured in a staggering final position among 176 countries. See Bacha and de Bolle (2013, pp. 3–4).
3. For a recent (re)statement of the trade liberalization–growth nexus which is explicitly assumed in the present chapter, see Estevadeordal and Taylor (2008).
4. I will return to the political economy of foreign trade policy in Brazil later in the chapter.
5. The classic account of the onset of this shift is Furtado (1970), chapter 32.
6. Abreu (1999) is the best analysis of Brazilian foreign economic relations during the Vargas Era (1930–45).
7. For the political motivations behind Dutra's foreign economic policy, see Bastos (2004).
8. Maintenance of a fixed exchange rate amid a marked difference between rates of inflation in Brazil and the United States further facilitated imports, which, of course, benefited from an increasingly overvalued currency.
9. A major exception to this general trend was the passing of Superintendency of Money and Credit (SUMOC) Instruction no. 113, in January 1955, which facilitated the internalization of foreign capital goods into Brazil and would play a pivotal role in the industrialization drive undertaken by President Juscelino Kubitschek (1956–61).
10. It is worth noting that Brazil kept in place a system of *specific* tariffs up until 1957, thus removing much of the protectionist force of this instrument of commercial policy.
11. Indeed, not only did the composition of its exports appear out of touch with the more sophisticated productive structure achieved by the country but its total value fell short of Brazil's weighting within world GDP: 0.6 percent versus 2.5 percent, respectively, as of 1973. Calculated from data in Maddison (2006), vol. 2, Appendix.

12. In practice, therefore—and from the standpoint of the international trading system— developing countries such as Brazil were "free riders" during most of the 1950s and 1960s, in the sense that they benefited from continuing tariff reductions agreed among industrialized economies and which were subsequently extended to poorer countries via the most favored nation (MFN) clause. Maddison (2006), vol. 2, p. 25.

13. For a more detailed account of trade liberalization and the relevant macroeconomic background in Brazil in the early 1990s, see Fritsch and Franco (1993).

14. Empirical evidence is provided by Ricardo Markwald, "The Political Economy of Foreign Trade Policy: the Brazilian case." In R. Bouzas, ed., *Domestic Determinants of National Trade Strategies: A Comparative Analysis of Mercosur Countries, Mexico and Chile.* Working Group on EU-Mercosur Negotiations, Chaire Mercosur de Sciences-Po/OBREAL. *Apud* Motta Veiga (2009).

15. In his view, it was, rather "parental, clan-based, and authoritarian." For a discussion of Vianna's ideas and his defense of "instrumental authoritarianism" as a means for the State to impose a liberal agenda on society, see Santos (1998).

16. For Sikkink (1991, pp. 51–52), developmentalism is best understood as a "compromise between the domestic demands for industrialization and state intervention on the one hand, and international demands for openness on the other." This might be true for the high tide of that ideology during the Kubitschek administration in the late 1950s (and which is the subject of Sikkink's book), but does not account for its emergence in the 1930s, when international demands for openness, except for a trade agreement signed with the United States in 1934, were non-existent.

17. In this regard, the famous "planning controversy," which opposed Eugenio Gudin and archprotectionist Roberto C. Simonsen in the closing days of the Vargas Era, is a potent reminder of how the overwhelming superiority of Gudin's liberal arguments ended up constituting, in practice, a pyrrhic victory for his cause, as the illiberal, anti-market, views of Simonsen would frame Brazilian trade and industrial policies for the next half century. For the controversy, see Simonsen (1977).

18. As noted by Pedro Motta Veiga, in Brazil's history, "the definition of foreign threats and the perception of external risks by the elites relates essentially to economic vulnerabilities rather than to security concerns" (Motta Veiga, 2009).

19. This is not meant to sound like a wholesale indictment of *dirigiste* policies pursued by the Brazilian government, to varying degrees, from the 1930s to the early 1990s. The intention, rather, is to point out that if these policies indeed helped transform a hitherto underdeveloped, agrarian country into the industrialized, middle-income economy it is today it did so at great cost in terms of efficiency, income distribution, and future growth potential (not to mention macroeconomic disarray from the early 1960s to the mid-1990s). For a more sanguine view of state-led development strategies, see Wade (1990) and Amsden (2001).

20. For a recent discussion, see Bacha and de Bolle (2013).

21. The predominance of *Paulista* interests in both parties is a further element accounting for the strength of protectionist sentiment and policies in Brazil no matter which party might eventually be in office.

22. This fact is vividly revealed, for instance, on rather prosaic occasions such as on the evening news on TV where the broadcaster will use the same (somber) demeanor and tone of voice to refer to a trade deficit—no matter its size—as he/she would reserve for the announcement, say, of the victim toll of an earthquake in China.

Afterword: Emerging Powers and the Future of the American-Led Liberal International Order

James Goldgeier

This outstanding volume highlights major dilemmas facing US foreign policy, as officials in Washington assess the rise of emerging powers such as Brazil and the challenge they pose to the US-led liberal international order that emerged after World War II and became the dominant organizing principle for global affairs after the collapse of the Soviet Union. As perceptions of US dominance change, Brazil's support for the rule of law, human rights, and the Global South coupled with its opposition to American hegemony provides the nation with opportunities to wield significant influence in the decades ahead.

A Changing World

Were we to take a snapshot of the world today, we would be very impressed with the US power to shape international outcomes. The United States is the only nation with global military reach and with command of the global commons. It remains the world's richest nation and is a source of tremendous innovation. The US dollar serves as the world's reserve currency. Youngsters around the world wish to learn English, and elites hope to send their children to universities in the United States. Its network of alliances is enviable, and its ability to monitor the activities of states and groups throughout the world is unparalleled.

While the United States faces demographic challenges, these pale in comparison to those of Europe, Japan, China, and India. After decades of handwringing about dependence on oil from the Middle East, the United States now speaks confidently about energy independence and is on track to become the world's largest energy exporter. A major asset remains its geographic distance from other major power centers: smaller nations in Asia and Europe continue to look to the United States to ensure regional stability against potential hegemons, fearing domination by those powers more than they fear the United States.

But we are not simply taking a snapshot. After the military debacle in Iraq, and inflicting further damage to its reputation by producing the debilitating global financial crisis and exhibiting deep domestic political gridlock, the United States has fostered the perception that it is a country in decline and that the rise of the rest is assured. No longer do we speak of the "end of history" (Fukuyama 1989) or the "unipolar moment" (Krauthammer 1990).

So which is it? A United States that remains the world's only true superpower or a United States that can no longer dominate emerging powers as it did in the 1990s? In fact, both are true. But it is the latter that has fundamentally changed the way people think about world politics.

One way to understand what has changed is to compare American actions in the 1990s with American actions today. Twenty years ago, Russian president Boris Yeltsin eagerly welcomed American and international officials proffering advice on how to develop a democratic market-oriented country that could join the West. Today, Russian president Vladimir Putin has gone beyond ignoring American calls to return Edward Snowden—annexing Crimea and assisting pro-Russian separatists in Ukraine, cracking down on civil society at home, and supporting the brutal regime of Bashar al-Assad in Syria. In 1999, *Time* magazine unabashedly featured Treasury officials Robert Rubin and Lawrence Summers alongside Federal Reserve Chairman Alan Greenspan on its cover, dubbing them "The Committee to Save the World" for their roles in combating a global financial crisis (Ramo 1999); the trio looked much less omnipotent (and omniscient) by 2008 when the US housing and banking policies they promoted and executed fueled a vicious worldwide financial meltdown. The United States fostered German unification in 1990, created the North American Free Trade Agreement (NAFTA) in 1993, and bailed out Mexico in 1995. Today, the United States seems powerless to stop crises and conflicts that have escalated across Africa and the Middle East, and has made little progress in securing major trade deals in Europe and Asia.

At the beginning of the 1990s, the United States forged a massive international coalition under United Nations (UN) auspices to easily reverse Saddam Hussein's invasion of Kuwait and, in the process, declared a New World Order;[1] at the end of the decade, the United States led North Atlantic Treaty Organization (NATO) on a bombing campaign of Serbia to protect civilians in Kosovo, ignoring Serb claims of national sovereignty and bypassing the UN, given the certainty of a Chinese and Russian veto. In 2003, the United States was so confident of its ability to dominate world affairs that President George W. Bush was unconcerned about convincing American allies of the need to invade Iraq. By 2011, however, the United States was "leading from behind" in the UN-authorized effort to protect the citizens of Benghazi, and subsequently played a clearly supporting role as the French intervened in Mali. Despite initial signs in late August 2013 that he planned a military strike on Syria in response to the Assad government's use of chemical weapons, President Barack Obama publicly indicated his hesitation and at the last minute gambled that a Russian proposal to remove those weapons through diplomacy would enable him to avoid punishing the Assad government for crossing an American "red line." Even as the United States escalated the use of force against the Islamic State of Iraq and Syria (ISIS) in 2014, the US president has sought to avoid anything approaching a major military commitment.

We know that perceptions of power are central to international politics. While the war in Iraq and the 2008 financial crisis have proven extremely costly in terms of lives and money lost, they have also proven costly to American legitimacy and therefore to the willingness of other countries like Brazil to accept American rule-making. When the United States advocated a Washington consensus on market economics in the early 1990s, countries seeking international financial assistance had no choice but to go along with US-imposed rules. No one today would regard officials in Washington as having a monopoly on an understanding of capitalism, and China has provided significant aid to countries in Africa and elsewhere that are not interested in the constraints imposed by the United States and its Western allies. Partisan political gridlock is not helping to foster the sense that democracy is the most effective form of government. What has changed the most since the 1990s is the ability of the United States to convince (or force) emerging powers to go along with its version of world politics, its understanding of international norms, and its definition of universal values. America's power to persuade has declined, and this means that global governance will be much harder to achieve today than when the United States could simply set the rules of the game and expect others to follow.

Different Ways of Thinking about American Power

As we consider the constraints and opportunities within which countries like Brazil operate in international affairs, we should examine first the relative capabilities of the United States to dominate the global order as it has in the past. In this regard, much depends on how the United States defines the requirements for its national security. Two very different views have existed since the Soviet Union's collapse: the first argues that the US national security establishment should focus primarily on preventing the rise of other major powers that challenge American military hegemony (relatively easy to address); the second argues that officials should try to manage the challenges produced by failed states, civil wars, and non-state actors (much harder to address). Following from this is the broader question of the type of international order that will exist in the future. The United States created and has dominated the liberal world order that came into existence after World War II.

What will the rise of other major power centers like Brazil mean for the continuation of that order? Over the past two decades, a seismic shift has occurred in the major fault lines of world affairs. Throughout the Cold War, the central conflict remained the global clash between the democratic West and the communist East, with the United States assuming its role as "leader of the Free World"; a smaller though related conflict was the effort of the Global South to seek resource reallocations from the wealthy nations of the North in order to address previous injustices.

Today, the central conflicts have emerged from within the Muslim world, with numerous governments and groups with competing ideologies attempting to wrest control of regions and states across the Middle East and North and Sub-Saharan Africa, and with the potential to expand into Central and South Asia. These conflicts vary widely, from the major cleavages between Sunni and Shia and tribal groups and more modern and at times secular groups, to the divergent interpretations of Islam resulting in large part from the varying state–religious leadership dynamics in different Muslim states. These phenomena have relegated the United States to a more peripheral role in a key region of the world, with less ability to shape events, as became clear in 2014 during the emergence of ISIS, which caused Washington to scramble in response to horrific violence and the unexpected capacity for regional expansion, fundraising, and militant recruitment by a group previously labeled by President Obama as a "junior varsity" squad.

Meanwhile, growth in countries such as India, Brazil, and South Africa has diminished the notion of a North–South economic divide.

America's Role in World Affairs and the Pursuit of National Security

At the end of the George H. W. Bush administration more than 20 years ago, two starkly different visions of America's role in the world emerged from the Pentagon and the State Department.[2] In early 1992, officials in the Office of the Secretary of Defense began work on the Defense Planning Guidance, the first since the collapse of the Soviet Union. Initial drafts caused a huge political firestorm, as they appeared to indicate an effort to ensure continued US dominance over potential foes and long-standing allies alike. "Our first objective," an early draft read, "is to prevent the re-emergence of a new rival, either on the territory of the former Soviet Union or elsewhere, that poses a threat on the order of that posed formerly by the Soviet Union." This objective was contentious for those who believed no such threat existed and saw little need to devote significant resources to combat it. A major controversy erupted around the draft document's concerns about allies such as Germany and Japan, which many touted as the real victors of the Cold War: "We must account sufficiently for the interests of the advanced industrial nations to discourage them from challenging our leadership or seeking to overturn the established political and economic order." The key goal for the United States, as the Pentagon saw it, was the preservation of American military hegemony globally and over every region of the world as the vehicle to ensure continued American dominance. In this view, a key benefit of its alliances in Europe and Asia was to ensure American oversight of security arrangements across the Atlantic and Pacific oceans.

Not surprisingly, officials at the State Department created an alternative vision, conveyed in a 22-page secret memo from Acting Secretary Lawrence Eagleburger to incoming Secretary Warren Christopher in January 1993. This document focused largely on the maintenance of American leadership through softer means. The United States should serve as "a provider of reassurance and architect of new security arrangements; an aggressive proponent of economic openness; an exemplar and advocate of democratic values; [and] a builder and leader of coalitions to deal with problems in the chaotic post-Cold War world." State Department officials feared that the US economic position was eroding in the face of competition from Germany and Japan, and that this would diminish American global leadership. In the State Department's view, the answer to this challenge was to rebuild the American economic infrastructure. The greatest fear centered not on a new potential rival, but rather on the chaos stemming from the disintegration of states, and the memo stated: "This is going to confront us with the dilemma of whether to take part in limited military interventions in situations which do not directly threaten our interests." Hence, a key goal for the United States, as the State Department saw it, was to forge multilateral coalitions under strengthened American leadership to respond to vexing political, military, and economic challenges and to maintain the liberal world order.

At times this debate has been cast in terms of "American exceptionalism," the notion that the United States has a special role to play in the world to promote democracy, market economies, human rights, and the rule of law.

But if we cast the challenge in terms of the Pentagon's ability to prevent a Soviet-type challenge or the State Department's efforts to forge coalitions to manage global problems, it is clear that the latter is what has been made most difficult with the rise of powers such as China, India, Brazil, and Turkey.

Two decades after the 1992 Defense Planning Guidance and the 1993 Eagleburger memo were written, the United States maintains its global military hegemony, but its ability to successfully lead coalitions to combat climate change, terrorism, the spread of weapons of mass destruction, piracy, cyber-crime, pandemics, and corruption varies widely. Moreover, cooperation often entails the involvement of states like China and Russia, frequent challengers of US positions and policies. The most discussed American strategic effort of recent years—the so-called pivot to Asia—is fundamentally about maintaining military and political dominance in the face of a rising China. The United States seeks to accommodate China's rise within a US-led order but hedges against a more militaristic and anti-American Chinese foreign policy. Ultimately, the United States will seek to ensure that China does not become a global rival that "poses a threat on the order of that posed formerly by the Soviet Union," as argued in the 1992 Defense Planning Guidance, and will continue to check China's ability to challenge US dominance of the Western Pacific. The ideal outcome for US policy—a China that accepts the fundamental premises of the liberal world order and competes with the United States within the rules of the post–Cold War international system—will become less likely over time. Moreover, the United States should anticipate China—alongside India, Brazil, and perhaps other emerging states—will push forward alternative conceptions of how the globe should be governed.

Continuation of the American Order?

Even as challenges have emerged to US political dominance, the United States possesses more resources to shape global outcomes than any other nation. Most importantly, the United States maintains an alliance network that no other nation can even imagine, particularly through NATO and its bilateral alliances across Asia. The challenge for US leaders is accepting that America's power is limited in ways that were not so clear 20 years ago. Fundamentally transforming other nations is in most cases too difficult and too costly. Convincing China, Russia, India, Brazil, Turkey, and others to go along with US policy is becoming and will continue to become increasingly difficult. The United States can no longer simply announce its position and expect others to adopt it, but must instead accept that other nations' approaches are valid, and demonstrate an ability to listen and occasionally to lose.

In the mid-1990s, Bill Clinton promoted the idea of the United States as the indispensable nation,[3] a notion his successors have championed as well: while the United States is not able to solve global issues on its own, no global issue is solvable without US engagement. But a bifurcation emerges in global governance between non-military and military issues, mirroring the questions of military and political dominance outlined in the 1992–93 visions articulated by the departments of State and Defense. On issues such as climate and economic governance, the emerging powers are demanding more voice and engaging in real debates. By contrast, on issues involving military intervention, the country that matters is the United States, and secondarily the United Kingdom and France. China, India, and Brazil have largely avoided international discussions concerning military intervention, and simply stating a preference for non-intervention does not involve them in the conversation. Russia is not able to intervene globally (although we have seen how much destruction Moscow can cause in its neighborhood) but actively seeks to prevent American military intervention against other states. Given American military dominance, the central actor on questions of use of force will remain the United States, even as other nations gain greater voice on non-military issues.

The Shift in Global Fault Lines

One of the reasons for the perception of American decline is that the United States has gone from being cast as the leading actor in a global ideological battle to a bystander to the central clashes of our time. After 1945, the fault line in world politics lay between democracy and communism. The United States took upon itself the mantle of "leader of the Free World" to combat communist forces in every part of the globe.

Although there is clearly an ideological difference between American- and Chinese-style capitalism, it is not (or not yet at least) a major global dividing line. The major dividing line today is not even between "Islam and the West," as many believed after the conclusion of the Cold War and in particular after the terrorist attacks of September 11, 2001. Rather, it is the frequent clashes of ideologies and sectarian interests within the Muslim world. The United States appears impotent in much of North Africa, Sub-Saharan Africa, and the Middle East, possessing little leverage to determine political outcomes. It cannot easily act to support one faction over another; it possesses little on-the-ground understanding in many places; and its military or financial support or the absence of such support is of less concern in a region where regional powers like Saudi Arabia can step in to serve in this role. Whereas the United States relied on military, political, and economic power to combat the

Soviet Union, these currencies of power have proven of limited value in shaping political outcomes in the broader Muslim world. The battle for regional domination between Iran and Saudi Arabia, and the broader clashes between states and militant groups taking shape, will occur largely irrespective of US influence.

For the first 15 years after the collapse of the Soviet Union, the United States believed it had the power to transform other societies, and that doing so served its interests. In some cases, notably formerly communist Eastern Europe, its policies succeeded. In others, such as Russia, Iraq, and Afghanistan, it failed miserably. In the latter three cases there existed great hope initially that American investment of time, resources, and guidance could help foster societal transformation. The United States no longer believes it possesses this kind of leverage in much of North Africa and the Middle East today.

In assessing US power, we should return to the question of what outcomes the United States is attempting to shape in world politics. At its core, the United States will continue to pursue the Pentagon's vision to prevent the rise of a peer competitor, and despite growing military spending in China, the United States should be able to maintain its extraordinary military supremacy well into the future, although China will increasingly challenge US pre-eminence in the Western Pacific. The broader global challenge to US dominance is not military, however; it is political and technological. The United States may be able to continue to foster free trade, but through trade pacts with groups of countries rather than through the World Trade Organization. It will promote democratic ideals abroad, though seldom through interventions to transform other societies. Like other states, it faces vexing challenges from non-state actors such as cyber-criminals and terrorists.

There is no other state that can do what the United States can do, but forging global coalitions is much harder than it was previously. In the 1990s, as the global order realigned after the conclusion of the Cold War, it was difficult for other nations to challenge American policies; today it is difficult for the United States to convince others to go along. While other states cannot do what the United States does, the United States cannot do as much as it used to do. Clashes in the Muslim world will continue to grab global headlines, as American influence remains peripheral to those ongoing struggles. Even as the United States remains the most powerful country in the world, with a formidable range of assets that others do not possess, the perception of decline will continue as efforts to forge global coalitions to respond to global challenges will increasingly founder. The changing international order will require the United States to share voice over rule-making, but it is unclear what country or group of countries will be willing to step up to prevent rule-breaking. The issue is not whether the United States is willing to share power with others but whether others are willing to develop and promote ideas about the future of global governance.

Brazil's Emerging Global Role

Unlike Russia and China, Brazil is a democratic state, and thus some have expected it to support the liberal international order fostered by the United States. This volume has demonstrated that while Brazil does not seek to upend that order, its values and interests are quite different than those of the United States. Therefore it will take positions, particularly regarding non-intervention, that often run counter to the American approach, and its main concern with the liberal international order, as Stuenkel and Taylor note, is its wariness toward American hegemony.

One of Brazil's most important divergences from US conceptions of the global order stems from different perspectives on economic issues that have long-standing roots in the old North–South debate. The United States has fostered open markets and free trade, but Brazil's overall philosophy, as demonstrated in the Porzecanski and Villela chapters (Chapters 8 and 9), has centered on a state capitalist ideology that originates from an inward-looking development model initiated in the 1930s. These authors note that, until recently, there existed a paucity of strong domestic proponents for greater economic liberalization, leading to insular economic policies that dramatically limit the potential for Brazilian influence on global affairs.

Potentially most interesting is Brazil's emphasis on state sovereignty and the equality of states. A major feature of US foreign policy after the Cold War, and even during the Obama administration, which was more reluctant to use force than its immediate predecessors, has been the willingness to intervene for humanitarian purposes. The chapters by Bosco and Stuenkel (Chapter 2), as well as Maia and Taylor (Chapter 3), make clear that Brazil seeks to uphold its philosophy of non-intervention and sovereignty. Tourinho argues that Brazil's support for the liberal international order stops with fears of American military hegemony, for example, in the case of the 2011 intervention in Libya, in which coalition forces went beyond protecting civilians to achieving regime change. Whereas the United States and the UK have promoted the "Responsibility to Protect," Brazil has articulated the notion of "Responsibility while Protecting."

This approach puts Brazil somewhere between the United States, which has sought to promote intervention against egregious human rights violators, and Russia and China, strong proponents of the Westphalian emphasis on state sovereignty (despite Russia's violation of these principles in Ukraine). Brazil is willing to support intervention against human rights violators but does not condone regime change, again limiting its acceptance of the liberal international order as currently practiced.

A key question going forward is the extent to which Brazil—and the other emerging powers—put forward new ideas for norms, rules, and institutions to manage global political, security, economic, health, and environmental challenges. The UN is the central international institution, but one with numerous structural weaknesses, including a permanent Security Council membership that no longer reflects the structure of global power and is unable to respond effectively to major military threats. The Group of 20 has been an important new global grouping, reflecting the inadequacies of the Group of 7 and Group of 8, but it has yet to develop institutionally. The major carbon emitters have not developed a successful arrangement for promoting a serious global effort to combat climate change, and as Bratman notes in her chapter (Chapter 6), Brazil faces problems similar to those of other states in fulfilling international environmental commitments in the face of domestic challenges.

Brazil is well positioned to develop a more powerful voice in global governance. It is a democratic state, and thus shares affinities with those nations that support the rule of law and protection of human rights, but its long-standing opposition to American hegemony and support for the Global South affords it credibility among countries not allied with the United States. As challenges to the liberal international order continue to emerge, Brazil thus has the potential to play an increasingly important role in the debate over the future of world affairs.

Notes

1. George H. W. Bush, Address Before a Joint Session of the Congress on the Cessation of the Persian Gulf Conflict, March 6, 1991.
2. The discussion of these two approaches draws on Chollet and Goldgeier (2008, pp. 44 ff.).
3. Clinton used the phrase in his acceptance speech at the 1996 Democratic National Convention and his second inaugural address, even though it became more closely associated later with Secretary of State Madeleine Albright.

References

Aall, Carlo, Kyrre Groven, and Gard Lindseth G. 2007. "The Scope of Action for Local Climate Policy: The Case of Norway." *Global Environmental Politics* 7(2): 83–101.

Abreu, Marcelo de Paiva. 1999. *O Brasil e a economia mundial, 1930–1945*. Rio de Janeiro: Civilização Brasileira.

———. 2004a. "The Political Economy of High Protection in Brazil before 1987." *Working Paper* 8A, INTAL.

———. 2004b. "Trade Liberalization and the Political Economy of Protection in Brazil since 1987." *Working Paper* 9A, INTAL.

———. 2007. "A quem beneficiam as políticas públicas no Brasil? Uma visão de longo prazo." *Working Paper* 554, Departamento de Economia, PUC-Rio.

Abrucio, Fernando Luiz, Paula Pedroti, and Marcos Vinicius Pó. 2010. "A Formação da Burocracia Brasileira: A trajetória e o significado das reformas administrativas." In *Burocracia e Política no Brasil: desafios para o Estado Democrático no século XXI*, eds. Maria Rita Loureiro, Fernando Luiz Abrucio, and Regina Silvia Pacheco. Rio de Janeiro: Editora FGV, pp. 21–71.

Acharya, Amitav. 2009. *Whose Ideas Matter? Agency and Power in Asian Regionalism*. Ithaca, NY: Cornell University Press.

———. 2013. *Rethinking Power, Institutions and Ideas in World Politics: Whose IR?* London: Routledge.

Acselrad, Henri. 2012. "Agronegócio e povos tradicionais." *Le Monde Diplomatique*, October 2, available at: http://www.diplomatique.org.br/artigo.php?id=1277

Adler, Emanuel. 1987. *The Power of Ideology*. Los Angeles, CA: University of California Press.

Afkhami, Artin. 2012. "Iran Says It is Building a Nuclear-Powered Submarine." *The New York Times*, June 12, http://www.nytimes.com/2012/06/13/world/middleeeast/iran-says-it-is-building-a-nuclear-powered-submarine.html?_r=0, A12

Agence-France Press. 2013. "Brazil's Azevedo Poised to Be Named WTO Chief." May 9, http://www.thenews.com.pk/Todays-News-3-176172-Brazils-Azevedo-poised-to-be-named-WTO-chief

Agrawal, Arun. 2005. *Environmentality: Technologies of Government and the Making of Environmental Citizens*. Durham, NC: Duke University Press.

Agyeman, Julian, Robert D. Bullard, and Bob Evans. 2002. "Exploring the Nexus: Bringing Together Sustainability, Environmental Justice and Equity." *Space & Polity* 6(1): 77–90.

Albuquerque, José Augusto Guilhon. 2002. "O Brasil e os chamados blocos regionais." *São Paulo em Perspectiva* 16(1): 20–36.

Alden, Chris, and Marco Antonio Vieira. 2005. "The New Diplomacy of the South: South Africa, Brazil, India and Trilateralism." *Third World Quarterly* 26(7): 1077–95.

Alimonda, Hector. 2000. "Brazilian Society and Regional Integration." *Latin American Perspectives* 27(6): 27–44.

Almeida, Paulo Roberto de. 1999. *O Brasil e o multilateralismo econômico*. Porto Alegre: Livraria do Advogado.

Almeida, Paulo Roberto de, and Miguel Diaz. 2009. "Brazil's Candidacy for Major Power Status." In *Powers and Principles: International Leadership in a Shrinking World*, eds. Michael Schiffer and David Shorr. Lanham: Lexington Books, 225–58.

Alonso, Angela. 2010. "O abolicionista cosmopolita: Joaquim Nabuco e a rede abolicionista transnacional." *Novos Estudos-CEBRAP* 88: 55–70.

———. 2012. "A teatralização da política: a propaganda abolicionista." *Tempo Social* 24(2): 101–22.

Alvarez, Alejandro. 1924. *The Monroe Doctrine: Its Importance in the International Life of the States of the New World*. New York: Oxford University Press.

Aly, Heba. 2010. "G20 Summit: Less-Developed Nations Still Struggle to Shape Agenda." *The Christian Science Monitor*, June 25, http://www.csmonitor.com/World/Americas/2010/0625/G20-summit-less-developed-nations-still-struggle-to-shape-agenda

Amazon Watch. 2013. "Massive Indigenous Rights Movement Launches Across Brazil." October 1, available at: http://amazonwatch.org/news/2013/1001-massive-indigenous-rights-movement-launches-across-brazil

Amorim, Celso. 1999. "Entre o desequilíbrio unipolar e a multipolaridade: o Conselho de segurança da ONU no período pós-Guerra Fria." In *O Brasil e as Novas Dimensões da Segurança Internacional*, eds. G. Dupas and T. Vigevani. São Paulo: Alfa-Omega, 87–98.

———. 2004. "O Brasil e os Novos Conceitos Globais e Hemisféricos de Segurança." In *Reflexões sobre Defesa e Segurança: Desafios para o Brasil*, eds. J. R. Almeida Pinto, A. J. R. Rocha, and R. D. P. Silva. Brasília: Ministério da Defesa, Secretaria de Estudos e Cooperação, 135–56.

———. 2008. "Os Brics e a reorganização do mundo." *Folha de S. Paulo*, June 8, http://www1.folha.uol.com.br

———. 2010a. "Brazilian Foreign Policy under President Lula (2003–2010): An Overview." *Revista Brasileira de Política Internacional* 53: 214–40.

———. 2010b. "Statement by His Excellency Ambassador Celso Amorim, Minister of External Relations of the Federative Republic of Brazil, at the Opening of the General Debate of the 65th Session of the United Nations General Assembly,"

September 23, available at: http://www.un.int/brazil/speech/10d-CA-65th-agnu. html

———. 2011a. "Reconciling Interests," Transcript of keynote address given at the 2011 Carnegie International Nuclear Policy Conference, Washington, DC, transcript by Federal News Service, available at: http://carnegieendowment.org/files/ Welcome_and_Keynote.pdf

———. 2011b. "Brazil and the Middle East," *Cairo Review of Global Affairs* 2 (Summer 2011): 48–63.

———. 2012. "Uma politica de defesa para um país pacífico," *Revista da Escola de Guerra Naval*, Rio de Janeiro, v. 18, n. 1 (January/June).

Amorim Neto, Octavio. 2011. *De Dutra a Lula: a condução e os determinantes da política externa brasileira*. Rio de Janeiro: Campus, Konrad Adenauer-Stiftung.

Amsden, Alice. 2001. *The Rise of 'the Rest': Challenges to the West from Late-Industrializing Economies*. Oxford: Oxford University Press.

Andrews, Christina W., and Edison Bariani. 2010. "Da década perdida à reforma gerencial: 1980–1998." In *Administração Pública no Brasil: Breve História Política*, eds. Christina W. Andrews and Edison Bariani. São Paulo: Editora Unifesp, 13–37.

Araújo, Gisele. 2010. "Tradição liberal, positivismo e pedagogia: a síntese derrotada de Rui Barbosa." *Perspectivas* 37: 113–44.

Araujo, Tavares de Jr., José da Costa, and Katarina Pereira da Costa. 2011. "Abertura comercial e inserção internacional: os casos do Brasil, China e Índia." *Textos Cindes* 14.

Arbix, Glauco, and Scott B. Martin. 2010. "Beyond Developmentalism and Market Fundamentalism in Brazil: Inclusionary State Activism without Statism." Paper presented at the Workshop on States Development and Global Governance, Global Legal Studies Center and the Center for World Affairs and the Global Economy. University of Wisconsin-Madison, March 12–13.

Armijo, Leslie Elliott. Forthcoming. "The Public Bank Trilemma: Brazil's New Developmentalism and the BNDES." Working Paper.

Armijo, Leslie Elliott, and Saori Katada, eds. 2014. *The Financial Statecraft of Emerging Powers*. New York: Palgrave Macmillan.

Armitage, David. 2002. "The Concepts of Atlantic History." In *The British Atlantic World: 1500–1800*, eds. D. Armitage and M. Braddick. New York: Palgrave Macmillan, 15–24.

Arnson, Cynthia, and Paulo Sotero. 2010. "Brazil as a Regional Power: Views from the Hemisphere." Brazil Institute Report. Washington, DC: Woodrow Wilson Center.

Avelar, Idelber. 2011. "Dilma Rousseff e a encruzilhada do desenvolvimentismo tecnocrata." *Revista Forum (Blog)*, November 22, http://www.revistaforum.com.br/ idelberavelar/2011/11/22/dilma-rousseff-e-a-encruzilhada-do-desenvolvimentismo-tecnocrata/

Bacha, Edmar, and Monica B. de Bolle. 2013. *O futuro da indústria no Brasil: desindustrialização em debate*. Rio de Janeiro: Civilização Brasileira.

Ban, Cornel. 2013. "Brazil's Liberal Neo-developmentalism: New Paradigm or Edited Orthodoxy?" *Review of International Political Economy* 20(2): 298–331.

Baptista, Fernando Mathias, and Kjersti Thorkildsen. 2011. "The Belo Monte Dam: A Camel in the Tent?" *Working Paper*, Norwegian Latin America Research Network.

Barma, Nazneen, Ely Ratner, and Steve Weber. 2007. "A World Without the West." *National Interest*, November 21, http://nationalinterest.org/article/report-and-retort-a-world-without-the-west-1658

Barraclough, Geoffrey. 1990. *An Introduction to Contemporary History*. Harmondsworth: Penguin.

Barrera, Mariano, Alejandro Inchauspe, and Eugenia Inchauspe. 2012. "Las 'translatinas' brasileñas: análisis de la inserción de petrobras en argentina (2003–2010)." *Sociedad y Economía* 22: 39–68.

Barros-Platiau, Ana Flávia. 2010. "When Emergent Countries Reform Global Governance of Climate Change: Brazil Under Lula." *Revista Brasileira de Política Internacional* 53 (special edition): 73–90, 78.

Bastos, Pedro Paulo Z. 2004. "O presidente iludido: a campanha liberal e o pêndulo da política econômica no governo Dutra (1942–1948)." *História Econômica e História de Empresas* 7(1): 90–135.

Baumann, Renato. 2009. "The Geography of Brazilian External Trade: Right Option for a BRIC?" *ECLAC Working Paper*, at http://www.cepal.org/brasil/publicaciones/sinsigla/xml/1/35271/The_Geography_of_Brazilian_External_Trade.pdf

Beck, Ulrich. 2005. *Power in the Global Age: A New Global Political Economy*. Translated Kathleen Cross. Malden, MA: Polity.

Becker, Berta. 2012. "Reflexões sobre hidrelétricas na Amazônia: agua, energia e desenvolvimento." *Bol. Mus. Para. Emílio Goeldi* 7(3): 783–90.

Becker, Bertha K., and Claudio A. G. Eckler. 1992. *Brazil: A New Regional Power in the Global Economy: A Regional Geography*. Cambridge: Cambridge University Press.

Bekerman, Marta, and Haroldo Montagu. 2009. "Impacto dos fatores macro e microeconômicos nas relações comerciais: o caso da Argentina e do Brasil." *Contexto Internacional* 31(1): 115–58.

Belém Lopes, Dawisson. 2013. *Política externa e democracia no Brasil: Ensaio de interpretação histórica*. São Paulo: Editora Unesp.

Bellamy, Alex J. 2011. *Global Politics and the Responsibility to Protect: From Words to Deeds*. New York: Routledge.

———. 2012. "R2P – Dead or Alive?" In *The Responsibility to Protect: From Evasive to Reluctant Action? The Role of Global Middle Powers*, ed. Malte Brosig. South Africa: Hanns Seidel Foundation, ISS, the Konrad-Adenauer-Stiftung, and SAIIA, 11–29.

Benevides, Maria Vitoria. 1981. *UDN e udenismo*. Rio de Janeiro: Ed Paz e Terra.

Bernal-Meza, Raúl. 1999. "Políticas exteriores comparadas de Argentina e Brasil rumo ao Mercosul." *Revista Brasileira de Política Internacional* 42(2): 40–51.

———. 2002. "A política exterior do Brasil: 1990–2002." *Revista Brasileira de Política Internacional* 45(1): 36–71.

Bernstein, Steven. 2000. "Ideas, Social Structure and the Compromise of Liberal Environmentalism." *European Journal of International Relations* December 6(4): 464–512.

———. 2002. "Liberal Environmentalism and Global Environmental Governance." *Global Environmental Politics* 2(3): 1–16.

Bersch, Katherine, Sérgio Praça, and Matthew M. Taylor. Forthcoming. "State Capacity and Bureaucratic Autonomy within National States: Mapping the Archipelago of Excellence in Brazil." In *State Building in the Developing World*, eds. Miguel Angel Centeno, Atul Kohli and Deborah Yashar.

Betsill, Michelle M., and Harriet Bulkeley. 2006. "Cities and the Multilevel Governance of Global Climate Change." *Global Governance* 12(2): 141–59.

Bexell, Magdalena, and Ulrika Wirth. 2010. "Conclusions and Directions." In *Democracy and Public-Private Partnerships in Global Governance*, eds. Magdalena Bexell and Ulrika Wirth. Basingstoke: Palgrave Macmillan, 213–27.

Bielschowsky, Ricardo. 1988. *Pensamento Econômico Brasileiro: O Ciclo Ideológico Do Desenvolvimentismo*. Rio de Janeiro: IPEA/INPES.

Blount, Jeb. 2013. "Analysis: Brazil's Once-Envied Energy Matrix a Victim of 'Hubris.'" *Reuters*, January 7, http://www.reuters.com/article/2013/01/07/us-brazil-energy-idUSBRE9060MS20130107

Blyde, Juan S. 2006. "Convergence Dynamics in Mercosur." *Journal of Economic Integration* 21(4): 784–815.

Blyth, Mark. 2003. "Structures Do Not Come with an Instruction Sheet: Interests, Ideas, and Progress in Political Science." *Perspectives on Politics* 1(4): 695–706.

Bonelli, Regis. 1996. *Ensaios sobre política econômica e industrialização no Brasil*. Rio de Janeiro: Senai.

Borchard, Edwin. 1928. *The Diplomatic Protection of Citizens Abroad: Or, the Law of International Claims*. New York: Banks Law Publishing.

Borges, André. 2013. "Ibama Notifica Construtoras de Belo Monte." *Valor*, February 17, http://www.ihu.unisinos.br/noticias/517681-ibama-notifica-construtoras-de-belo-monte

Bosco, David. 2009. *Five to Rule Them All: The United Nations Security Council and the Making of the Modern World*. Oxford: Oxford University Press.

———. 2011. "Abstention Games on the Security Council." *Foreign Affairs*, March 17, http://bosco.foreignpolicy.com/posts/2011/03/17/abstention_games_on_the_security_council

Bouzas, Roberto. 2001. "El Mercosur diez años después. ¿Proceso de aprendizaje o déjà vu?" *Desarrollo Económico* 41(162): 179–200.

Bowen, A., and S. Fankhauser. 2011. "The Green Growth Narrative: Paradigm Shift or Just Spin?" *Global Environmental Change* 21(4): 1157–59.

Brandão, Gildo Marçal. 2001. "Idéias e intelectuais: modos de usar." *Lua Nova* 54: 5–34.

———. 2007. *Linhagens do Pensamento Político Brasileiro*. São Paulo: Aderaldo & Rothschild.

Brands, Hal. 2010. "Dilemmas of Brazilian Grand Strategy." *Strategic Studies Institute Monograph*, August.

Bratman, Eve. 2014. "Through the Green Looking Glass: Activism, Environmental Justice, and the Belo Monte Dam." *International Environmental Agreements, Law, and Policy*, "Passive Revolution in the Green Economy: Activism and the Belo Monte Dam." *International Environmental Agreements: Politics, Law and Economics.* ISSN: 1567-9764 DOI: 10.1007/s10784-014-9268-z.

Bremmer, Ian. 2010. *The End of the Free Market: Who Wins the War Between States and Corporations?*. New York: Portfolio.

Bresser-Pereira, Luiz Carlos. 2009. "From Old to New Developmentalism in Latin America." In *Handbook of Latin American Economics*, ed. José Antonio Ocampo. Oxford: Oxford University Press, 108–219.

Brigagão, Clóvis. 2001. *Estratégias de negociações internacionais: uma visão brasileira.* Rio de Janeiro: Aeroplano.

———. 2011. "Brasil: Relações internacionais com os Estados Unidos e a América do Sul." *Relações Internacionais* 29: 83–90.

Brown, Lawrence T. 2013. "Restoring the 'Unwritten Alliance': Brazil-U.S. Relations." *Joint Forces Quarterly* 69 (2nd Quarter): 42–8.

Bulkeley, Harriet. 2005. "Reconfiguring Environmental Governance: Towards a Politics of Scales and Networks." *Political Geography* 24(8): 875–902.

Bulkeley, Harriet, and Michele M. Betsill. 2003. *Cities and Climate Change: Urban Sustainability and Global Environmental Governance.* New York: Routledge.

Bulkeley, Harriet, and Susanne Moser. 2007. "Responding to Climate Change: Governance and Social Action Beyond Kyoto." *Global Environmental Politics* 7(2): 1–10.

Bull, Hedley. 1984. "The Revolt Against the West." In *The Expansion of International Society*, eds. Hedley Bull and Adam Watson. Oxford: Oxford University Press, 217–28.

———. 2000. "Justice in International Relations: The 1983 Hagey Lectures." In *Hedley Bull on International Society*, eds. Kai Alderson and Andrew Hurrell. New York: St. Martin's Press, 229–30.

Bull, Hedley, and Adam Watson, eds. 1984. *The Expansion of International Society.* Oxford: Oxford University Press.

Burges, Sean W. 2005. "Auto-Estima in Brazil: The Logic of Lula's South-South Foreign Policy." *International Journal* 60(4): 1133–51.

———. 2006. "Without Sticks or Carrots: Brazilian Leadership in South America During the Cardoso Era, 1992–2003." *Bulletin of Latin American Research* 25(1): 23–42.

———. 2007. "Building a Global Southern Coalition: The Competing Approaches of Brazil's Lula and Venezuela's Chávez." *Third World Quarterly* 28(7): 1343–58.

———. 2009. *Brazilian Foreign Policy After the Cold War.* Gainesville: University Press of Florida.

———. 2013. "Brazil as a Bridge Between Old and New Powers?" *International Affairs* 89(3): 577–94.

Burges, Sean W., and Jean Daudelin. 2007. "Brazil: How Realists Defend Democracy." In *Promoting Democracy in the Americas*, eds. Thomas Legler, Sharon F. Lean, and Dexter S. Boniface. Baltimore: Johns Hopkins University Press, 107–31.

Burns, E. Bradford. 1970. *A History of Brazil*. New York: Columbia University Press.

Cabral, Lídia. 2011. "Cooperação Brasil-África para desenvolvimento: caracterização, tendências e desafios." *Textos Cindes 26*.

Callahan, Michael D. 1999. *Mandates and Empire: The League of Nations and Africa, 1914–1931*. Brighton: Sussex Academic Press.

Camarotto, Murillo. 2013. "Dilma: Brasil pode ser o maior produtor de plataformas de petróleo," *Valor Econômico*, December 17.

Cameron, David, Barack Obama, and Nicolas Sarkozy. 2011. "Libya's Pathway to Peace." *The New York Times*, April 14, http://www.nytimes.com/2011/04/15/opinion/15iht-edlibya15.html

Canuto, Otaviano, Matheus Cavallari, and José Guilherme Reis. 2013. "The Brazilian Competitiveness Cliff." *Economic Premise (The World Bank Poverty Reduction and Economic Management Network)* 105: 1–8.

Cardoso, Eliana. 2009. "A Brief History of Trade Policies in Brazil: From ISI, Export Promotion and Import Liberalization to Multilateral and Regional Agreements." Paper presented at the Conference on the Political Economy of Trade Policy in the BRICS. New Orleans, March 27–28.

Cardoso, Fernando H. 2006. *The Accidental President of Brazil: A Memoir*. New York: Public Affairs.

Cardoso, Fernando Henrique, and Faletto Enzo. 2004. *Dependência e desenvolvimento na América Latina: Ensaio de interpretação sociológica*, 8th edition. Rio de Janeiro: Civilização Brasileira.

Carothers, Thomas. 1997. "Think Again: Democracy." *Foreign Policy* 107, Summer: 11–12.

Carvalho, José Murilo de. 1975. "Elite and State-Building in Imperial Brazil." Unpublished Ph.D. dissertation, Stanford University.

———. 2009. "Radicalismo e Republicanismo." In *Repensando o Brasil do Oitocentos: Cidadania, política e liberdade*, eds. J. M. de Carvalho and L. M Bastos Pereira das Neves. Rio de Janeiro: Civilização Brasileira, 19–48.

Carvalho, Maria Alice Rezende de. 1998. *O Quinto Século: André Rebouças e a construção do Brasil*. Rio de Janeiro: Revan.

Cason, Jeffrey. 2000. "On the Road to Southern Cone Economic Integration." *Journal of Interamerican Studies and World Affairs* 42(1): 23–42.

Cason, Jeffrey, and Jennifer Burrell. 2002. "Turning the Tables: State and Society in South America's Economic Integration." *Polity* 34(3): 457–77.

Cason, Jeffrey W., and Timothy J. Power. 2009. "Presidentialization, Pluralization, and the Rollback of Itamaraty: Explaining Change in Brazilian Foreign Policy Making in the Cardoso-Lula Era." *International Political Science Review* 30(2): 117–40.

Castañeda, Jorge G. 2010. "Not Ready for Prime Time: Why Including Emerging Powers at the Helm Would Hurt Global Governance." *Foreign Affairs* 89(5): 109–22.

Castello Branco, Marta, Pedro da Motta Veiga, and Sandra Polónia Rios. 2011. "Cenários para a nova configuração da ordem econômica internacional e seus impactos sobre as estratégias brasileiras." *Textos Cindes 29*.

Cervo, Amado Luiz. 1997. "Política de comércio exterior e desenvolvimento: a experiência brasileira." *Revista Brasileira de Política Internacional* 40(2): 5–26.

Chollet, Derek, and James Goldgeier. 2008. *America Between the Wars: From 11/9 to 9/11*. New York: Public Affairs.

Christensen, Steen Fryba. 2013. "Brazil's Foreign Policy Priorities." *Third World Quarterly* 34(2): 271–86.

Clements, B. 1997. "The Real Plan, Poverty and Income Distribution in Brazil." *Finance and Development* 34(3): 44–6.

Coatsworth, John H. 2005. "Structures, Endowments, and Institutions in the Economic History of Latin America." *Latin American Research Review* 40(3): 126–44.

Coatsworth, John H., and Jeffrey G. Williamson. 2004. "Always Protectionist? Latin American Tariffs from Independence to the Great Depression." *Journal of Latin American Studies* 36 (May): 205–32.

Cohen, Stephen Philip. 2002. *India: Emerging Power*. Washington, DC: Brookings Institution Press.

Comparato, Fabio Konder. 2001. "Saber combinar o específico e o universal." *Lua Nova* 54: 97–101.

Cornago, Noé. 2010. "On the Normalization of Sub-State Diplomacy." *The Hague Journal of Diplomacy* 5(1/2): 11–36.

Costa, Emília Viotti da. 1977. *Da Monarquia à República: momentos decisivos*. São Paulo: Grijalbo.

Costa Vaz, Alcides. 1999. "Parcerias estratégicas no contexto da política exterior brasileira: implicações para o Mercosul." *Revista Brasileira de Política Internacional* 42(2): 52–80.

Dantas, Francisco Clementino de San Tiago. 2007. "Discurso de posse do Ministro das Relações Exteriores, Francisco Clementino de San Tiago Dantas em 11 de Setembro de 1961." In *Documentos da Política Externa Independente*, ed. Alvaro da Costa Franco. Brasília: Fundação Alexandre de Gusmão, 159–64.

Daudelin, Jean. 2013. "Coming of Age?: Recent Scholarship on Brazilian Foreign Policy." *Latin American Research Review* 48(2): 204–17.

Davutoğlu, Ahmet and Celso Amorim. 2010. "Giving Diplomacy a Chance." *New York Times*, May 26.

Davis, Sonny B. 1996. *A Brotherhood of Arms: Brazil-United States Military Relations, 1945–1977*. Boulder, CO: University of Colorado Press.

Defense News. 2013. "Brazil to Get Its First Nuclear Subs." March 2, at http://www.defensenews.com/article/20130302/DEFREG02/303020009/Brazil-Get-Its-First-Nuclear-Subs

Deutsche Presse-Agentur. 2007. "Brazil Criticizes Selection Process at World Bank, IMF." May 27.

Diniz, Eli. 1978. *Empresário, estado e capitalismo no Brasil: 1930–1945*. São Paulo: Paz & Terra.

Dow Jones Newswire. 2013. "Brazil to Hold First Pre-salt Oil Exploration Auction in October." May 23, http://www.rigzone.com/news/oil_gas/a/126640/Brazil_to_Hold_First_PreSalt_Oil_Exploration_Auction_in_October

DuBois, Frank, and Marcos Primo. 2013. "State Capitalism and Economic Development: The Case of Brazilian Shipbuilding." Working paper presented at workshop on "Brazil and the Liberal Order: Brazil's Influence on Global Norms and Institutions," School of International Service, American University, September 2013.

Duchacek, Ivo. 1990. "Perforated Sovereignties: Towards a Typology of New Actors in International Relations." In *Federalism and International Relations: The Role of Subnational Units*, eds. H. J. Michelman and Panayitos Soldatos. Oxford: Clarendon Press, 1–33.

Dulci, Otavio Soares. 1986. *A UDN e o anti-populismo no Brasil*. Belo Horizonte: UFMG.

Einaudi, Luigi R. 2011. "Brazil and the United States: The Need for Strategic Engagement." *Strategic Forum 266*. Washington, DC: National Defense University, 1–16.

Empresa de Pesquisa Energética (EPE). 2013. "Brazilian Energy Balance, 2013 (2012 data)." https://ben.epe.gov.br/downloads/Relatorio_Final_BEN_2013.pdf

Estevadeordal, Antoni, and Alan M. Taylor. 2008. "Is the Washington Consensus Dead? Growth, Openness, and the Great Liberalization, 1970s–2000s." *NBER Working Paper Series*, no. 14264, August.

Estevadeordal, Antoni, Junichi Goto, and Raul Saez. 2001. "The New Regionalism in the Americas: The Case of Mercosur." *Journal of Economic Integration* 16(2): 180–202.

Evans, Gareth. 2012. "The Responsibility to Protect in Action." *The Stanley Foundation Courier* 74 (Spring), available at: http://www.stanleyfoundation.org/articles.cfm?id=721

Faleiros, Gustavo. 2011. "Brazilian President's Promises Crumble Under Weight of Belo Monte Dam." *The Guardian*, February 1, http://www.theguardian.com/environment/blog/2011/feb/01/brazil-dilma-rousseff-hydroelectric-dam

Faoro, Raymundo. 1975 [2000]. *Os donos do poder: formação do patronato político brasileiro*. São Paulo: Globo Livro.

Faust, Jorg, and Christian Wagner. 2010. "India: A New Partner in Democracy Promotion?" *DIE Briefing Paper 3*. Bonn, Germany: German Development Institute.

Fearnside, Philip. 2012. "Brazil's Amazon Forest in Mitigating Global Warming: Unresolved Controversies." *Climate Policy* 12(1): 70–81.

Feldman, Luiz. 2009. "Soberania e modernização no Brasil: Pensamento de política externa no Segundo Reinado e na Primeira República." *Contexto Internacional* 31(3): 535–92.

Fernandes, Florestan. 1975. *A revolução burguesa no Brasil*. Rio de Janeiro: Zahar.

Feu Alvim, Carlos, Leonam dos Santos Guimarães, Frida Eidelman, and Olga Mafra. No date. "Brazil and Argentina Experience in Non-Proliferation." Available at: http://www.academia.edu/3821904/Brazil_and_Argentina_experience_in_non_Proliferation

Fisch, Jörg. 1992. "Law as Means and as an End: Some Remarks on the Function of European and Non-European Law in the Process of European Expansion." In *European Expansion and Law: The Encounter of European and Indigenous Law in 19th- and 20th-Century Africa and Asia*, eds. W. J. Mommsen and J. A. De Moor. New York: Berg, 15–38.

Fishlow, Albert. 2011. *Starting Over: Brazil since 1985*. Washington, DC: The Brookings Institution Press.

Flemes, Daniel. 2006. "Brazil's Nuclear Policy: From Technological Dependence to Civil Nuclear Power." *Working Paper* 23, Berlin: German Institute for Global and Area Studies.

Florini, Ann. 2011. "Rising Asian Powers and Changing Global Governance." *International Studies Review* 13(1): 24–33.

Florini, Ann, and Benjamin K. Sovacool. 2011. "Bridging the Gaps in Global Energy Governance." *Global Governance* 17 (February): 57–74.

Forero, Juan. 2013. "Power-Hungry Brazil Builds Dams, and More Dams, Across the Amazon." *The Washington Post*, February 9, http://www.washingtonpost.com/world/the_americas/brazil-building-more-dams-across-amazon/2013/02/09/f23a63ca-6fba-11e2-b35a-0ee56f0518d2_story.html

Franco, Maria Sylvia de Carvalho. 1976. "As idéias estão em seu lugar." *Cadernos de Debate*, 1: 61–64.

Franko, Patrice. 2013. "The Defense Acquisition Trilemma: The Case of Brazil." *Working Paper*, Institute for National Security Studies of the National Defense University.

Frechette, Myles, and Frank Samolis. 2012. "A Tentative Embrace: Brazil's Foreign and Trade Relations with the United States." *Política Externa* (March/April/May). English reprint, available at: http://www.gwu.edu/~clai/working_papers/Frechette_03_2012.pdf

Freitas, Any. 2014. "China and Brazil: Growing Together or Apart?" *Cheung Kong Graduate School of Business*, June 2, http://knowledge.ckgsb.edu.cn/2014/06/02/finance-and-investment/china-and-brazil-growing-together-apart/

Friedman-Rudovsky, Jean. 2012. "The Bully from Brazil." *Foreign Policy*, July 20, available at: http://foreignpolicy.com/2012/07/20/the-bully-from-brazil/

Friedman, Thomas. 2000. *The Lexus and the Olive Tree: Understanding Globalization*. New York: Farrar, Straus and Giroux.

Fritsch, Winston, and Gustavo H. B. Franco. 1993. *The Political Economy of Trade and Industrial Policy Reform in Brazil in the 1990s*. Santiago: ECLAC.

Fryba Christensen, Steen. 2007. "The Influence of Nationalism in Mercosur and in South America – Can the Regional Integration Project Survive?" *Revista Brasileira de Política Internacional* 50(1): 139–58.

Fukuyama, Francis. 1989. "The End of History?" *The National Interest* 16 (Summer): 3–18.

Furtado, Celso. 1970. *Formação Econômica Do Brasil*, 10th edition. São Paulo: Companhia Editora Nacional.

———. 1984. "Rescuing Brazil, Reversing Recession." *Third World Quarterly* 6(3): 604–23.

Gaspari, Elio. 2005. *A ditadura encurralada: O sacerdote e o feiticeiro*, São Paulo: Companhia das Letras.

Gasparre, Richard. 2009. "What is Brazil's Real Nuclear Aim?" *Power Technology*, January 27, www.power-technology.com/features/feauture48542

Geddes, Barbara. 1994. *Politician's Dilemma: Building State Capacity in Latin America*. Berkeley: University of California Press.

Genna, Gaspare M., and Taeko Hiroi. 2007. "Brazilian Regional Power in the Development of Mercosul." *Latin American Perspectives* 34(5): 43–57.

Geyer, Martin H., and Johannes Paulmann. 2001. *The Mechanics of Internationalism: Culture, Society, and Politics from the 1840s to the First World War*. Oxford: Oxford University Press.

Goffredo, Gustavo Sénéchal de. 2005. *Entre poder e Direito: A tradição grotiana na política externa brasileira*. Brasília: Fundação Alexandre de Gusmão.

Goldstein, Judith, and Robert O. Keohane. 1993. "Ideas and Foreign Policy: An Analytical Framework." In Judith Goldstein and Robert O. Keohane, eds. *Ideas and Foreign Policy: Beliefs, Institutions, and Political Change*. Ithaca: Cornell University Press, 3–30.

Gomes, Ângela Maria de Castro. 1993. "A práxis corporativa de Oliveira Vianna." In *O Pensamento de Oliveira Vianna*, eds. Elide R. Bastos and João Q. de Moraes. Campinas: Ed. Unicamp, 43–57.

Gomez-Mera, Laura. 2005. "Explaining Mercosur's Survival: Strategic Sources of Argentine-Brazilian Convergence." *Journal of Latin American Studies* 37(1): 109–40.

———. 2007. "Macroeconomic Concerns and Intrastate Bargains: Explaining Illiberal Policies in Brazil's Automobile Sector." *Latin American Politics and Society* 49(1): 113–40.

Gonzalez, C. G. 2012. "China's Engagement with Latin America: Partnership or Plunder?" In *Natural Resources and the Green Economy: Redefining the Challenges for People, States and Corporations*, eds. E. Merino-Blanco and J. Razzaque. London: Brill, 37–80.

Graeff, Bibiana. 2012. "Should We Adopt a Specific Regulation to Protect People That are Displaced by Hydroelectric Projects?: Reflections Based on Brazilian Law and the 'Belo Monte' Case." *Florida A&M University Law Review* 7(2): 261–85.

Granberg, Mikael, and Ingemar Elander. 2007. "Local Governance and Climate Change: Reflections on the Swedish Experience." *Local Environment* 12(5): 537–48.

Grandgirard, Agnes. 2007. "Towards a New Leader of Water Policy in France?" *European Water* 19/20: 25–35.

Granovsky, Martin. 2013. "Entrevista Exclusiva a Celso Amorim, Ministro de Defensa de Brasil." *Página 12*, 16.

Greenpeace. 2010. "Mar, Petróleo e Biodiversidade: A geografia do conflito." http://go.nature.com/g5xwcw

Grewe, Wilhelm. 2000. *The Epochs of International Law*. New York: De Gruyter.

Haber, Stephen. 1997. *How Latin America Fell Behind: Essays on the Economic Histories of Brazil and Mexico, 1800–1914*. Stanford: Stanford University Press.

Hage, Altahyde, and José Alexandre. 2010. "Reflexões sobre a política externa brasileira e a integração regional." *Cadernos Adenauer* 11(4): 14–22.

Hakim, Peter. 2014. "A New Normal for U.S.-Brazil Relations." *O Estado de S. Paulo*, June 30. English translation at http://www.thedialogue.org, accessed July 7, 2014.

Hall, Anthony, and Sue Branford. 2012. "Development, Dams and Dilma: The Saga of Belo Monte." *Critical Sociology* 38(6): 851–62.

Hall, Peter. 2001. "Global City-Regions in the 21st Century." In *City-Regions: Trends, Theory, Policy*, ed. Allen John Scott. New York: Oxford University Press, 59–77.

Hall, Peter A. 1989. *The Political Power of Economic Ideas: Keynesianism across Nations*. Princeton: Princeton University Press.

Hammond, Phillip. 2013. "Working Towards Nuclear Disarmament." Ministry of Defence, March 25, available at: https://www.gov.uk/government/policies/working-towards-nuclear-disarmament

Harrison, Glenn W., Thomas F. Rutherford, David G. Tarr, and Angelo Gurgel. 2004. "Trade Policy and Poverty Reduction in Brazil." *The World Bank Economic Review* 18(3): 289–317.

Harvey, Fiona. 2007. "Beware the Carbon Offsetting Cowboys." *Financial Times*, 26 April, http://www.ft.com/cms/s/0/dcdefef6-f350-11db-9845-000b5df10621.html#axzz2vbclCK8K

Hecht, Susanna B. 2011a. "From Eco-Catastrophe to Zero Deforestation? Interdisciplinarities, Politics, Environmentalisms and Reduced Clearing in Amazonia." *Environmental Conservation* 39(1): 4–19.

———. 2011b. "The New Amazon Geographies: Insurgent Citizenship, 'Amazon Nation' and the Politics of Environmentalisms." *Journal of Cultural Geography* 28(1): 203–23.

Herz, Monica. 2010. Concepts of Security in South America. *International Peacekeeping* 17: 598–612.

Hibbs, Mark. 2011. "New Global Rules for Sensitive Nuclear Trade." *Nuclear Energy Brief*. Washington, DC: Carnegie Endowment for International Peace.

———. 2013. "The IAEA Additional Protocol after the 2010 NPT Review: Status and Prospects." United Nations Institute for Disarmament Research (UNIDIR). Available at: http://www.unidir.org/files/publications/pdfs/the-iaea-additional-protocol-after-the-2010-npt-review-status-and-prospects-en-373.pdf, No date, available at: www.unidir.org/publications

Hobson, Kersty. 2013. "On the Making of the Environmental Citizen." *Environmental Politics* 22(1): 56–72.

Hochstetler, Kathryn. 2011. "The Politics of Comparatively Good Times: Brazil in the Global Financial Crisis." Paper presented at the the Annual Meeting of the International Studies Association, Montreal, Canada, March 16–19.

Hochstetler, Kathryn, and Alfred P. Montero. 2013. "The Renewed Developmentalist State: The National Development Bank and the Brazil Model." *Journal of Development Studies*, 49(11): 1484–99.

Hochstetler, Kathryn, and Margaret E. Keck. 2007. *Greening Brazil: Environmental Activism in State and Society*. Durham, NC: Duke University Press.

Holanda, Cristina Buarque de. 2008. "A questão da representação política na Primeira República." *Cadernos CRH* 21(52): 25–35.

Holanda, Sérgio Buarque de. 1985. *O Brasil Monárquico: Do Império À República*. São Paulo: Difel.

Holgate, Claudia. 2007. "Factors and Actors in Climate Change Mitigation: A Tale of Two South African Cities." *Local Environment* 12(5): 471–84.

Human Rights Center. 2007. *The Responsibility to Protect (R2P): Moving the Campaign Forward*. Berkeley, CA: University of California.

Humphreys, David. 2006. *Logjam: Deforestation and the Crisis of Global Governance*. London: Earthscan.

Huntington, Samuel P. 1968. *Political Order in Changing Societies*. New Haven and London: Yale University Press.

Huntington, William. 2005. "Brazilian Regulator Denies Uranium Claims." *Arms Control Today*, September 28, https://www.armscontrol.org/act/2005_11/NOV-Brazil

Hurrell, Andrew. 2006. "Hegemony, Liberalism and Global Order: What Space for Would-Be Powers?" *International Affairs* 82(1): 1–19.

———. 2008. "Lula's Brazil: A Rising Power, but Going Where?" *Current History* 107(706): 51–7.

———. 2010. "Brazil and the New Global Order." *Current History* 109(724): 60–6.

Hurwitz, Zachary. 2011. "IBAMA President Resigns over Belo Monte Licensing." *International Rivers Network (Blog)*, January 13, http://www.internationalrivers.org/blogs/258/ibama-president-resigns-over-belo-monte-licensing

Husar, Joerg, and John Best. 2013. "Energy Investments and Technology Transfer Across Emerging Economies." Paris, France: International Energy Agency.

Ignatieff, Michael. 2012. "How Syria Divided the World." *The New York Review of Books*, July 10, http://www.nybooks.com/blogs/nyrblog/2012/jul/11/syria-proxy-war-russia-china/

Ikenberry, G. John. 1999. "Why Export Democracy? The 'Hidden Grand Strategy' of American Foreign Policy." *The Wilson Quarterly* 23(2): 56–65.

———. 2001. *After Victory: Institutions, Strategic Restraint, and the Rebuilding of Order After Major Wars*. Princeton: Princeton University Press.

———. 2007. "American Grand Strategy in the Age of Terror." *Survival* 43(4): 19–34.

———. 2008. "The Rise of China and the Future of the West – Can the Liberal System Survive." *Foreign Affairs* 87(1): 23–37.

———. 2009. "Liberal Internationalism 3.0: America and the Dilemmas of Liberal World Order." *Perspectives on Politics* 7(1): 71–87.

———. 2010. "The Liberal Order and Its Discontents." *Millennium* 38(3): 509–21.

———. 2011a. *Liberal Leviathan: The Origins, Crisis, and Transformation of the American World Order*. Princeton: Princeton University Press.

———. 2011b. "The Future of the Liberal World Order." *Foreign Affairs* 90(3): 56–68.

Inside U.S. Trade. 2013. "Azevedo Rode to WTO Victory Mainly Due to Developing World Support." May 8.

Inter-American Commission on Human Rights. 2011. "Precautionary Measure PM 382/10 – Indigenous Communities of the Xingu River Basin." Pará, Brazil. April 1 and July 29. http://www.oas.org/en/iachr/indigenous/protection/precautionary.asp

IPEA. 2011. *Sistema de Indicadores de Percepção Social: Defesa Nacional*. Brasília: Instituto de Pesquisa Econômica Aplicada.

Jacobi, Pedro Roberto, and Paulo Antonio de Almeida Sinisgalli. 2012. "Environmental Governance and the Green Economy." *Ciência & Saúde Coletiva* 17(6): 1469–78.

Johnston, Alastair Iain. 2003. "Is China a Status Quo Power?" *International Security* 27(4): 5–56.

Jonsson, Christer. 2013. "The John Holmes Memorial Lecture: International Organizations at the Moving Public-Private Borderline." *Global Governance* 19(1): 1–18.

Kahl, Colin H. 1998. "Constructing a Separate Peace: Constructivism, Collective Liberal Identity, and Democratic Peace." *Security Studies* 8(2/3): 94–144.

Kahler, Miles. 2013. "Rising Powers and Global Governance: Negotiating Change in a Resilient Status Quo." *International Affairs* 89(3): 711–29.

Kassenova, Togzhan. 2014. *Brazil's Nuclear Kaleidoscope: An Evolving Identity*. Washington, DC: Carnegie Endowment for International Peace.

Kasturi, Charu Sudan. 2013. "Brazil Snubs Tri-Meet Invite." *The Telegraph (India)*, July 11, http://www.telegraphindia.com/1130711/jsp/nation/story_17104373. jsp#.U9k4-oBdXs4

Kern, Kristine, and Harriet Bulkeley. 2009. "Cities, Europeanization and Multi-Level Governance: Governing Climate Change through Transnational Municipal Networks." *Journal of Common Market Studies* 47(2): 309–32.

King, Sir David, Megan Cole, Sally Tyldesley, and Ryan Hogarth. 2012. "The Response of China, India, and Brazil to Climate Change: A Perspective for South Africa." Smith School of Enterprise and the Environment, University of Oxford.

Kooiman, Jan. 1993. *Modern Governance: New Government-Society Interactions*. London: Sage.

Kowitt, Beth. 2009. "For Mr. BRIC, Nation Meeting a Milestone." *CNN Money*, June 17, http://money.cnn.com/2009/06/17/news/economy/goldman_sachs_jim_ oneill_interview.fortune/index.htm

Krasner, Stephen D. 1985. *Structural Conflict: The Third World Against Global Liberalism*. Berkeley: University of California Press.

Krauthammer, Charles. 1990. "The Unipolar Moment." *Foreign Affairs* 70(1): 23–33.

Kupchan, Charles. 2010. *How Enemies Become Friends: The Sources of Stable Peace*. Princeton: Princeton University Press.

Kutchesfahani, Sara. 2010. "The Path Towards the Creation of ABACC." Unpublished Ph.D. dissertation, University College London.

Laird, Sam. 1997. "Mercosur: Objectives and Achievements." *Staff Working Paper TPRD9702*, World Trade Organization: Trade Policy Review Division, available at https://www.wto.org/english/res_e/reser_e/ptpr9702.pdf

Lamounier, Bolivar. 1977. "Formação de um pensamento político autoritário na Primeira República: uma interpretação." In *História Geral da Civilização Brasileira; O Brasil Republicano*, ed. Boris Fausto. São Paulo: Difusão Européia do Livro, 345–75.

Lampreia, João, Maria Silvia Muylaert de Araújo, Christiano Pires de Campos, Marcos Aurélio V. Freitas, Luiz Pinguelli Rosa, Renzo Solari, Cláudio Gesteira,

Rodrigo Ribas, and Neílton F. Silva. 2011. "Analyses and Perspectives for Brazilian Low Carbon Technological Development in the Energy Sector." *Renewable and Sustainable Energy Reviews* 15(7): 3432–44.

Landim, R., R. Leopoldo, and T. Irany. 2013. "BNDES decide abandonar a política de criação de 'Campeãs' Nacionais." *O Estado de S.Paulo*, April 22, http://economia.estadao.com.br/noticias/geral,bndes-decide-abandonar-a-politica-de-criacao-de-campeas-nacionais,151356e

Landsberg, Chris. 2010. "Pax South Africana and the Responsibility to Protect." *Global Responsibility to Protect Journal* 2(4): 436–57.

Layne, Christopher. 2006. "The Unipolar Illusion Revisited." *International Security* 31(2): 7–41.

Lazzarini, Sérgio G. 2010. *Capitalismo de Laços: Os donos do Brasil e suas conexões*. Rio de Janeiro: Elsevier – Campus.

Lazzarini, Sérgio G., Aldo Musacchio, Rodrigo Bandeira-de-Mello, and Rosilene Marcon. 2011. "What Do Development Banks Do? Evidence from Brazil, 2002–2009." *Working Paper*, Harvard Business School, available at: http://www.hbs.edu/faculty/Publication%20Files/12-047.pdf

Lee, Taedong. 2013. "Global Cities and Transnational Climate Change Networks." *Global Environmental Politics* 13(1): 108–28.

Lefèvre, Benoit. 2012. "Incorporating Cities into the Post-2012 Climate Change Agreements." *Environment & Urbanization* 24(2): 575–95.

Leigh, Monroe. 2001. "The United States and the Statute of Rome." *The American Journal of International Law* 95(1): 124–31.

Leipziger, Danny, Claudio Frischtak, Homi J. Kharas, and John F. Normand. 1997. "Mercosur: Integration and Industrial Policy." *The World Economy* 20(5): 585–603.

Leitão, Miriam. 2012. "Ministra Izabella Teixeira Em Um Barraco Ambiental." *O Globo.com*, June 22, https://www.google.com/webhp?sourceid=chrome-instant&rlz=1C5CHFA_enUS551US551&ion=1&espv=2&ie=UTF-8#q=Ministra%20Izabella%20Teixeira%20Em%20Um%20Barraco%20Ambiental

Leopoldi, Maria Antonieta P. 2000. *Política e interesses: as associações industriais, a política econômica e o Estado na industrialização brasileira*. São Paulo: Paz e Terra.

Lessa, Renato. 1988. *A Invenção Republicana*. Rio de Janeiro: Vértice and IUPERJ.

Liyu, Lin. 2009. "G20 Ministers Tackle Economic Crisis." *China View*, March 15, http://news.xinhuanet.com/english/2009-03/15/content_11014440.htm

Lorca, Arnulf Becker. 2006. "International Law in Latin America or Latin American International Law? Rise, Fall and Retrieval of a Tradition of Legal Thinking and Political Imagination." *Harvard International Law Journal* 47(1): 283–306.

———. 2011. "Sovereignty beyond the West: The End of Classical International Law." *Journal of the History of International Law* 13(1): 7–73.

Louis, William Roger. 1984. "The Era of the Mandates System and the Non-European World." In *The Expansion of International Society*, eds. Hedley Bull and Adam Watson. Oxford: Oxford University Press, 201–13.

Love, Joseph L. 1996. "Economic Ideas and Ideologies in Latin America since 1930." In *Ideas and Ideologies in Twentieth Century Latin America*, ed. Leslie Bethell. Cambridge: Cambridge University Press, 207–74.

Luke, Timothy W. 2003. "Global Cities vs. "Global Cities: Rethinking Contemporary Urbanism as Public Ecology." *Studies in Political Economy* 70: 11–22.

Lynch, Christian. 2008. "O pensamento conservador ibero-americano na era das Independências (1808–1850)." *Lua Nova* 74: 59–92.

———. 2009. "Liberal/liberalismo." In *Léxico da história dos conceitos politicos no Brasil*, ed. João Feres Junior. Belo Horizonte: UFMG, 141–60.

MacAskill, Ewen. 2013. "Iran Faces Fresh sanctions as Russia and China Support UN Resolution." *The Guardian*, May 18.

Macfarquhar, Neil. 2010. "U.N. Approves New Sanctions to Deter Iran." *The New York Times*, June 9.

Machado, Maíra Rocha, and Evaldo Cabral de Mello. 2004. *A outra independência: o federalismo Pernambucano de 1817 a 1824*. São Paulo: Editora, 34.

Maddison, Angus. 2006. *The World Economy*. Paris: OECD.

Malamud, Andrés. 2005. "Presidential Diplomacy and the Institutional Underpinnings of Mercosur: An Empirical Examination." *Latin American Research Review* 40(1): 138–64.

———. 2011. "A Leader without Followers?: The Growing Divergence between the Regional and Global Performance of Brazilian Foreign Policy." *Latin American Politics & Society* 53: 1–24.

Malan, Pedro S. 1986. "Relações Econômicas Internacionais Do Brasil (1945–1964)." In *História Geral Da Civilização Brasileira*. ed. Boris Fausto, Vol. III. São Paulo: Difel, 51–106.

Manela, Erez. 2007. *The Wilsonian Moment: Self-determination and the International Origins of Anticolonial Nationalism*. Oxford: Oxford University Press.

Manzetti, Luigi. 1994. "The Political Economy of Mercosur." *Journal of Interamerican Studies and World Affairs* 35(4): 101–41.

Vieira, Marco Antonio, and Chris Alden. 2011. "India, Brazil, and South Africa (IBSA): South-South Cooperation and the Paradox of Regional Leadership." *Global Governance: A Review of Multilateralism and International Organizations*. 17(4): 507–28.

Mariano, Passini, Marcelo Júnior, and Haroldo Ramanzini Júnior. 2012. "Uma análise das limitações estruturais do Mercosul a partir das posições da política externa brasileira." *Revista de Sociologia e Política* 20(43): 23–41.

Marinis, Alexandre. 2010. "Bank Gone Wild in Brazil Distorts Market." *Bloomberg*, August 18, http://www.bloomberg.com/news/2010-08-19/bank-gone-wild-in-brazil-distorts-market-alexandre-marinis.html

Markwald, Ricardo. 2006. "The Political Economy of Foreign Trade Policy: The Brazilian case." In *Domestic Determinants of National Trade Strategies: A Comparative Analysis of Mercosur Countries, Mexico and Chile*, ed. R. Bouzas. Working Group on EU-Mercosur Negotiations, Chaire Mercosur de Sciences-Po/OBREAL, 85–143.

Marques, Gerusa. 2009. "Governo mantém data para leilão de Belo Monte." *O Estado de S. Paulo*, November 2, http://economia.estadao.com.br/noticias/geral,governo-mantem-data-para-leilao-de-belo-monte,460109

Marques, Joseph. 2013. "Sweet Sixteen: Brazil and the CPLP." Paper presented at the Annual Meeting of the Latin American Studies Association. Washington, DC, May 30–June 1.

Martins Filho, João, and Daniel Zirker. 2007. "The Brazilian Armed Forces in the Post-Cold War Era: What Has Changed in Military Thinking?" *Working Paper* CBS-85-07, Centre for Brazilian Studies, University of Oxford.

Mattos, Hebe Maria. 2000. *Escravidão e cidadania no Brasil monárquico*. Rio de Janeiro: Zahar.

Mattos, Ilmar Rohloff. 1987. *O tempo Saquarema: formação do Estado Imperial*. São Paulo: Hucitec.

Mazower, Mark. 2012. *Governing the World: The History of an Idea*. London: Allen Lane.

McCann, Frank D. 1973. *The Brazilian-American Alliance, 1937–1945*. Princeton: Princeton University Press.

McConnell, Fiona, Terri Moreau, and Jason Dittmer. 2012. "Mimicking State Diplomacy: The Legitimizing Strategies of Unofficial Diplomacies." *Geoforum* 43(4): 804–14.

Meadowcroft, James. 2002. "Politics and Scale: Some Implications for Environmental Governance." *Landscape and Urban Planning* 61(2–4): 169–79.

Mecham, Michael. 2003. "Mercosur: A Failing Development Project?" *International Affairs* 79(2): 369–87.

Melo, Evaldo Cabral de. 2001. *Frei Joaquim do Amor Divino Caneca*. Rio de Janeiro: Editora, 34.

Messner, Dirk, and John Humphrey. 2006. "China and India in the Global Governance Arena." Paper presented at the Seventh Annual Global Development Conference: At the Nexus of Global Chance, Pre-conference Workshop on Asian and Other Drivers of Global Change. St. Petersburg, Russia, January 19–21, 2006.

Milani, Carlos R. S., and Maria Clotilde Meirelles Ribeiro. 2011. "International Relations and the Paradiplomacy of Brazilian Cities: Crafting the Concept of Local International Management." *Brazilian Administration Review* 8(1): 21–36.

Ministry of Defense. 2008. *Brazil's National Strategy of Defense*, at www.defesa.gov.br/projetosweb/estrategia/arquivos/estrategia_defesa_nacional_ingles.pdf

———. 2012. *Livro Branco de Defesa Nacional*, at www.defesa.gov.br/arquivos/2012/mes07/lbdn.pdf

Ministry of National Defense of the People's Republic of China. "Arms Control and Disarmament," http://eng.mod.gov.cn/Database/ArmsControl/, accessed September 2013.

Moreira, Mauricio Mesquita. 2009. "Brazil's Trade Policy: Old and New Issues." In *Brazil as an Economic Superpower? Understanding Brazil's Changing Role in the Global Economy*, eds. Lael Brainard and Leonardo Martinez-Diaz. Washington, DC: Brookings Institution Press, 137–56.

Motta Veiga, Pedro da. 2009. "Brazil's Trade Policy: Moving Away From Old Paradigms?" In *Brazil as an Economic Superpower? Understanding Brazil's Changing Role in the Global Economy*, eds. Lael Brainard and Leonardo Martinez-Diaz. Washington, DC: Brookings Institution Press, 113–35.

Motta Veiga, Pedro da, Sandra Polónia Rios, and Leane Cornet Naidin. 2013. "Políticas comercial e industrial: o hiperativismo do primeiro biênio Dilma." *Textos Cindes* 35.

Muggah, Robert, and Gustavo Diniz. 2013. "Securing the Border: Brazil's 'South America First' Approach to Transnational Organized Crime." *Strategic Paper* 5. Rio de Janeiro, Brazil: Igarapé Institute.

Musacchio, Aldo, and Sergio G. Lazzarini. 2014. *Reinventing State Capitalism: Leviathan in Business, Brazil and Beyond.* Cambridge, MA: Harvard University Press.

Narlikar, Amrita. 2008. "Bargaining for a raise? New Powers in the International System." *Internationale Politik*, September, available at https://ip-journal.dgap.org/en/ip-journal/topics/bargaining-raise.

Neves, Lúcia Maria Bastos P. 2002. "Cidadania e participação política na época da Independência do Brasil." *Cadernos Cedes* 22(58): 47–64.

Nogueira Batista Jr., Paulo. 1994. "O Mercosul e os interesses do Brasil." *Estudos Avançados* 8(21): 79–95.

———. 2008. "A América do Sul em movimento." *Revista de Economia Política* 28(2): 226–38.

Novaes, Roberto Leonan Morim, and Renan de França Souza. 2013. "Legalizing Environmental Exploitation in Brazil: The Retreat of Public Policies for Biodiversity Protection." *Tropical Conservation Science* 6(4): 477–83.

Nunes, Edson. 1997. *A Gramática Política No Brasil: Clientelismo E Insulamento Burocrático.* 2003 edition. Rio de Janeiro: Jorge Zahar Editor.

Nye, Joseph. 2011. *The Future of Power.* Washington, DC: Public Affairs.

Obregón, Liliana. 2012. "Regionalism Constructed: A Short History of 'Latin American International Law'." In *5th Biennial Conference European Society of International Law*, eds. Nico Krisch, Anne van Aaken, and Mario Prost. Valencia: European Society of International Law, at http://www.academia.edu/3285991/Regionalism_Constructed_A_Short_History_of_a_Latin_American_International_Law_

Ocampo, José Antonio. 2012. "The Transition to a Green Economy: Benefits, Challenges and Risks from a Sustainable Development Perspective." In *The Transition to a Green Economy: Benefits, Challenges and Risks from a Sustainable Development Perspective: Report by a Panel of Experts*, UN-DECA, UNEP, UNCTAD, 3–13.

O Eco (blog). 2012. "Izabella Bate Boca Com Manifestantes." June 22, http://www.oeco.org.br/salada-verde/26148-ministra-izabella-rebate-criticas-de-manifestantes

O Estado de S.Paulo. 2010. "Jobim Vê 'Com Reservas' Atuação da Otan no Atlântico Sul." *Estado do São Paulo*, available at: www.estado.com.br/noticias/internacional, jobim-ve-com-reservas-atuacao-da-otan-no-atlantico-sul,609597,0.htm

Olarreaga, Marcelo, and Isidro Soloaga. 1998. "Endogenous Tariff Formation: The Case of Mercosur." *The World Bank Economic Review* 12(2): 297–320.

Oliveira, Francisco de. 2001. "Pensar com radicalidade e com especificidade." *Lua Nova* 54(1): 89–95.

Onuki, Janina. 2010. "Interesses comerciais brasileiros na América do Sul." *Cadernos Adenauer* 11(4): 90–6.

Paikin, Zach. 2012. "Responsibility to Protect and the New Calculus of Genocide." *iPolitics*, December 18, http://www.ipolitics.ca/2012/12/18/responsibility-to-protect-and-the-new-calculus-of-genocide/

Parmer, Inderjeet, and Michael Cox. 2010. *Soft Power and US Foreign Policy.* New York: Routledge.

Parracho, Lunae, and Caroline Stauffer. 2014. "Brazil Land Disputes Spread as Indians Take on Wildcat Miners." *Reuters*, February 17, 2014.

Patrick, Stewart. 2010. "Irresponsible Stakeholders?: The Difficulty of Integrating Rising Powers." *Foreign Affairs* 89(6): 44–53.

Patriota, Antônio. 2012. "Sabatina da Folha com Antônio Patriota." *Folha de S. Paulo*, May 17, http://www1.folha.uol.com.br/paineldoleitor/agendafolha/1061028-ministro-antonio-patriota-cancela-sabatina-na-folha.shtml

Patriota, Antonio de Aguiar. 2013. "Statement by H.E. Ambassador Antonio de Aguiar Patriota, Minister of External Relations of the Federative Republic of Brazil." Open Debate of the Security Council on the Protection of Civilians in Armed Conflict, November 9.

Patti, Carlo. 2010. "Brazil and the Nuclear Issues in the Years of the Luiz Inácio Lula Da Silva Government." *Revista Brasileira de Política Internacional* 53(2): 178–97.

———. 2012. "Brazil in Global Nuclear Order." Unpublished Ph.D. dissertation, University of Florence.

Pereira da Costa, Katarina, and Pedro da Motta Veiga. 2011. "O Brasil frente à emergência da África: comércio e política comercial." *Textos Cindes* 24.

Pereira, Leandro. 2013. "As origens da política nuclear brasileira (1945–57)." Unpublished M.A. thesis, Fundação Getulio Vargas.

Perkovich, George, and James Acton, eds. 2009. *Abolishing Nuclear Weapons: A Debate*. Washington, DC: Carnegie Endowment for International Peace.

Piccone, Ted. 2011. "The Multilateral Dimension." *Journal of Democracy* 22(4) (October): 139–52.

Pinheiro, Armando Castelar, and Fabio Giambiagi. 2006. *Rompendo o marasmo: a retomada do desenvolvimento no Brasil*. São Paulo: Elsevier.

Porter, Keith. 2012. "Marking Ten Years of the Responsibility to Protect." *The Stanley Foundation Courier* 74(2).

Prebisch, Raúl. 1983a. *Accumulation and Development: The Logic of Industrial Civilization*. Oxford: Martin Robertson.

———. 1983b. "Centro y periferia en el origen y maduración de la crisis." *Pensamiento Iberoamericano* 3: 27–40.

Proença Júnior, Domício, and Érico Esteves Duarte. 2010. "Brazilian Strategic Context: An Offensive Realist Assessment." Paper delivered at the Congress of the Latin American Studies Association, Toronto, Canada, October 6–9.

Quadros, Jânio. 1961. "Brazil's New Foreign Policy." *Foreign Affairs* 40(1): 19–27.

Rabello, Tânia. 2013. "Deforestation Brings Along Poverty." *Amazônia Pública*. São Paulo: Pública.

Rachman, Gideon. 2008. "Is America's New Declinism for Real?" *Financial Times*, November 24, http://www.ft.com/cms/s/0/ddbc80d0-ba43-11dd-92c9-0000779fd18c.html#axzz38ykLb4J9

Ramo, Joshua Cooper. 1999. "The Three Marketeers." *Time* 153(6) (February 15): 34–43.

Rapoza, Kenneth. 2014. "Was Brazil's Belo Monte Dam a Bad Idea?" *Forbes*, March 7.

Register, Richard. 2006. *Ecocities*. Gabriola Island, BC: New Society Publishers.

Reuters. 2012. "Brazil's BNDES Approves $10.8 Bln Loan for Amazon Belo Monte Dam." November 26, http://www.reuters.com/article/2012/11/26/bndes-belomonte-idUSL1E8MQ76I20121126

Ricupero, Bernardo. 2007. *Sete Lições sobre as Interpretações do Brasil.* São Paulo: Alameda.

Ritcher, Melvin. 2011. "Reconstructing the History of Political Languages: Pocock, Skinner and the Geschichtliche Grundbegriffe." *History and Theory* 29(1): 38–70.

Roberts, Adam. 2006. "The United Nations and Humanitarian Intervention." In *Humanitarian Intervention and International Relations*, ed. Jennifer M. Welsh. Oxford: Oxford University Press, 71–97.

Rocky Mountain Institute. 1998. *Green Development: Integrating Ecology and Real Estate.* New York: John Wiley and Sons.

Rodogno, Davide. 2012. *Against Massacre: Humanitarian Interventions in the Ottoman Empire, 1815–1914.* Princeton: Princeton University Press.

Rodrigues, José Honório. 1962. "The Foundations of Brazil's Foreign Policy." *International Affairs* 38(3): 324–38.

Rojas, Shunko. 2013. "Understanding Neo-Developmentalism in Latin America: New Industrial Policies in Brazil and Colombia." In *Law and the New Developmental State: The Brazilian Experience in Latin American Context*, eds. David M. Trubek, Helena Alviar Garcia, Diogo R. Coutinho, and Alvaro Santos. Cambridge: Cambridge University Press, 65–113.

Rosenbaum, H. Jon, and Glenn M. Cooper. 1970. "Brazil and the Nuclear Non-Proliferation Treaty." *International Affairs* 46(1): 74–90.

Roseneau, James, and Ernst-Otto Czempiel, eds. 1992. *Governance without Government: Order and Change in World Politics.* Cambridge: Cambridge University Press.

Roth, Patrick H. 2001. "From the Brazil Squadron to USNAVSO: Significant Aspects of U.S. Navy Forward Presence in Latin American Waters." Unpublished paper prepared for the U.S. Navy Forward Presence Bicentennial Symposium, Alexandria VA, The CNA Corporation, June 21.

———. 2009. The U.S. Navy in Brazil: The First Fourth Fleet: Duas Grandes Nações – Uma Causa Comum. Unpublished Powerpoint brief shared with Ralph Espach in May 2010.

Rousseff, Dilma. 2011. "Dilma Rousseff Inauguration Speech: Brazil's First Female President Addresses Congress in Brasilia." *Huffington Post*, January 3, http://www.huffingtonpost.com/2011/01/03/dilma-rousseff-inaugurati_1_n_803450.html

Rubenfeld, Jed. 2003. "The Two World Orders." *Wilson Quarterly* 27(4) (Autumn): 22–37.

Ruggie, John G. 1982. "International Regimes, Transactions, and Change: Embedded Liberalism in the Postwar Economic Order." *International Organization* 36(2): 379–415.

———. 2008. "Introduction: Embedding Global Markets." In *Embedding Global Markets: An Enduring Challenge*, ed. John Gerard Ruggie. Aldershot: Ashgate Publishing Company, 1–9.

Ruiz, Briceño, José Saraiva, and Miriam Gomes Saraiva. 2010. "Las diferentes percepciones sobre la construcción del Mercosur en Argentina, Brasil y Venezuela." *Foro Internacional* 50(1): 35–62.

Salm, Rodolfo. 2009. "Belo Monte: A farsa das audiências públicas." *Correio da Cidadania*, October 5, http://www.correiocidadania.com.br/index.php?option=com_content&view=article&id=3827:submanchete061009&catid=28:ambiente-e-cidadania&Itemid=57

Salomon, Monica. 2011. "Paradiplomacy in the Developing World: The Case of Brazil." In *Cities and Global Governance: New Sites for International Relations*, ed. Mark M. Amen. Surrey: Ashgate Publishing Company, 45–68.

Santos, Resende. 2002. "The Origins of Security Cooperation in the Southern Cone." *Latin American Politics and Society* 44(4): 89–126.

Santos, Wanderley Guilherme dos. 1978a. *A Práxis Liberal no Brasil: propostas para reflexão e pesquisa*. São Paulo: Duas Cidades.

———. 1978b. *Ordem burguesa e liberalismo político*. São Paulo: Duas Cidades.

———. 1992. *Razões da desordem*. Rio de Janeiro: Rocco.

———. 1998. *Décadas de Espanto e uma apologia democrática*. Rio de Janeiro: Rocco, 9–61.

Saraiva, José Flávio Sombra. 1996. *O lugar da África: A dimensão Atlântica da política externa brasileira (de 1946 a nossos dias)*. Brasília: Ed. Univ. Brasília.

———. 2012. *África parceira do Brasil Atlântico: Relações Internacionais do Brasil e da África no início do Século XXI*. Belo Horizonte: Editora Fino Traço.

Saraiva, Miriam Gomes. 2008. "As diferentes percepções na Argentina sobre o Mercosul." *Contexto Internacional* 30(3): 735–75.

———. 2010a. "A diplomacia brasileira e as visões sobre a inserção externa do Brasil: institucionalistas pragmáticos X autonomistas." *Mural Internacional* 1(1): 45–52.

———. 2010b. "Brazilian Foreign Policy Towards South America During the Lula Administration: Caught between South America and Mercosur." *Revista Brasileira de Política Internacional* 53: 151–68.

———. 2014. "The Brazilian Soft Power Tradition." *Current History* 1994(113): 64–9.

Sassen, Saskia. 2006. *Cities in a World Economy*, 3rd edition. Thousand Oaks, CA: Pine Forge Press.

Scarano, Fabio, Guimarães, André, and da Silva, José Maria. 2012. "Rio+20: Lead by example." *Nature* 486(7 June): 25–6.

Schiff, Maurice, and L. Alan Winters. 1998. "Dynamics and Politics in Regional Integration Arrangements: An Introduction." *The World Bank Economic Review* 12(2): 177–95.

Schreurs, Miranda A., and Elizabeth Economy, eds. 1997. *The Internationalization of Environmental Protection*. New York: Cambridge University Press.

Schwarz, Roberto. 1973. "As ideias fora do lugar." *Estudos CEBRAP* 3: 150–61.

———. 1992a. "As idéias fora do lugar." In Roberto Schwarz, ed. *Ao vencedor as batatas: forma literária e processo social nos inícios do romance brasileiro*, São Paulo: Livraria Duas Cidades.

———. 1992b. *Misplaced Ideas: Essays on Brazilian Culture*, ed. John Gledson. London, New York: Verso.

Schweller, Randall. 2011. "Emerging Powers in an Age of Disorder." *Global Governance* 17: 285–97.

Schweller, Randall, and Xiaoyu Pu. 2011. "After Unipolarity: China's Visions of International Order in an Era of U.S. Decline." *International Security* 36(1): 41–72.

Seabra de Cruz Junior, Ademar, Antonio Ricardo F. Cavalcante, and Luiz Pedone. 1993. "Brazil's Foreign Policy under Collor." *Journal of Interamerican Studies and World Affairs* 35(1): 119–44.

Serfaty, Simon. 2011. "Moving into a Post-Western World." *The Washington Quarterly* 32(2): 7–23.

Shankland, Alex, and Leonardo Hasenclever. 2011. "Indigenous Peoples and the Regulation of REDD+ in Brazil: Beyond the War of the Worlds?" *IDS Bulletin. Special Issue: Political Economy of Climate Change* 42(3): 80–8.

Sharp, Paul. 2009. *Diplomatic Theory of International Relations*. Cambridge: Cambridge University Press.

Shea, Donald Richard. 1955. *The Calvo Clause: A Problem of Inter-American and International Law and Diplomacy*. Minneapolis: University of Minnesota Press.

Shifter, Michael. 2012. "The Shifting Landscape of Latin American Regionalism." *Current History* 111(742): 56–61.

Sikkink, Kathryn. 1991. *Ideas and Institutions: Developmentalism in Brazil and Argentina*. Ithaca and London: Cornell University Press.

Sikri, Rajiv. 2007. *India's Foreign Policy Priorities in the Coming Decade*. Singapore: National University of Singapore, Institute of South Asian Studies.

Silva, Antônio Marcelo J. F. da. 2005. "Tavares Bastos: biografia do liberalismo brasileiro." Unpublished Ph.D. dissertation, IUPERJ.

Simonsen, Roberto C. 1977. *A controvérsia do planejamento na economia brasileira: Coletânea da polêmica Simonsen X Gudin, desencadeada com as primeiras propostas formais de planejamento da economia brasileira ao final do Estado Novo*. Rio de Janeiro: IPEA/INPES.

Simpson, Gerry J. 2004. *Great Powers and Outlaw States: Unequal Sovereigns in the International Legal Order*. Cambridge: Cambridge University Press.

Sjoberg, Laura. 2008. "Scaling IR Theory: Geography's Contribution to Where IR Takes Place." *International Studies Review* 10(3): 472–500.

Skidmore, Thomas. 1988. *The Politics of Military Rule in Brazil, 1964–85*. Oxford: Oxford University Press.

Skinner, Quentin. 1969. "Meaning and Understanding in the History of Ideas." *History and Theory* 8(1): 3–53.

Soares de Lima, Maria Regina. 2005. "A política externa brasileira e os desafios da cooperação Sul-Sul." *Revista Brasileira de Política Internacional* 48(1): 24–59.

———. 2013. "Relações Interamericanas: A nova agenda sul-americana e o Brasil." *Lua Nova* 90: 167–201.

Soares de Lima, Maria Regina, and Mônica Hirst. 2006. "Brazil as an Intermediate State and Regional Power: Action, Choice and Responsibilities." *International Affairs* 82(1): 21–40.

Solingen, Etel. 1993. "Macropolitical Consensus and Lateral Autonomy in Industrial Policy: The Nuclear Sector in Brazil and Argentina." *International Organization* 47(2): 263–98.

Soltis, Katie. 2011. "Brazil Disregards Charges from the Inter-American Commission on Human Rights." *Council on Hemispheric Affairs*, June 9, http://www.coha.org/brazil-disregards-charges-from-the-inter-american-commission-on-human-rights/

Sørensen, Georg. 2006. "Liberalism of Restraint and Liberalism of Imposition: Liberal Values and World Order in the New Millennium." *International Relations* 20(3): 251–72.

Sotero, Paulo. 2012. "The Brazilian Challenge: How to Manage Asymmetrical Regional Relations Beyond the OAS." *Revista CIDOB d'afers internacionales* 97/98: 101–16.

———. 2013. "Brazil and the BRICS: A Challenging Space for Global Relevance and Reform of an Obsolete World Order." In *Laying the Brics of a New Global Order: From Yekaterinburg 2009 to Ethekwini 2013*, eds. Kornegay Jr., Francis A. and Narnia Bohler-Muller. Pretoria: Africa Institute of South Africa, 279–94.

Sousa, Carolina Hermann Coelho de. 2013. "The Resistance Against the Giant Vale Mining Company Is Growing Worldwide." *ejolt*, available at: http://www.ejolt.org/2013/04/the-resistance-against-the-giant-vale-mining-company-is-growing-worldwide/

Souto Maior, Luiz A. P. 2004. "A crise do multilateralismo econômico e o Brasil." *Revista Brasileira de Política Internacional* 47(2): 163–90.

Spanakos, Anthony Peter, and Joseph Marques. 2014. "Brazil's Rise as a Middle Power: The Chinese Contribution." In *Middle Powers and the Rise of China*, eds. Bruce Gilley and Andrew O'Neil. Washington, DC: Georgetown University Press, 213–36.

Spektor, Matias. 2004. "Origens e direção do Pragmatismo Ecumênico e Responsável (1974–1979)." *Revista Brasileira de Política Internacional* 47(2): 191–222.

———. 2009. *Kissinger e o Brasil*. São Paulo: Zahar.

———. 2011. "Brazil the Hemisphere Rises: Eyes on the Global Prize." *Americas Quarterly* 5(2): 56–61.

———. 2012. "Humanitarian Interventionism Brazilian Style?" *Americas Quarterly* 6(3): 54–5.

———. 2014. "O projeto autonomista na política externa Brasileira." In *Política externa, espaço e desenvolvimento*, ed. Aristides Monteiro Neto. Brasília: IPEA, 17–58.

Starling, Heloísa M. Murgel. 2006. "Onde só vento se semeava outrora: a tradição do republicanismo e a questão agrária no Brasil." In *Sentimento de Reforma Agrária, Sentimento de República*, eds. Delsy G. de Paula, Heloísa M. M. Starling, and Juarez R. Guimarães. Belo Horizonte: UFMG, 31–71.

Stepan, Alfred. 1971. *The Military in Politics: Changing Patterns in Brazil*. Princeton, NJ: Princeton University Press.

Stephens, Philip. 2010. "Rising Powers Do Not Want to Play by the West's Rules." *Financial Times*, May 20, https://www.google.com/webhp?sourceid=chrome-instant&rlz=1C5CHFA_enUS551US551&ion=1&espv=2&ie=UTF-8#q=%22Rising%20Powers%20Do%20Not%20Want%20to%20Play%20by%20the%20West%E2%80%99s%20Rules%22

Stuenkel, Oliver. 2010. "Towards the 'Greater West' or a 'Post-Western World'? International Institutions, Integration and Confrontation in India's and Brazil's Foreign Policy Strategy." Unpublished Ph.D. dissertation, Universitat Duisburg-Essen.

———. 2011. "Identity and the Concept of the West: The Case of Brazil and India." *Revista Brasileira de Política Internacional* 54(1): 178–95.

———. 2012. "Can the BRICS Co-operate in the G-20? A View from Brazil." *Occasional Paper* 123. Capetown, South Africa: South African Institute of International Affairs (SAIIA).

Stuenkel, Oliver, Daniel Gros, Nikita Maslennikov, and Pradumna B. Rana. 2012. *The Case for IMF Quota Reform*. Washington, DC: Council on Foreign Relations.

Swan, Alan C. 2000. "The Dynamics of Economic Integration in the Western Hemisphere: The Challenge to America." *The University of Miami Inter-American Law Review* 31(1): 1–8.

Taylor, Alan M. 1998. "On the Costs of Inward-Looking Development: Price Distortions, Growth, and Divergence in Latin America." *The Journal of Economic History* 58(1): 1–28.

Taylor, Paul D. 2009. "Why Does Brazil Need Nuclear Submarines?" *Proceedings Magazine*, June 2009, 136/6/1.

Teixeira, Isabella. 2010. "A Review of Brazil's Environmental Policies and Challenges Ahead." Webcast. Wilson Center, October 20, http://www.wilsoncenter.org/event/review-brazils-environmental-policies-and-challenges-ahead

Thielmann, Greg, and Wyatt Hoffman. 2012. "Submarine Nuclear Reactors: A Worsening Proliferation Challenge." *Threat Assessment Brief*. Washington, DC, Arms Control Association, available at http://www.armscontrol.org/files/TAB_Submarine_Nuclear_Reactors.pdf

Tollefson, Scott D. 1997. "National Security." In Rex Hudson, ed., *The Library of Congress Country Study: Brazil*. Washington, DC: The Library of Congress.

———. 1998. *A Country Study: Brazil*. Washington, DC: Library of Congress.

Toly, Noah. 2008. "Transnational Municipal Networks in Climate Politics: From Global Governance to Global Politics." *Globalizations* 5(3): 341–56.

———. 2011. "Cities, the Environment, and Global Governance: A Political Ecological Perspective." In *Cities and Global Governance: New Sites for International Relations*, ed. Michael Mark Amen. Farnham, Surrey: Ashgate Publishing Company, 137–50.

Tourinho, Marcos. 2013. "The Devil in the Details. Brazil and the Global Implementation of RtoP." *Working Paper*, Fundação Getulio Vargas.

Trindade, Alexandro Dantas. 2011. *André Rebouças – um engenheiro do Império*. São Paulo: Hucitec.

Tulchin, Joseph S., and Ralph H. Espach. 2000. *Latin America in the New International System*. Boulder, CO: Lynne Rienner Publishers.

Turcotte, Sylvain F., and Félix G. Mostajo. 2008. "La política de Brasil hacia Sudamérica: Entre voluntarismo y resistencias." *Foro Internacional* 48(4): 785–806.

UN-DESA. 2012. "A Guidebook to the Green Economy Issue 1: Green Economy, Green Growth, and Low-Carbon Development – History, Definitions and a Guide to Recent Publications." http://sustainabledevelopment.un.org/index.php?page=view&type=400&nr=634&menu=35, accessed September 2013.

UNEP. 2011. "Towards a Green Economy: Pathways to Sustainable Development and Poverty Eradication." http://www.unep.org/greeneconomy/Portals/88/documents/ger/GER_synthesis_en.pdf, accessed July 1, 2013.

Vadell, Javier A. 2013. "The North of the South: The Geopolitical Implications of 'Pacific Consensus' in South America and the Brazilian Dilemma." *Latin American Policy* 4(1): 36–56.

Vadell, Javier A., Bárbara Lamas, and Daniela M. de F. Ribeiro. 2009. "Integração e desenvolvimento no Mercosul: Divergências e convergências nas políticas econômicas nos governos Lula e Kirchner." *Revista de Sociologia e Política* 17(33): 39–54.

Valenzuela, Arturo. 1997. "Paraguay: The Coup That Didn't Happen." *Journal of Democracy* 8(1): 43–55.

Valor Econômico. 2013. "Múltis brasileiras perdem ânimo com o país e investimento desaba." August 26, available at: http://www2.valor.com.br/brasil/3246254/multis-brasileiras-perdem-animo-com-o-pais-e-investimento-desaba

———. 2014. "Venezuela deve US$ 2 bi a empreiteiras brasileiras." March 5, available at: http://www2.valor.com.br/internacional/3450136/venezuela-deve-us-2-bi-empreiteiras-brasileiras

VanDeveer, Stacy D., and Geoffrey D. Dabelko. 2001. "It's Capacity, Stupid: International Assistance and National Implementation." *Global Environmental Politics* 1(2): 18–29.

Vervaele, John A. E. 2005. "Mercosur and Regional Integration in South America." *The International and Comparative Law Quarterly* 54(2): 387–409.

Vianna, Oliveira. 1954. *Instituições políticas brasileiras*. São Paulo: Cia. Editora Nacional.

Vianna, Sá. 1912. *De La Non Existence D'un Droit International Americain*. Rio de Janeiro: L. Figueredo.

Vieira de Jesus, Diego Santos. 2012. "In the Search for Autonomy: Brazil's Foreign Policy on Nuclear Issues." *Global Change, Peace & Security* 24(3): 365–84.

Vieira, Martins, Norberto Marília, Fátima Marília, and Andrade de Carvalho. 2009. "O setor agroexportador brasileiro no contexto da integração Mercosul/UE." *Revista de Economia e Sociologia Rural* 47(2): 311–34.

Vigevani, Tullo, and Gabriel Cepaluni. 2009. *Brazilian Foreign Policy in Changing Times: The Quest for Autonomy from Sarney to Lula*. Translated by Leandro Moura. Lanham, MD: Lexington Books.

Vigevani, Tullo, and Haroldo Ramanzini Júnior. 2009. "Mudanças da inserção brasileira na América Latina." *Lua Nova* 78: 37–75.

Vigevani, Tullo, Eric Hershberg, and Andrés Serbin. 2013. "Introdução: Dossiê Hemisfério Americano em Transformação." *Lua Nova* 90: 167–201.

Villela, André A. 1993. "Política comercial e importações na Primeira República: 1889–1930." Unpublished Ph.D. Dissertation, Pontifícia Universidade Católica, Rio de Janeiro.

Viola, Eduardo, Matías Franchini, and Thaís Lemos Ribeiro. 2012. "Climate Governance in an International System under Conservative Hegemony: The Role of Major Powers." *Revista Brasileira de Política Internacional* 55: 9–29.

Viotti, Maria Luiza Ribeiro. 2010. "Statement by H.E. Ambassador Maria Luiza Ribeiro Viotti, Permanent Representative of Brazil to the United Nations Security Council." At http://www.un.int/brazil/SC_2013.html

Wade, Robert. 1990. *Governing the Market: Economic Theory and the Role of Government in East Asian Industrialization.* Princeton and Oxford: Oxford University Press.

Wall Street Journal. 2012. "BNDES Aims for 25% Increase in Infrastructure Lending in 2012," February 14.

Wapner, Paul K. 1996. *Environmental Activism and World Civic Politics.* Albany: SUNY Press.

Watson, Adam. 1984. "New States in the Americas." In *The Expansion of International Society,* eds. Hedley Bull and Adam Watson. Oxford: Oxford University Press, 127–41.

Watts, Jonathan, and Liz Ford. 2012. "Rio+20 Earth Summit: Campaigners Decry Final Document." *The Guardian,* June 22, http://www.theguardian.com/environment/2012/jun/23/rio-20-earth-summit-document

Weidner, Glenn R. 1996. "Operation Safe Border: The Ecuador-Peru Crisis." *Joint Forces Quarterly* 11 (Spring): 52–8.

Weinstein, Barbara. 2008. "Erecting and Erasing Boundaries: Can We Combine the 'Indo' and the 'Afro' in Latin American Studies?" *EIAL: Estudios Interdisciplinarios de America Latina y el Caribe* 19(1): 129–44.

Weis, W. Michael. 1993. *Cold Warriors & Coups D'Etat: Brazilian-American Relations, 1945–1964.* Albuquerque: University of New Mexico Press.

Weiss, Edith Brown, and Harold K. Jacobson, eds. 1998. *Engaging Countries: Strengthening Compliance with International Environmental Accords.* Cambridge, MA: MIT Press.

Weiss, Thomas G., and Rama Mani. 2011. "R2P's Missing Link, Culture." *Global Responsibility to Protect* 3: 451–72.

Wendt, Alexander. 1999. *Social Theory of International Politics.* Cambridge: Cambridge University Press.

Werneck Vianna, Luiz J. 1997. *A Revolução Passiva: Americanismo E Iberismo No Brasil.* Rio de Janeiro: Revan.

———. 2001. "O pensar e o agir." *Lua Nova* 54: 35–42.

Wertheim, Stephen. 2012. "The League of Nations: A Retreat from International Law?" *Journal of Global History* 7(2): 210–32.

Wight, Colin. 2006. *Agents, Structure, and International Relations.* Cambridge: Cambridge University Press.

Wilson, Dominic, Alex L. Kelston, and Swarnali Ahmed. 2010. "Is This the BRICS Decade?" *Goldman Sachs Global Economics* 10(3): 1–4.

Wolfensohn, James D., Julia E. Sweig, and Samuel W. Bodman. 2011. "Global Brazil and U.S.-Brazil Relations: Independent Task Force Report No. 66." Washington, DC: Council on Foreign Relations.

World Bank and IPEA. 2011. *Bridging the Atlantic: Brazil and Sub-Saharan Africa, South–South Partnering for Growth*, available at http://siteresources.worldbank.org/AFRICAEXT/Resources/africa-brazil-bridging-final.pdf

World Nuclear Association. 2013. "World Uranium Mining Production." Available at: www.world-nuclear.org/info/Nuclear-Fuel-Cycle/Mining-of-Uranium/World-Uranium-Mining-Production/#.ugJyqqAkjTo

Wrobel, Paulo. 1996. "Brazil and the NPT: Resistance to Change?" *Security Dialogue* 27: 337–47.

Yeats, Alexander J. 1998. "Does Mercosur's Trade Performance Raise Concerns about the Effects of Regional Trade Arrangements?" *The World Bank Economic Review* 12(1): 1–28.

Yeh, Emily. 2012. "Transnational Environmentalism and Entanglements of Sovereignty: The Tiger Campaign Across the Himalayas." *Political Geography* 31(7): 408–18.

Zaluar, Achilles. 2010. Remarks at Panel on *Brazil as a Regional Power: Views from the Hemisphere*, at http://www.wilsoncenter.org/event/brazil-regional-power-views-the-hemisphere.

About the Contributors

David Bosco is an Assistant Professor at the School of International Service, American University. Bosco is a past Fulbright Scholar and senior editor at *Foreign Policy* magazine. Formerly an attorney at Cleary, Gottlieb, Steen & Hamilton, he focused on international arbitration, litigation, and antitrust matters. He also served as a political analyst and journalist in Bosnia and Herzegovina and as deputy director of a joint United Nations/NATO project on repatriating refugees in Sarajevo. He is author of *Five to Rule Them All* (2009) and *Rough Justice* (2014). He writes the *Multilateralist* blog for *Foreign Policy* magazine.

Eve Z. Bratman is an Assistant Professor at the School of International Service, American University. Dr Bratman's research involves sustainable development politics in the Brazilian Amazon. Her major research projects focus on the links between environmental policy, agriculture, and human rights in Brazil and beyond. Her book-in-progress focuses on infrastructure, sustainability, and human rights in the Brazilian Amazon, and is based on nearly a decade of research and work in Brazil. Dr Bratman holds a PhD from American University's School of International Service, and was a Fulbright Scholar in Brazil.

Ralph Espach is Director of CNA's Latin American Affairs program. CNA is a not-for-profit center for policy and operational analysis based in Alexandria, Virginia, in the United States. Espach has recently directed projects and published papers on criminal organizations in Central America, Brazil's strategic and security interests and relations with the United States, the implications of China's growing presence in Latin America for the United States and regional security, and the security implications of climate change for the countries of Latin America. Espach holds a PhD in Political Science from the University of California, Berkeley.

James Goldgeier is Dean of the School of International Service at American University. Prior to American University, his career includes stints at George

Washington University, Cornell University, Stanford University's Center for International Security and Cooperation, the State Department, the National Security Council, the Brookings Institution, the Council on Foreign Relations, the Library of Congress, the Woodrow Wilson Center, the Hoover Institution, and the German Marshall Fund's Transatlantic Academy. His books include *America between the Wars: From 11/9 to 9/11* (co-authored with Derek Chollet, 2011), *Power and Purpose: U.S. Policy toward Russia after the Cold War* (co-authored with Michael McFaul, 2003), and *Not Whether but When: The U.S. Decision to Enlarge NATO* (1999).

Eric Hershberg is Director of the Center for Latin American and Latino Studies and Professor of Government at American University. From 2007–2009 he was Professor of Political Science and Director of Latin American Studies at Simon Fraser University in Vancouver, Canada. He received his PhD from the University of Wisconsin–Madison, and has taught at New York, Southern Illinois, Columbia, Princeton, and The New School Universities. He served for 15 years as Program Director at the Social Science Research Council in New York City. His research focuses on the comparative politics of Latin America, and on the politics of development. Current research projects analyze the state of democracy and emerging development strategies in South America, and the ways in which elites exercise power in Central America. From 2011 to 2013 he coordinated, with Andres Serbin and Tullo Vigevani, a multiyear research project entitled "Hemisphere in Flux: Regionalism, Multilateralism and Foreign Policies in the Americas," which resulted in special issues of journals in Spanish (*Pensamiento Propio*, No. 39, Spring 2014) and Portuguese (*Lua Nova,* No. 90, 2013).

Togzhan Kassenova is an Associate in the Nuclear Policy Program at the Carnegie Endowment. She currently works on issues related to the role of emerging powers in the global nuclear order, weapons of mass destruction non-proliferation issues, nuclear security, and strategic trade management. Kassenova serves on the UN Secretary General's Advisory Board on Disarmament Matters. She is the author of *From Antagonism to Partnership: The Uneasy Path of the U.S.-Russian Cooperative Threat Reduction* (2007). Her latest publications include "Iran Nuclear Talks in Kazakhstan: Remember When Diplomacy Worked," "A Regional Approach to WMD Nonproliferation in the Asia-Pacific," "Global Non-Proliferation and the Taiwan Dilemma," and a contribution on Kazakhstan's nuclear disarmament and non-proliferation policy in *Slaying the Nuclear Dragon: Disarmament Dynamics in the Twenty-First Century* (2012).

João M. E. Maia is an Assistant Professor at Fundação Getulio Vargas in Rio de Janeiro, Brazil, where he directs the undergraduate program in Social Sciences at the Social Science and History School (CPDOC). Prof. Maia holds a PhD in Sociology (IUPERJ, 2006) and a Master's Degree in Sociology (IUPERJ, 2001). His main areas of research include Brazilian social thought, history of sociology, and social theory in the Global South. Prof. Maia's most recent article in English is "Space, Social theory and Peripheral Imagination: Brazilian Intellectual History and De-colonial Debates" (*International Sociology*, 2011).

Arturo C. Porzecanski is Distinguished Economist in Residence at the School of International Service at American University. He previously taught at Columbia University, New York University, and Williams College. Dr. Porzecanski spent most of his professional career working as an international economist on Wall Street, as chief economist for emerging markets at ABN AMRO Bank (2000–2005), chief economist for the Americas at ING Bank (1994–2000), chief emerging-markets economist at Kidder, Peabody & Co. (1992–1993), chief economist at Republic National Bank of New York (1989–1992), senior economist at J.P. Morgan Bank (1977–1989), research economist at the Center for Latin American Monetary Studies in Mexico City (1975–1976), and visiting economist at the International Monetary Fund (1973). His research focuses largely on themes in international finance.

Oliver Stuenkel is an Assistant Professor of International Relations at the Getúlio Vargas Foundation (FGV) in São Paulo, where he coordinates the São Paulo branch of the School of History and Social Science (CPDOC), and the executive program in International Relations. He is also a non-resident Fellow at the Global Public Policy Institute (GPPi) in Berlin. His research focuses on rising powers, specifically on Brazil's, India's, and China's foreign policy and their impact on global governance. He is the author of *IBSA: The Rise of the Global South?* (2014) and *BRICS and the Future of Global Order* (2014). He holds a BA from the Universidad de Valencia in Spain, a Master's in Public Policy from the Kennedy School of Government at Harvard University, where he was a McCloy Scholar, and a PhD in political cal science from the University of Duisburg-Essen in Germany.

Matthew M. Taylor is an Associate Professor at the School of International Service at American University. He has lived and worked extensively in Brazil, most recently as an assistant professor at the University of São Paulo, from 2006–2011. Taylor is the author of *Judging Policy: Courts and Policy Reform in Democratic Brazil* (2008), and co-editor with Timothy J. Power of *Corruption and Democracy in Brazil: The Struggle for Accountability* (2011).

His scholarly work has been published in a variety of journals, including *Comparative Politics*, *Journal of Latin American Studies*, *Latin American Politics and Society*, and *World Politics*.

Marcos Tourinho is a Researcher and Lecturer at the Getulio Vargas Foundation in São Paulo, where his work focuses on the history and practices of international norms transformation and dialogue. Previously, he was at the Programme for the Study of International Governance (PSIG) in Geneva, and was a main researcher at the Targeted Sanctions Consortium, a multiyear and multinational study of the impacts and effectiveness of UN Targeted Sanctions. The product of this research is forthcoming from Cambridge University Press. He is also a PhD candidate at the Graduate Institute of International and Development Studies (IHEID), Geneva, where his dissertation takes a global history approach to the emergence of international society and its fundamental norms.

André Villela has been an Assistant Professor at the Graduate School of Economics of the Getulio Vargas Foundation (EPGE/FGV) since 2002, where he teaches and conducts research on the economic history of Brazil. He holds a BA and MSc in economics, and earned his PhD in Economic History at the London School of Economics. Villela has experience as a private consultant and has worked in several Brazilian governmental agencies, including IPEA, BNDES, and IBGE. He is the co-editor of the book *Economia Brasileira Contemporânea: 1945–2010* (2004).

Index

CPSIA information can be obtained
at www.ICGtesting.com
Printed in the USA
LVHW042300130119
603787LV00005B/394/P